D1564285

# The Short Life and Elusive
# Legend of a Texas Desperado

By
Chuck Parsons and Thomas C. Bicknell

University of North Texas Press
Denton, Texas

10  9  8  7  6  5  4  3  2  1

Permissions:
University of North Texas Press
1155 Union Circle #311336
Denton, TX  76203-5017

The paper used in this book meets the minimum requirements of the
American National Standard for Permanence of Paper for Printed Library
Materials, z39.48.1984. Binding materials have been chosen for durability.

Library of Congress Cataloging-in-Publication Data

Parsons, Chuck, author. | Bicknell, Thomas C., 1952- author.
  King Fisher : the short life and elusive legend of a Texas desperado / by
  Chuck Parsons and Thomas C. Bicknell.
      Pages cm
  Includes bibliographical references and index.
  ISBN-13 978-1-57441-861-3 (cloth)
  ISBN-13  978-1-57441-872-9 (ebook)
  1. LCSH: Fisher, King, 1854–1884. 2. Outlaws—Texas—Biography.
3. Peace officers—Texas—Biography. 4. Frontier and pioneer life—Texas.
5. LCGFT: Biographies.

  F391 .P2635 2022
  364.1092 [B]–dc23

                        2021061650

The electronic edition of this book was made possible by the support of the
Vick Family Foundation. Typeset by vPrompt eServices.

"As a young man, he cowboyed in south Texas, where he broke horses, chased Mexican bandits, and learned to shoot. A gaudy dresser, Fisher sported fringed shirts, crimson sashes, and bells on his spurs. He became a colorful and dominant figure in the nearby border town of Eagle Pass, and he was feared as a rustler.... Fisher admitted to killing seven men ..."

Bill O'Neal, *Texas Gunslingers*

"He was the incarnation of desperadoism."
*San Antonio Daily Express*, March 12, 1884

This work is dedicated to the memory of two dear friends of the Wild West: Gary P. Fitterer (July 7, 1946–June 28, 2016), who willingly and earnestly dug deeply into the lives of various personages of Texas history, such as Alfred Y. Allee, John King Fisher, and others among their contemporaries. His research is ongoing, even though, sadly, his life has ended; and Robert G. McCubbin (February 17, 1937–April 9, 2020) who amassed the most wonderful collection of first-edition books and original photographs dealing with the American West. He most obligingly shared his knowledge, friendship, and expertise with all who asked.

*Requiescat in pace.*

# Contents

# Illustrations

# Preface

In 2018 our biography of Ben Thompson was released by the University of North Texas Press. *Ben Thompson: Portrait of a Gunfighter* was the result of years of research, the majority of which had been done by Thomas Bicknell before coauthor Chuck Parsons joined the effort. We felt that the successful result was the combination of two writers who had a passion for accuracy in preserving the history of the gunfighter-gambler breed of America's Wild West. In many ways Ben Thompson was the quintessential gunfighter-gambler. Our work was based on searching through available court records, newspapers, memoirs, Civil War records, and many secondary sources, to name just the essential sources. We were also fortunate in two highly respected historians accepting and recommending our work for publication—prolific Texas author Mike Cox and Emeritus Professor Gary L. Roberts. We were also grateful that the prominent Old West author Robert K. DeArment contributed the Foreword.

We both felt that, with *Ben Thompson: Portrait of a Gunfighter* behind us, the next logical effort should be a biography of the man who was killed alongside Ben Thompson, John King Fisher. Our effort in researching the life of Ben Thompson had already begun. To be sure, we were familiar with the man, his life, his places of action, his gunfights, and his tragic death, which remains controversial to this day—nearly a century and a half later. Surprisingly, there have been only a few biographies of King Fisher. One is *King Fisher: His Life and Times*, coauthored by O. C. Fisher and J. C. Dykes and published by the University of Oklahoma Press in 1966. Later, G. R. Williamson published a dual biography entitled *The Texas Pistoleers: The True Story of Ben Thompson and King Fisher—Two of the Most Feared Pistol Fighters of the American West*. Larry G. Shaver of Roanoke, Virginia wrote a fascinating study on King Fisher, which he chose not to publish, although he generously shared the results of his research with us. Of course, there have been countless articles published throughout the years, from disappearing (and, in many cases, disappointing) pulp magazines to more respectable publications. An excellent example is the article by Jack DeMattos published in the *Real West* series "Gunfighters of the Real West." This brief background of the publications dealing with John King Fisher does not claim to be exhaustive, but it is representative of why we felt John King Fisher deserved a fresh study.

At times King Fisher was a desperado, perhaps a terror to many citizens of southwest Texas. Certainly in the mid-seventies, he was outwardly such a man, developing a reputation as a rustler and a man-killer. It is impossible to determine exactly how many men did die at the barrel-end of his six-shooter. As in the cases of Longley and Hardin, one could not always stick around the site of the gunfight to determine the answer to that question, and sometimes a man died fighting against a small group of men, all shooting. King Fisher admitted he had killed men. Yet, he remained in Texas in the Nueces Strip area, never becoming a hunted fugitive scurrying to other states as had Hardin and Longley before their capture. After his marriage in 1876, as a husband and father, he became a lawman, determined to set a positive example for his family and neighboring citizens.

However, for all his efforts at respectability, many writers still list him in the same category as the most notorious man-killers of the Wild West, a class of men in which he would have felt uncomfortable if placed there during his brief life. Few remember him as a deputy sheriff of Uvalde County during the early 1880s—or that, in all likelihood, he would have become county sheriff at the upcoming election. His life therefore can rightly be described as ambiguous, for he lived the life of both a desperado and a law officer sworn to uphold the constitution and the law of the land.

King Fisher was an exceptional man for his times, but his attitude toward minorities was typical of white settlers in that period. To a young Bonnet he stated, supposedly in all seriousness, that he had killed seven men but didn't count Mexicans as men. Those he killed include the Black Seminole scout George Washington, William Donovan, perhaps Estanislado and Pancho, and either Thomas or John Hannahan. If we accept that he also killed three Mexicans (whether or not we accept that they were intent on killing him), that is a total of eight human beings. We are left with only

William Donovan and possibly one Hannahan. Some writers have considered him a deadly gunfighter, striking terror throughout the Nueces Strip. Especially since he was never convicted of murder in any case, some might even wonder why he is considered a gunfighter at all.

To reinforce the idea that his life and career were filled with qualities both admirable and repulsive, it should be considered that King Fisher is one of the few gunfighters to have a Texas State Historical Marker erected in his memory. The event took place on June 6, 1967 at the Pioneer Rest Cemetery in Uvalde. United States Congressman O. C. Fisher was the principal speaker at the ceremonies. The announcement came from William Alex Kincaid, chairman of the Uvalde County Historical Committee. County Judge Lee Darley presided as Master of Ceremonies, and Melvin Roland, the Uvalde mayor, gave the welcoming address. According to the press release, Congressman Fisher, described as "a distant cousin" of King Fisher, highlighted "the events and colorful history surrounding his legend."

Fisher had coauthored the book *King Fisher: His Life and Times* with J. C. Dykes, a "noted authority on 'Billy the Kid.'" As the press release pointed out, the life of King Fisher paralleled that of Billy the Kid, as "both fell in with bad crowds at a tender age and both gained reputations for expert handling of guns." However, as the press release continued to explain, the similarities were few, for King Fisher "reformed his ways after he was arrested by Texas Ranger Captain L. H. McNelly and 'given a mighty good talk.'" King Fisher was quoted as having said that the Captain was on the right road and that he realized that it would be a lot better for himself to be on the King's highway.[1]

The marker at Fisher's grave has received frequent attention in the Uvalde newspaper. Looking back twenty years, the March 23, 1980 issue reprinted a brief article from March 10, 1960 reporting that the grave had a new granite marker inscribed with the wording, "John King Fisher, 1856–1884." Further, the iron fence which enclosed the grave "had been repaired and put in place." The body had been "disinterred from the spot where it was buried 75 years earlier under a large oak tree, about half a block west of where it is now buried."[2]

John King Fisher earned a great deal of respect during his early years as a desperado of the Nueces Strip, but he had little opportunity to develop a reputation as a lawman due to his untimely death. The existing court records suggest he was fearless and active while working as a deputy sheriff of Uvalde County. A perusal of the fee book in the Uvalde County Clerk's office reveals the variety of crimes and misdemeanors Fisher dealt with. Fisher frequently arrested men charged with "Gaming," typically earning $4.50 or $5.00 per arrest. Most of the men arrested are of little consequence historically, but on August 8, 1883 Fisher arrested John Baylor, who was fined $10.00 for gambling. Other infractions included selling goods or merchandise on a Sunday, assault and battery, being drunk and disturbing the peace, assault with intent to kill, stealing a horse, burning a store, and fighting. Each arrest was accomplished peacefully. Fisher had earned the job of deputy because of the reputation he had made, and, knowing that reputation, few would care to challenge him.[3]

Certainly Fisher had rightfully earned his reputation as a "gunfighter," but the word is not necessarily synonymous with criminal. Rather, its meaning denotes a man who is not afraid to use his guns to defend his life or his property. As such, James Butler Hickok, Wyatt Earp, and Pat Garrett were rightfully termed "gunfighters." Perhaps John King Fisher should be thought of as an effective gunfighter-lawman, and in this sense in a class apart from John Wesley Hardin or William Preston Longley.

# Acknowledgments

**K**aren Bicknell and Natalie Bicknell-Argerious, Seattle, WA; Marjorie Bicknell-Shapiro, Philadelphia, PA; John Boessenecker, San Francisco, CA; Donaly E. Brice, Senior Reference Archivist Retired, Lockhart, TX; Norman Wayne Brown, Snyder, TX; Mary Burke, Hardin-Simmons University, Abilene, TX; Charles C. Caney, Westlake, OH; Jack DeMattos, Independent Historian and wonderful artist, North Attleboro, MA; Doug Dukes, Lieutenant, South Central Area Command Retired, Liberty Hill, TX; Doug Ellison, Medora, ND; Richard Gilreath, Reference & Research Assistant, Texas State Library & Archives, Austin, TX; Tillie Gonzales, Deputy District Clerk, Goliad County, Goliad, TX; Kurt House, Independent Historian, San Antonio; Laurie Jasinski, editor of *New Handbook of Texas* online, New Braunfels, TX; David D. Johnson, Independent Historian, Indianapolis, IN; Caroline Jones, Reference & Research Assistant, Texas State Library & Archives, Austin, TX; Rick Miller, Belton, TX; William A. "Billy" Mills, Independent Historian, Perry, GA; Madeline Moya, Austin History Center, Austin, TX; Larry G. Shaver, Roanoke, VA; Lisa A. Struthers, Director, Albert and Ethel Herzstein Library, San Jacinto Museum of History, La Porte, TX; Gail M. Turley, District Clerk, Goliad County, Goliad, TX; Harold J. Weiss Jr, Leander, TX; Jackie Wilson, Archivist and Dustin Dewey, University of Western Florida Historic Trust, Pensacola, and Roy B. Young, Apache, OK.

Virginia Davis, Archivist, El Progreso Memorial Library, and Mendell D. Morgan Jr, Director El Progreso Memorial Library, Uvalde, Texas, receive our heartiest thanks. They willingly went beyond the expected in assisting us with the research papers the late Frank L. Hobart had collected over the years. Born in Anderson County, Kansas, Hobart was a glider pilot during World War II. He crashed during the Battle of Bastogne in Belgium in 1944 and endured the horrors of a POW camp until the end of the war. He left the service in 1960 and then went to the Uvalde area where he continued working as a crop duster pilot. He retired from flying in 1977. For many years he was fascinated by the story of King Fisher and whenever able he researched the life of John King Fisher. His widow later donated the Frank L. Hobart Research Collection to the El Progreso Memorial Library.

# Prologue

The humidity was heavy on the banks of Espantosa Lake that night in October 1876. The recent heavy rains had made the ground soggy, and the night air was damp with mist. Here was a good spot to camp, as the livestock the men had stolen needed rest. King Fisher and his small group had gathered some fifty head of horses and twenty-two yoke of oxen, which would all be sold later.

It was easy to stay there and rest for a while, as the tales about the ghostly lake kept most people away. In spite of the many disappearances and frightening screams at night, King had felt it prudent to stop there for now. Although he had business elsewhere, he could depend on his men. So here the four rustlers were camped, resting somewhat peacefully in their bedrolls. The silence was broken when someone shouted. "Hands up!"

They tried to roll out of their blankets as they grabbed their weapons and began firing toward the sound of unknown figures advancing in the dark and mist. Who were they? the men wondered. Were they the sheriff and a posse? Those whose cattle they had stolen? Texas Rangers? No matter. It was time to shoot. The fiery exchange was over quickly.

In the midnight hour, the four members of King Fisher's gang fired at the ghostlike figures firing back. They were Sergeant John B. Armstrong and a squad of his rangers, a small detachment on the scout for outlaws—especially John King Fisher.

The lively exchange of gunfire in the dark was brief. Armstrong had the advantage of surprise, as the rangers held their six-shooters in their hands. The result of the deadly exchange was one-sided: John Martin, Jim Roberts, and George Mullen lay on the ground, shot to death while resisting arrest; a fourth member, Jim McAllister, screamed in agony due to his several wounds.

Sergeant Armstrong was disappointed, for he had hoped to capture King Fisher among the rustlers. But that would have to wait for another day, and perhaps for another gun battle.

# Chapter 1

# The Call of the Pendencia

The fiery exchange on the shores of Espantosa Lake in northern Dimmit County, Texas was only one example of bloody shootouts between recognized outlaws and legitimate law enforcement officers. These violent exchanges did not bring about peaceful conditions in the wild southwest. They represented only a small step forward in the progress of what would eventually be the establishment of law and order.

Some would contend that law and order has not yet been established. Dimmit County is situated along the Rio Grande, the entire length of which—by reputation, certainly—remains a dangerous place today. Dimmit, and its neighboring counties—Maverick, Zavala, and Webb—are in the region known as the Nueces Strip, the land south of the Nueces River of Texas, stretching to the Rio Grande. The entire area was once wild, termed by early cartographers and explorers as the "Wild Horse Desert." Nature ruled, as thousands of mustangs roamed the land, descendants of the breed brought to this continent and used by sixteenth-century Spanish explorers. The vast numbers of wild horses were gradually reduced, just as the vast herds of American bison that once roamed the Great Plains were reduced nearly to extinction.

Even the end of the Mexican-American War in 1848 did not eliminate the wildness of the area. Some influential leaders from Mexico still considered the area south of the Nueces River part of Mexico. They refused to accept the Rio Grande (known in Mexico as the Rio Bravo) as the legitimate border between the two countries in spite of the terms of the Treaty of Guadalupe-Hidalgo. The American Civil War resulted in continued conflict. Reconstruction followed with hatreds deepened between the Anglo ranchers, Hispanic ranchers, and remnants of the once powerful Comanche Nation and other tribes. According to a descendant of King Fisher, O. C. Fisher, who was familiar with the situation on both sides of the Rio Grande, "conditions were intolerable. Cattle thieves, cutthroats, and other outlaws and gamblers and homesteaders wormed their way through the chaparral, all vying for supremacy and survival."[1]

In this no-man's-land John King Fisher rose to become a dominant figure in the decade of the seventies, much like Texas Ranger Leander Harvey McNelly did, as well as the partisan Mexican leader Juan Nepomuceno Cortina. The decade of the 1870s had all the right elements for men with fiery leadership skills to emerge. These three fighting men also contributed to what collateral descendant Ovie Clark Fisher termed "the terrible seventies."[2] Of course the trio's origins were far removed from the Wild Horse Desert. Fisher came down from Collin County, Texas in northeast Texas—not from Kentucky as numerous writers have claimed, while L. H. McNelly was from Virginia and Juan N. Cortina was a native of Camargo, Tamaulipas, Mexico.

Collin County is located in northeast Texas, some thirty miles south of the Red River. The Caddo tribe inhabited the area when white settlers began arriving, and generally the relationship between the white settler and the Caddo was a peaceful one, but gradually the encroachment of the settlers forced the Caddo to move elsewhere. In 1846, Collin County was demarked from Fannin County, and McKinney became the county seat, in memory of Collin McKinney, a signer of the Texas Declaration of Independence. One might think Collin County was similar to the rest of the South, but on the contrary most settlers were from the upper South. Hence, their livelihood was different and they held fewer slaves. These settlers were engaged not on huge plantations but smaller farms based on raising different crops, not cotton or tobacco but wheat and corn. When the Civil War loomed, the county voted against seceding with the Confederacy. In Collin County amidst the post-war violence there was hatred between followers of Confederate veteran Robert Lee and those of his enemy Lewis Peacock of the Union League, culminating in what is known as the Lee-Peacock Feud.[3]

The Fisher family had entered bravely and willfully into this new land and developing conflict. King's grandfather, James Fisher Sr., had left his home in Illinois and slowly traveled through the territories, not reaching Texas, then part of Mexico, until 1835. His days were numbered, but he stopped on Sister Grove Creek in what was then Fannin County but later Collin County. How the creek obtained that unusual name is unknown. It rises in extreme southeastern Grayson County, then flows southeast for some twenty miles to its mouth in Pilot Grove Creek.[4] Here James Fisher decided to stop in order "to build a log house and carve out a homestead on Sister Grove Creek."[5] The name and setting suggest he had found a peaceful site to establish his home. Fisher had brought with him his family, which included his wife Anna Ladd Fisher, a native of Virginia, and their children: son Jobe, daughter S. A., sons John and James, and another daughter Delila. His time in Texas was brief as he died two years later in 1837. His son Jobe (sometimes recorded as Job) had been born in Arkansas, before the family continued on to northeast Texas. Widow Anna Fisher, having arrived in Texas before March 1836, qualified to apply for and receive a "league and labor of land" grant from the new Republic of Texas, which amounted to 4,605 acres of land.[6]

In 1851, Jobe Fisher married Lucinda Warren, a native of Kentucky and the daughter of Hiram Warren, a fellow Collin County resident.[7] Born in 1832, she was nineteen when she became Mrs. Jobe Fisher. Their first child was a son whom they named John King Fisher. Most likely, King—the actual middle name by which he became best known—was born in 1855 in Collin County, but the exact date of his birth is uncertain. King's first biographer, O. C. Fisher, states that he "was born in 1854, of humble parentage."[8] Florence Fisher Kellogg, King's daughter, possessed the family Bible showing he was born in October of 1855, but without a specific date.[9] Amanda Gardner, a great-great-granddaughter of King, records he was born in Collin County in

1853 or possibly 1854.[10] At his gravesite, a replacement stone in the Pioneer Rest Cemetery in Uvalde, Texas gives his birth date as 1856. It is doubtful his exact date of birth will ever be confirmed.

In 1856, Jobe and Lucinda had a second son whom they named Jasper but, sadly, Lucinda did not survive Jasper's birth. After Lucinda died, Jobe and his two children moved to Jack County where widower Fisher met a woman and then remarried, perhaps due to love. However, reality may have encouraged the match since he needed help in raising his two very young sons.[11] We know very little about the second Mrs. Fisher, except that her name was Minerva Coffee, and she was born about 1836 in Kentucky, the daughter of Alfred and Sarah Coffee.[12] The Coffee family moved frequently. The 1860 Karnes County, Texas census shows this family's makeup, with Jobe as thirty-three years old and Minerva, twenty-six. Census taker S. Sheppard recorded King as age seven; Jasper, six years; John, three years old; and infant Sarah, two months of age.[13] The three-year-old John was the biological son of Minerva by her first husband.

Sources indicate the Fisher family moved to central Texas and lived in several locations. Traveling directly from Collin County, they resided for a short time in adjacent Denton County before locating in Jack County and then Karnes County south of San Antonio. Jobe next moved his family up to Williamson County, about fifty miles north of the state capital, Austin in Travis County. Not many years later, King Fisher, while living in Goliad County, became friendly with numerous other young men who hailed from the Karnes-Goliad region, some of whom also contributed to the lawlessness of western Texas.

Goliad County has a fascinating history, partly because it is one of the oldest counties in the state. It was established in 1836 but not organized until the following year. One of the most tragic and atrocious events of the War of Texas Independence took place in Goliad County when the advancing Mexican army slaughtered the forces of Colonel James Fannin's command after they had surrendered.

When the Civil War came, Jobe Fisher enlisted in the Texas State Troops in October 1861 under Captain J. L. Whittenberg. He was now an infantry soldier in the 27th Brigade under General E. S. C. Roberson.[14]

It remains uncertain how long the family remained in Karnes County or when they relocated in Williamson County, but meanwhile, the head of household fought for the Stars and Bars. Regardless of where the family was, the children now were denied a father's presence and influence. Jobe Fisher's army career ended on February 1, 1864, as he was mustered out. He then returned to Florence, Williamson County, where his family anxiously waited.[15] The family apparently intended to remain there, since Jobe Fisher registered to vote on August 5, 1867. He had resided in the state for twelve months, thirty days in Williamson County and thirty days in Precinct No. 4. He gave Arkansas as his place of birth.[16] However, the family's fortunes were to change again, as Fisher did not remain long in Lampasas County. Minerva Fisher's health was failing and in Lampasas County, a two-day ride away, there were mineral springs which supposedly held medicinal waters. The Fishers traveled there in an attempt to improve her condition, but apparently the springs did not improve Minerva's health. An unidentified doctor recommended that the climate further south might be beneficial for Mrs. Fisher, so again the Fisher family packed up and moved to Goliad County. During these moves, the Fisher boys had responsibilities. In addition to personal belongings to move, there were livestock to drive, and King Fisher, now a teenaged boy and no doubt becoming an excellent horseman, was old enough to help keep the cattle together. Jobe, feeling King was associating with "bad company," then sent his son to Williamson County to avoid the negative influences of certain Goliad County residents, especially the Bruton boys. According to O. C. Fisher, during the period when Jobe was finding success with the freighting business, his second wife died, having given two children, Laura and John, to the family. Minerva Fisher passed away from an unknown disease (exactly when is uncertain, but sometime in the late 1860s). Where she is buried is also a mystery—perhaps in an unmarked grave in Goliad. Unlike today, there was no grief counseling available for the Fisher family. Jobe never remarried but did bring down his widowed mother Anna Ladd Fisher from Williamson County to help him keep house, raise the children, and perhaps provide a modicum of stability for the children while their father was away on his frequent freighting trips.

The Fisher family contributed to the importance of the town and county of Goliad. Citizens began constructing new buildings as they kept the old ones in good repair. People were soon to enjoy eight stores offering affordable goods freighted in from the seaports on the Gulf. Two blacksmith shops, two schools, two churches and another frontier necessity, two gin shops, were operating. Edward Seeligson was a prominent merchant, and he and his brother Henry A. established the first bank there which suffered a robbery in August of 1876. King Fisher, among several other individuals, would be charged with aiding and abetting the robbers, although just how he aided and abetted was never determined. Fortunately, the robbery did not end the bank's ability to continue to serve the business community and local farmers and ranchers. Farmland produced profitable crops such as corn and cotton. A variety of vegetables, including both Irish and sweet potatoes, grew all year long and quality land was still affordable for new immigrants to purchase. By 1870, Jobe Fisher had established a home for his family. In addition to raising cattle, he began a successful freighting business which moved goods from the Powder Horn depot serving the Gulf port town of Indianola in Calhoun County back to Goliad, San Antonio, and other points in central Texas. Census enumerator S. Sheppard identified Mr. Fisher as a "Stock Raiser." As his freighting business thrived, he spent longer and longer periods away from his home and family.[17]

It was sometime around 1867 in Goliad that King Fisher met a member of the prominent Vivian family. Young and pretty, eleven-year-old Sarah Elizabeth, caught the eye of thirteen-year-old King Fisher. She was destined to become King's wife. Sarah was the daughter of John Thomas and his remarkable wife Elizabeth Jane O'Neal Vivian who was born September 17, 1836. Jane's father had fought in the Battle of San Jacinto and received a league and labor of land for his service. Jane O'Neal and John T. Vivian were married in Goliad on February 12, 1857. John Vivian served in the Confederate Army and rose to the rank of corporal in Captain William M. Blair's Company D of Waller's Regiment in the Texas Cavalry. He had enlisted on April 25, 1862 in Victoria County and mustered into the service at Hempstead on May 14, 1862.[18] After the Civil War, Jane and John T. ventured into the Pendencia Creek area with their three children (they would eventually have six). John Vivian died on May 25, 1894. After his death Jane lived with daughter Sarah, the widow of King Fisher. When Texas celebrated its Centennial in 1936, Jane O'Neal Vivian celebrated her 100th birthday as well. She had lived to "witness the growth of a frontier State into a thriving empire of progress," according to a Fort Worth reporter.[19] Jane Vivian died March 20, 1937 in the home of her granddaughter Florence Fredonia Fisher Kellogg and is buried in Mount Hope Cemetery at Carrizo Springs.[20]

Another new arrival in Goliad was a man with a mouthful of a name, French Strother Grey White. As soldiers-to-be, he and John T. Vivian enlisted in the same company on the same day and remained friends throughout the war and for years afterward.[21] His well-known veterinarian skills in nursing sick and injured livestock resulted in his name being shortened to "Doc" White.[22] Though greatly separated in age, King and Doc White struck a close friendship, though it was destined to be interrupted. Doc, with his family, began to organize a wagon train of settlers in the late fall of 1867. They planned on relocating from Goliad to the wild Pendencia Creek region in Dimmit County. According to White family lore, Grey White heard how beautiful the Pendencia country was. He had heard "such glowing tales of this country, of how pretty it was, that he decided to make up a wagon train and come out here, which he did ... right after the Civil War about '69, some-where in there."[23] The Pendencia Creek was one of several creeks that had continuous fresh running water. Joining this group were many members of the large Vivian clan.[24] Besides the prominent John T. Vivian, his wife Jane and their daughter Sarah Elizabeth, there were Caroline, the widow of Lloyd Vivian, and James, William, Lafayette, Richard, and Wesley Vivian, as well as Simon Love, their ex-slave. Lafayette "Fate" Vivian would marry Alpha Idania White,[25] a sister of Doc White.[26] They too prepared to leave for the Pendencia.

Pendencia Creek, pronounced "Pendench," rises west of Carrizo Springs in northwestern Dimmit County and flows to its mouth on Comanche Creek. The Spanish word *pendencia* refers to a quarrel, fight, or brawl. First efforts to settle the land occurred before the Civil War when John Townsend, a Black man from Nacogdoches, led a number of black families there. Native Americans forced these early settlers to abandon their efforts, and, instead of returning to east Texas, they found success on the Rio Grande above Eagle Pass.[27] In 1865, Captain Levi English, a cattleman whose family modernized their name from "Inglish," led a band of fifteen families to settle on Pendencia Creek. This settlement grew, mostly due to English's leadership based upon his firsthand experience with living on the Texas frontier. Family tradition states that in his youth he lived for almost a half a year with the Comanche and later in the 1850s was effective in fighting Native Americans as the captain commanding a company of Bexar County mounted volunteers. During the Civil War, English served in the Texas State Troops as an officer in another group of mounted volunteers, this time recruited from Frio County. In a personal feud over the affections of his former wife and mother of their eleven children, Matilda Jane Burleson, the tough Levi English shot and killed Major Ross Byers with one shot to the heart. Levi and Matilda later remarried.[28]

As Doc White prepared the wagon train to leave, King approached Doc and begged to go along with the other immigrants bound for Pendencia Creek. Friendship aside, White immediately refused, considering young Fisher as lacking maturity and likely adding to his responsibility. King reluctantly remained behind while the White-Vivian wagon train moved on. Ben C. White, a son of Doc White, later explained that "King Fisher wanted to come with Dad and Dad told him he didn't want any damn kids along with him! But it got so tough out here that Dad wrote to King to come out here too. ... He was just a boy at the time so he came out and settled here and stayed with them on 'Pendench' Creek. ... Dad and Mother thought the world of King Fisher—they said he was the finest man they ever saw but he just got off on the wrong foot."[29] There were a few houses on the Pendencia: "It wasn't any village—they built little rock houses—one-room. Most of the families that came brought a little furniture from Goliad with them in wagons but they had dirt floors and their living was very primitive."[30]

Young George P. Durham, while serving as a Texas Ranger under Captain McNelly, got to know King firsthand and developed great respect for Fisher. Years later, the old ranger who adored McNelly and lived out his life on the King ranch stated to frequent coauthor Clyde Wantland: "King stayed in camp all that last night, and when they pulled off from him at daybreak, they say King had tears in his eyes and looked like he had lost his last friend."[31] No doubt King would have wanted the adventure of settling on the Pendencia, but perhaps he was already smitten with Sarah Vivian and the tears were due to her leaving. As young as they both were, to King and Sarah it probably seemed like spending forever apart, but they would not remain separated for long, for in reality it was less than a year. He knew she was with her family to the south, somewhere along the stream called the Pendencia.[32] The group arrived on the Pendencia on Christmas Day, 1867.

In response, Jobe sent King back to live with first cousins in Florence, Williamson County and attend school. It was upon his arrival that King had his first brush with the law, a matter of horse theft, something for which he would later become famous. The lack of official records makes it impossible to determine the exact date of this event. Exploring the countryside, King decided to step down from his horse to rest. The young rider foolishly failed to hobble his own mount. King's horse wandered away while he slept. Not wanting to walk while in search of his mount, he borrowed one belonging to thirty-nine-year-old Andrew Jackson Turnbow, a local farmer and rancher. When Turnbow later discovered what Fisher had done without his permission, in his initial anger he chose to file charges against King for theft. According to Fisher family lore, King "didn't take time to ask permission, since he was in a hurry and he was friendly with the Turnbows, including the two sons—Hugh and Bill. He found his wandering horse, then turned Turnbow's animal loose where he had found him without reporting to Turnbow what he had done." Within days Fisher was arrested, but before he was brought before a court, Turnbow regretted the thought of young Fisher possibly being jailed for an apparently innocent act and allowed Fisher to escape.[33]

This was probably the last time that John King Fisher was in Williamson County. He now returned to his family in Goliad after apologizing to his cousins for the embarrassment he had caused them with the incident involving Turnbow's horse. When King got to Goliad his father, grandmother, and siblings awaited. How long his father Jobe lived is unknown, but while he did Anna Ladd Fisher was there as well. When Jobe died, she went to Llano County and remained there until her death.[34]

The Turnbows had one impression of King Fisher from their experience: horse thief. Mrs. Benjamin C. White thought he was only guilty of the company he kept: later, King Fisher "was always at war with them Outlaws. He did it more for the protection of the [Pendencia] settlement than anything else but, there's no doubt, that it's a recorded fact that he got into quite a bit of trouble himself ... it's hard not to—in a country like that where the people depended on him for protection—to come up with anything that's very detrimental to his character!" King Fisher would, Mrs. White continued, "gather up a bunch of pretty tough men himself and follow them across the river at times."[35]

Soon King Fisher would find additional associates and make new friends, but, in spite of some people depending on him for protection, he again found himself in trouble with the law.

# Chapter 2

# The Walls of Huntsville

In spite of Jobe's and Anna's best intentions, teenager King Fisher did get into trouble. What drew him to burglarize a Goliad storehouse in the summer of 1870 remains a mystery, but he did, and he was arrested, jailed, and charged. He may have acted with an older man variously identified as Willis Fulcrod or Philip Fulcro.[1] The faded record from the Goliad courthouse states that King Fisher did "feloniously, fraudently, unlawfully and willfully" take items from James H. Greenly's possession.[2] Both Fisher and Fulcrod were indicted and charged with breaking into the storehouse on June 12 and again on June 19, 1870.[3] State Policeman Christopher Columbus Simmons arrested King on October 5, 1870, and Fisher was charged with "theft & robbery."[4] Fulcrod was arrested on October 10 by Simmons and charged with "assault with intent to murder."[5] Who Fulcrod may have attacked is unknown, and no details of the store burglary, nor of what evidence authorities used to determine who the guilty parties were, have been discovered. King was found guilty of stealing tobacco, candy, a knife, and a pair of pants.[6] In spite of the loss of some court documents, we are fortunate that the "Minutes of District Court Book A, October Term 1870" have survived. It shows that on October 5 the Grand Jury met and found a true bill (meaning there was sufficient evidence to establish a case) against King Fisher, case # 622, State of Texas vs King Fisher for "theft from house."[7] The record shows the following:

> The defendant in This Cause having been arrested and placed in Custody of the Sheriff came into Open Court and acknowledged himself indebted to the State of Texas, in The full sum of Five hundred dollars to be levied of his goods and Chattles, lands and Tenements, but to be void on Condition that he makes his personal appearance before the Hon District [Court] of Goliad County, now being held at the Court house, and there remain from day to day, and from term to term until discharged by due Course of law, and then and there to answer an indictment to be exhibited against him, charging him with Theft from a house, and thereupon at the same Time came into open Court Richard Vivian and Charles Bruton, sureties of the said King Fisher and severally acknowledged themselves indebted to the State of Texas, in full Sum of Two hundred and fifty dollars each, to [be] levied of their goods and chattels lands and Tenements: [sic] respectively, but to be void however on Condition that their principal the said King Fisher shall make his personal appearance before the Hon Distriact Court of the County of Goliad, now being held at the Court House there of, and There remain from day to day, and from Term to Term, until discharged by due Course of law, and there to answer an indictment to be exhibited against him charging him with Theft from a house.[8]

King Fisher was not the only one brought before Judge David D. Claiborne during that October term of District Court. Kendle Lewis and William Brooking were charged with assault to murder. William Brooking was also charged with theft and murder. Brothers Madison "Matt" and Christopher "Chris" Peace were charged with the murder of Goliad County Sheriff Andrew J. Jacobs. Jack Friar and Edward Upshur Brooking were charged with theft, and Brooking was also charged with betting at monte. Mike O'Meara and William Campbell faced the vague charge of "malicious mischief." On October 8, the sixth day of the court's meeting, a jury had been empanelled consisting of Charles Goff, foreman, and jury members Joseph Stewart, Norman Conn, Ferdinand Albrecht, Henry Shaper, John A. Middleton, George N. Spence, Harry Rouse, William R. Jones, John Thigpen, J. F. Reneau, and Michael Schewitz. They were all farmers or stock raisers. Their verdict: "We the jury find the defendant Guilty and fix his punishment at two years Confinement in the Penitentiary." King Fisher was temporaroily confined to the county jail.

On October 12, 1870 Fisher through his attorney made a motion for a new trial, which Judge Claiborne denied. He gave notice of appeal. On October 14 sentence was to be pronounced. In this case justice was swift: Sheriff Isaac Franklin was allowed three persons to act as guard while he delivered prisoners to the penitentiary in Huntsville. They were George W. Simmons, W. C. Cartwright and Colby Q. Ragland. They were to deliver Fisher and Willis Fulcrod. Fulcrod was facing a term of seven years, having been found guilty of assault with intent to kill.

The arresting officer, State Policeman Christopher Columbus Simmons, had created quite a stir in neighboring DeWitt County in late August of that same year when he and three deputies, obeying the orders of Sheriff Jack Helm, arrested four brothers with the surname Kelly. Two of the brothers, William B. who had married Elizabeth (Day) Rivers and Henry who had married Amanda Jane Taylor, were killed by a Sutton posse working *la ley de fuga*, the unwritten law which allowed prisoners to be shot if attempting to escape. In fact, as defenseless prisoners, they were gunned down by Simmons and his fellow lawmen. This was just one of many violent acts during the raging Sutton-Taylor Feud which impacted nearly everyone in the area during the 1870s. Fisher and Fulcrod may have been aware of this double killing which happened only a few miles away.

The indictments of Fisher and Fulcrod in Goliad County were among a total of seventy-six filed, an obvious result of citizens determined to drive those they deemed as undesirable from the community. King was able to make the bond of $500 thanks to Richard Vivian and Charles Bruton. On October 30, guards William C. Cartwright, George Washington Simmons, and Colby Q. Ragland delivered the pair to Huntsville. G. W. Simmons was the much younger brother of C. C. Simmons.[9] Some may have wondered if the prisoners would attempt to escape.

King Fisher became Prisoner Number 1658. His physical description indicates he was only sixteen years of age (suggesting his birth year was 1854), was five feet and nine inches tall, weighed one hundred and fifty-five pounds, had a fair complexion with dark eyes, was single, used tobacco, and was "temperate." His education was described as "common" and his occupation given as "laborer." He was recorded as being born in Texas and having in his possession $4.53. Huntsville housed nearly five hundred inmates during this time. The man who would later play a prominent role in King Fisher's life and death, gambler, gunfighter, and lawman Ben Thompson, may have been incarcerated there when Fisher arrived. It is not known if they met for the first time while in prison. Thompson was pardoned in the Fall of 1870, but the exact date of his release is not recorded in the prison's records.[10] Fulcrod was Prisoner Number 1659, described as twenty-two years of age; complexion, copper; and hair and eyes, black. He also was single, temperate, and a laborer. He had no money.[11]

Within a short time, numerous petitions were forwarded to Governor E. J. Davis requesting King Fisher be pardoned due to his youth—a lengthy process. At the same time, as the Texas Supreme Court ruled that the prosecution had proved him guilty for the felony committed on the one day, evidence was introduced for another charge committed on a different day. The injustice in the court's decision was apparent to E. H. Wheeler, the judge who stated and signed the opinion: "It may have been for the alleged theft of the nineteenth of June, or it may have been for that of the twelfth of June; or, which is more plausible, the jury may have taken both charges into an account, and have considered that one or the other was not sufficiently made out to warrant a conviction, but that both together convinced them of the guilt of the defendant; and in either case we think the verdict incorrect, and a new trial should have been granted."[12] That questionable decision, and the numerous petitions for his pardon, resulted in freedom for John King Fisher.[13] No second trial took place, but Governor Davis issued Fisher's pardon on January 26, 1871.[14] Noted attorney Trevanion Theodore Teel, who would successfully defend Fisher numerous times, stated later that Fisher "was pardoned by the governor on account of his extreme youth."[15] Fulcrod was not so fortunate, for he was sentenced to a longer term, and, not having the friends or means to appeal the verdict, he remained in prison where he died in November, 1874.[16]

Released from Huntsville after four months as Number 1658, we do not know if anyone was there to greet King Fisher at the prison gate. Huntsville and Goliad are nearly two hundred and fifty miles apart. O. C. Fisher offers no explanation as to how he returned to Goliad, writing that King Fisher "could see no future in which he considered an unfriendly community."[17] His friend Charles Bruton, who earlier helped to provide bond for Fisher, was shortly to flee Goliad County. Supposedly he was headed for Mexico, leaving his father William Wesley Bruton and family wondering what would become of him.[18] He had been indicted on June 9, 1871 for using an unrecorded brand, for violating the estray law, and worst of all for "seduction and rape." Bruton was later acquitted of all these charges.[19]

Besides feeling unwanted by the community of Goliad, King missed his friends, the White and Vivian families, who had gone to the Pendencia Creek Settlement in Dimmit County. King Fisher decided to renew his friendship with Grey "Doc" White.[20] Doc needed drovers to help with his cattle-raising and knew of King's capabilities with livestock. White's ranch was on Pania Creek near the settlement on Pendencia Creek. King, with so many friends in Dimmit County, wanted to leave Goliad County behind, and with companion Edward A. "Bud" Thompson,[21] headed to new adventures on the Pendencia. He bid adieu to his father and siblings. His little sister Delila apparently had died while he was in prison, as had stepmother Minerva Coffee Fisher. It would not be long before Jobe Fisher would pass on as well. The last known record concerning Jobe is a bill of sale he made, dated December 5, 1870, for $190. He had sold thirty-seven head of cattle to William Wesley Bruton, the father of William, Charles, and Wiley.[22]

Edward A. "Bud" Thompson remains a mysterious figure. Historian Crystal S. Williams wrote in her history of Dimmit County that Thompson had "built a house near Presidio Crossing and put in a pasture between the river and the Espantosa [lake], fencing in several sections with skeletal fences and brush. A man named MacElroy worked with Thompson and used his pasture to make up herds to take to Kansas. King Fisher came from Goliad at the same time as Thompson and the Pendencia settlers and worked with the cowmen in the area."[23]

The tiny Pania Creek settlement of Dimmit County was close to another settlement, which soon would become better known due to the presence of King Fisher and his friends and associates. Pendencia was never an actual town, but merely a group of families living along the banks of Pendencia Creek. George P. Durham, a Texas Ranger serving under Captain McNelly and later one of the managers of the huge King Ranch and who had taken part in an arrest of King Fisher, remembered fondly the early settlement. "Them four or five families moved onto Pendencia and built them thatched houses and turned their herds loose there on what, I reckon was the best range to be found on the American continent," he recalled nearly eighty years after the fact. He went on to say, "If there ever was a wilderness paradise, Pendencia must have been it. ... Anyhow, them old pioneers built their homes in a bunch; and they organized for protection, according to the law as they saw it. They elected Uncle Doc White their Justice of the Peace."[24] In 1870 Dimmit County was on the edge of the Texas frontier. The census taken that year lists a total of one hundred and eight individuals making up the county's population. To give an idea of the emptiness of their situation: their post office was located in far-off Laredo, Webb County. Among the hardy Anglo families populating Dimmit County were those of Levi English, John R. Burleson, Simpson McCoy, Silas Hay, the Bell Brothers, Grey White, and the Vivian clan. It was an unforgiving land, but Durham called it the best range to be found, having toiled as a foreman on the massive eight hundred thousand-acre King Ranch.

Sarah Vivian remembered when King Fisher arrived on Pendencia Creek. "He started in the ranching business near us and lived with my cousin," she recalled. Clearly infatuated with the handsome young cowboy, she admitted: "He would have disappointed me if he did not soon drop by our house." On her fifteenth birthday, Sarah's social life began. Described by Mary Brock as "a wide-awake young lady" who "loved to dance," Sarah later enjoyed "reliving ... the hours of her square dance, waltz, Schottische and polka. She went on horseback to the dances. The journey, if distant, began in the early afternoon and her destination was reached by dark. After a night of dancing the trip home started with daybreak and ended by noon." Sarah explained, "Many's the time I danced from sundown to sunup. … The next morning we'd horseback home in our long riding skirts, and begin work as soon as we got there."[25] Energetic, pretty, and fun-loving, it is easy to see why King Fisher, in return, became infatuated with her. Knowing the potential dangers that were not uncommon in those days, one must conclude she returned home with a group of men and family members to assure her safety.

King Fisher's name in the early 1870s would have been unrecognized outside his immediate area. Within a few years he would become notorious to many, but to others he would become a heroic figure. Frontier historian Paul S. Taylor wrote, "history and legend in Dimmit [County] combine to contribute a colorful character to the lore of the southwestern frontier in the person of King Fisher."[26] Riding through the rough mesquite and chaparral while working for Doc White, King perfected his riding skills on top of his favorite horse, "Yellow Lightnin'," and with practice he honed the art of handling a six-shooter. Youthful as he was, King became more than just another drover and began serving his neighbors living along the Pendencia, Pania, and Comanche Creeks as a range detective providing them with protection from livestock thieves. His first biographer later recalled with a touch of romanti-cism how "King broke and trained the best horses obtainable. Irrepressible, he moved about in the shadows of night, chasing Mexican bandits across the river, often retrieving stolen horses and cattle to be returned to their owners on the Pendencia. The settlers soon developed a genuine respect and admiration for the youthful cowboy."[27] All were grateful for what stock he could recover, since it was a constant complaint coming from settlers that there was no frontier protection from "Eagle Pass to the mouth of the Rio Grande [because] not a single company of United States cavalry was stationed there."[28] Shortly, in response to the call for protection, the government staffed Fort Duncan in Eagle Pass and Fort McIntosh at Laredo.

Many exciting episodes in the life and career of King Fisher remain only tantalizing stories told and retold without any contemporary record to verify when and if they actually occurred. One such incident involved Joel Clinton Fenley, his son George W., and King Fisher, and perhaps took place in Zavala County in 1871. O. C. Fisher tells the following story as true.[29] In a remote part of Zavala County, King encountered a group of Mexican *vaqueros* with a herd of stolen cattle headed for the Rio Grande. Rather than challenging the group alone, Fisher fortunately met up with Joel Fenley and his son George who by sheer chance were also on the trail of the same stolen cattle. The trio believed that together they could recover the stolen property. Amazingly the three overtook the *vaqueros* and the stolen herd about noon and, after cautiously riding into their camp, Joel Fenley with King Fisher demanded to be allowed to "inspect" the herd. Son George Fenley remained close by with his Winchester across the saddle, his armed presence apparently sufficient persuasion to allow the herd to be inspected. The result was that Fisher and Fenley were allowed to cut out the cattle bearing their brands and then the trio returned home, leaving the *vaqueros* to continue on their way.[30]

Thus is the incident recorded by O. C. Fisher and J. C. Dykes. The authors place it as happening about 1871. Something similar to this may have happened, but if son George W. Fenley was involved, it was a most unusual happening, even in south Texas. At that time young George, born December 2, 1866, would have been only four, or possibly five, years of age.[31] No responsible father would take along so young a child on a hunt to recover stolen cattle. Quite possibly O. C. Fisher was mistaken as to when this event took place. If it happened closer to 1878 or 1879, when George was closer to being a teenager, then he could have handled a Winchester, or held one "across the saddle."[32]

A variation of this story was recorded by Frank L. Hobart during his research into the life of King Fisher. Hobart conducted an interview with Joel C. Fenley's son Guy. According to this version, Joel Fenley had large ranch holdings and ran many head of cattle on his land. Cattle rustling was a common occurrence in those days ... and on one occasion after a large number of his cattle had been drivn off by stock thieves, Mr. Fenley started out horseback alone to track down and if possible recover the stolen animals. ... Somewhere out in the brush, Mr. Fenley met up with John King Fisher. ... At the time Mr. Fenley met Fisher, he was also on the trail of the same bunch of stock thieves who had come up through the country from the South of the Border. As they moved to the north, they picked up cattle at every opportunity and threw them into their growing herd of stolen stock. The cattle would be sold at Fort Clark or points on north.

Guy Fenley further stated that "it was a common practice for victims of rustlers to each pitch in $50.00, a hundred or whatever each of them could afford, depending on how many head he'd lost … into a 'pot' that would sometimes amount to 3 or 4 hundred dollars and King Fisher would take the trail and recover these rancher's cattle from the thieves." It was on such a mission that day that Fisher and Joel C. Fenley met. The two hunters continued on the trail of the rustlers and finally overtook them in the rough canyon country of the Anacacho Mountain range in Kinney County. The men they were hunting looked rough and were "captained" by an even "rougher-looking" outlaw. King Fisher rode directly up to the "boss rustler" and made his identity known. He stated he intended to "cut the herd" for the brands which he had been employed to recover. The rustler chief was well aware of Fisher's reputation and immediately agreed to let him and Mr. Fenley cut out all the cattle in the brands that Fisher named. When Fisher was through recovering those cattle with the brands he was seeking, he informed the rustler chief that he was done and that they would leave the rustlers to do what they wished with the remaining cattle.[33]

An additional note to this account enforces the idea that King Fisher was a valuable man to have as a friend. Joel told his son Guy "that he considered King Fisher a brave man and a true Friend. He stated that King Fisher would 'rob a robber' but that he would never rob an honest man nor a poor man. It seems that King Fisher was a frequent visitor at the Murlo [sic] Settlement while on his way from Eagle Pass to Uvalde or vice versa. Joel Fenley said that King Fisher was a fearless Peace Officer, respected and well-liked by all who knew him!" In 1880, according to the Maverick County census, the settlement mentioned was known as "La Muela" and was made up of forty-nine inhabitants, including the Joel C. Fenley family.[34]

Like most Texans who were described as desperadoes, legend claims that they killed a man early in their lawless career. For King Fisher it was supposed to have happened when he was but sixteen years of age. However, no known record exists that he killed anyone then. One intriguing incident, which has become legendary, is that King Fisher and noted newspaperman Horace Greeley met and visited briefly as the newspaper man was traveling through Texas. The story goes that King Fisher was the man who was presented to Horace Greeley in 1870 or 1871, when the venerable editor was in Brenham for the purpose of delivering an address before the Agricultural Society. Mr. Greeley had expressed a desire to see a typical Texas desperado, and Fisher good-humoredly posed before him in this character. Mr. Greeley looked at him searchingly, and said he did not like to ask an improper question, but he would really like to know how many men Fisher had killed.[35]

This may have started the rumor that King Fisher had indeed killed a man when he was still a teenager, following in the footsteps of Texas killers like John Wesley Hardin or William Preston Longley. A search of Washington County, Texas newspapers failed to provide any information as to a possible visit by King Fisher to Brenham at any time in his life. However, the idea that Fisher had, like Hardin and Longley, killed a man while still a teenager remained. A. H. Gregory submitted an article for the *Texas Argus* of San Antonio in which he clearly states: "When he killed his first man down in Goliad County, back in 1873, he was then 16 years of age, but showed that same meticulous care and precision that was to mark his life for the next few years." Gregory does not offer an explanation as to how the "meticulous care and precision" had any bearing in this 1873 killing, nor does he give any evidence of who was killed "back in 1873." Finding no reference to an 1873 killing by King Fisher we reject his claim.[36]

The decade of the 1870s was the period of the great cattle drives to the railheads in Kansas, and although it is certain that King Fisher was involved in the movement of the thousands upon thousands of longhorns, details of his involvement are again lacking. Among the famous shipping points from Kansas to the eastern cities were Abilene, Ellsworth, Wichita, and Dodge City. Once the herd had been sold in one of these towns, the cowboy did not have to return home immediately, but could venture out on his own. King Fisher likely did just that, going to Lawrence in eastern Kansas, since his name appears in a list of letters waiting to be picked up at the Lawrence post office. His name appears "Fisher, King" following the Lawrence, Kansas *Tribune's* heading, which reads: "The following is a List of Letters remaining uncalled for at Lawrence, Kansas Territory, for the week ending Wednesday,

November 20, 1872." The names of the ladies appear first, and then the list continues with the names of the gentlemen.

An additional bit of evidence of Fisher going up the trail to Kansas must not be ignored. During the declining years of Wyatt Earp, the old lawman yearned to have his life story in print.[37] Journalist Stuart N. Lake found him and they created a biography which became a best-selling book, printed in many editions and still easily available. Although not accepted as a quality biography today, due to containing much created conversation and lacking supportive endnotes, it continues to be valuable. When describing the period when Earp was a lawman in the state of Kansas, Lake includes a list of well-known (and not so well-known) frontier figures. Lake provides the following for later historians to ponder, naming "a partial roster of gunmen who made headquarters in Dodge during the summer of '77. Among them were … Cal Polk … King Fisher, and John Culp, professional fighting men for the great cattle outfits."[38] We have omitted the names of numerous individuals listed on this roster who had an association with Billy the Kid and Pat Garrett. The name of Cal Polk is included perhaps to give some taste of verity to Lake's list, as Polk is known to have helped track the desperado Billy the Kid as well as driving cattle. Lake includes the names of King Fisher and Fisher's friend, John Culp, perhaps because Lake is aware of the photograph of the two of them together. No other historian of the Old West has ever suggested John Culp was among the "professional fighting men for the great cattle outfits." King Fisher could only be considered a professional fighting man in the broadest sense of the term. Although at times considered a rustler, he was known to fight for his own property as well as that of his friends, but did that make him a professional fighting man? A gunfighter or a gunslinger? In truth we can only wish that there was a complete roster of cowboys who trailed herds to the northern markets in the 1870s, but there is not. Perhaps Lake merely threw together a bunch of recognizable names for dramatic effect.

Not only was the period of the 1870s the time of the great cattle drives to Kansas, it was also when raiding parties of fierce Lipan Apache, Comanche, and Kickapoo warriors were still eager to go on the warpath, either for plunder, captives, or scalps. Newspapers such as the *Daily Express* and the *Daily Herald* of San Antonio frequently carried reports of attacks on south Texas towns and ranches. Colonel Ranald S. "Bad Hand" Mackenzie of the 4th Cavalry reported to General C. C. Augur that in mid-July 1873 a band of Lipans with some Mexicans had actually camped within two or three miles of San Antonio and had gone into the town and bought ammunition. He did not speculate as to what the ammunition was for and why a merchant of San Antonio would provide it to a potential enemy.[39] Only days later a J. H. Hicklin of Nuecesville, Uvalde County described in a letter to the *Daily Herald* that some "red fiends" were still "doing their nefarious work of carnage and stealing." He claimed that on July 23 thirty of them went down the Nueces Canyon and attacked a rancher identified only as Mr. Wells, killing him. He left "a widow with a large family to mourn his loss." On July 21 the town of Frio City was "invaded ... by the largest and most daring party of Indians ever known in this Western country."[40] Also according to this letter, the party numbered between thirty-five and forty and captured three horses before attacking a pair of Mexicans, wounding one as they attempted to escape. Apparently, a Captain Massey was murdered in his home, but the rest of the family managed to reach safety by escaping across the Frio River. The author of the letter writes that, after some time, the settlers were able to raise the alarm and, with some citizens and soldiers, began a pursuit. The party reached within rifle range and fired upon the fleeing Indians, but no skirmish occurred. Blood found on the trail indicated a few of the shots were effective.[41] Similar raids were reported as frequently happening in the Nueces Strip.[42]

Circuit-riding preacher Andrew Jackson Potter was at Frio City then and witnessed how fearful those settlers were. He also reported on the terror occurring all around him. Potter concluded his report to the *Daily Herald*'s editor by stating that the "most intense excitement prevails among the suffering people of this community. They are leaving their homes and crops exposed, and rushing into this place from almost every direction. Ten families came in on last Saturday night, and others are expected today."[43] Potter later gained fame as a "Fighting Parson," fearlessly preaching the Gospel in the frontier communities.

It is certain that during this time King became a cowboy in the modern sense and on this basis would someday become a rancher. In the eyes of many of his contemporaries, the term "cow boy"—usually spelled in two words—was synonymous with the term "rustler" or, more broadly, a thief. As described in chapter 1, King's first run-in with the law over a horse had been in Williamson County beginning in late 1867, but he may have had an additional scrape with the law in neighboring Coryell County. In October 1872, an individual using the name of King Fisher was wanted there for "theft of a gelding." This bit of information is recorded in the listing of fugitives printed in 1878 for the benefit of sheriffs and Texas Rangers, but no further details have been uncovered and it appears he never faced a judge and jury in Coryell County.[44] A thief may have been using the name of King Fisher as an alias, as did many individuals.

If King Fisher was starting to throw a long rope, he had little to fear from the legal system in 1872. Dimmit County was well below the Nueces River, where law enforcement was almost nonexistent, and the county court system of the 24th District, which was attached to Maverick County for judicial purposes, was ineffective. In March, where the spring court session was to take place, the county clerk noted how the prosecutor, Thomas M. Paschal, was absent because of illness and that, because of this, no court proceedings could be held. District Attorney Paschal would eventually play several roles in King Fisher's future legal troubles, serving as one of his defense counsels and later as the judge in charge of one of King's murder trials. In July, both the prosecutor and judge failed to appear. Judge J. J. Thornton carried a reputation as a fine jurist. However, once again court could not be held and was adjourned without doing any business. During the November session, Thornton was absent a second time due to health issues. In his stead Judge George H. Noonan of the 23rd Judicial Distrct traveled to Maverick County and managed to empanel a grand jury. This body included the friends and future in-laws of King Fisher.[45] Not surprisingly, there is no mention of Fisher in the court records for the entire year of 1872. His luck in avoiding the legal system could not possibly last forever.

# Chapter 3

# Gathering at
# *El Paso del Aguila*

Cortina and his followers caused at least part of the Mexican-Texan border problems of the 1870s, as he had for some years before and would continue to do for years after. Although the Rio Grande was officially the border between Mexico and the U.S., whoever wished to ignore it could easily do so. The long twisting river literally had a thousand places which were easily crossed. For example, a Texan could commit an illegal act and, if fearful of arrest or getting caught by a mob, could choose to cross the river and be relatively safe from pursuit. Likewise, if a Mexican wished to obtain cattle or horses from Texas illegally, a swift raid with some daring companions could easily be accomplished.

United States authorities were prohibited by law from crossing the river to recover stolen livestock. Anglo desperadoes knew this; *bandidos* from south of the Rio Bravo knew this; Kickapoo, Comanche, and Apache warriors, as well as those of other tribes, knew this too.[1]

It was a dangerous time and place for any individual, especially for a settler trying to make an honest living raising cattle, sheep, or horses. Livestock became a popular target of theft, not only to drive to a market but to slaughter and then sell the hides. Texans and Mexicans were both accused of skinning the cattle of the other. By early January 1873, skinning was recognized as a regular and very profitable business. This was becoming more and more a concern for stockmen in the coastal region. The *Corpus Christi Gazette* reported that the stockmen were "desirous of having a finger in the pie themselves, and are scouring the country in their own interests."[2] Nature was also a contributing factor, as the *Indianola Bulletin* reported that "the late severity of the weather has resulted fatally to the stock on the prairies. Cattle are dying fast, and many persons are engaged in skinning the hides from the dead animals."[3]

Raising livestock and driving herds to market could be a profitable business, but as the correspondent identified as "Seventy-Six" reported, writing a lengthy letter from Brownsville, "[the] skinning of dead cattle has become a business." Seventy-Six continued, claiming that there were *several thousand* head of cattle roaming between the Rio Bravo or Rio Grande and the Nueces Rivers. Many had died due to the weather, and now there were "hundreds of men roaming the country in search of carcasses in order to take off hides. They skin cattle belonging to their neighbors also." To convey the idea of the vastness of the business, Seventy-Six concluded that the "hide and cattle trade of Texas covers millions of dollars per year. This branch of business has received serious drawbacks for many years by interruptions and robberies committed by armed bands of Mexicans and Indians."[4]

Fisher became a sort of "range detective" working for Doc White.[5] Thus, he had free rein of the territory, beyond the borders of Dimmit County. In so doing, he became familiar with the neighboring counties—Zavala and Maverick, especially—and the men who worked there. As we will see, King was developing some bad habits, or at least was accused of unacceptable behaviors. Naturally, working for White would not have been as satisfactory for King as the idea of having his own ranch. With thousands of cattle roaming the Nueces Strip, gathering a herd would not have been difficult. If he could acquire his own ranch (King may have thought), men could work for him, have a place to stay, rest, and even avoid the law if necessary. Indeed, some nefarious individuals took advantage of the opportunity to lay low on Fisher's ranch. King may have known he was harboring criminals, and he may have even felt a desire to help out a wanted man, since it was not so long ago that he was an inmate of Huntsville prison experiencing the other side of the law-and-order coin.

On March 3, 1873 Judge J. J. Thornton was again well enough to serve, and with a new 24th District Attorney, A. A. Dial,[6] court was reopened and business conducted. The summer session found the court closed again, and no trials took place. On December 1, the court convened again, but there was no mention of King Fisher. However, during the next decade Fisher would deal with the court system again and again, spending time in jails waiting to face a jury of his peers.

Barely stepping out of his teenage years, King Fisher seemed to attract both good men and bad to be his companions. Both Anglo and Mexican could easily become his friends. To all he revealed his natural charisma, inherent charm, and leadership skills. "The [King Fisher] ranch," according to O. C. Fisher, "became a sort of headquarters for renegades and thieves. Many were fugitives wanted for various crimes, and 'on the dodge' as it was called in those days. Fisher treated them well, never turned them in, and gave them employment, perhaps often of a dubious nature. Gradually a sizeable gang was formed, all loyal to the King, and always available at his beck and call."[7] Certainly the image of a young man characterized as likeable to desperadoes as well as law-abiding citizens was emerging. It was a fascinating personality which appealed to all sorts of men—and women.

Suffering from illness for most of the past two years, February 12, 1874 Judge J. J. Thornton was finally deemed unfit to hold the office. His mental faculties had reached such a low point that the newspapers callously reported he was suffering from "mental imbecility."[8] Later in the spring, the court was once again not in session. In response, the Texas legislature acted with Governor Richard Coke and replaced Thornton with Captain James A. Ware. The editor of a Dallas newspaper said that he knew Ware, describing him as "a good lawyer, a man of strict integrity, and has been tried in the crucible which detects the true metal."[9] This announcement came on April 3, 1874. The news of the legal system changing judges certainly reached authorities in the Nueces Strip counties. In a more dramatic move, less than a month later, the governor selected John B. Jones of Corsicana as Major of the newly formed Frontier Battalion. An adjunct to this group was that of Leander H. McNelly, captain of the Washington County Volunteer Militia Company A, although those men were thought of as Texas Rangers no different than those serving under Major Jones. They all had the same general orders: to curb the lawlessness on the Texas frontier. On August 3, 1874 the 24th District Court was officially reopened, although it conducted very little business.[10]

The danger that was seemingly omnipresent during these years along the border cannot be overstated. A casual reading of the contemporaneous press suggests that an attack by white, red, or brown men, or any combination thereof, could occur at any moment. News reached San Antonio about a "horrible Indian outrage" committed at Frio City. The "red devils" had invaded Frio City on July 21 and killed Mr. Massey, "an old and respected citizen, near his own house, and destroyed his household furniture."[11] Citizens believed the raiding party was composed of Lipans, Mescalero Apaches, and Mexicans.[12] A later report stated that this party numbered about thirty-five or forty, stealing horses and murdering. After destroying nearly everything Old Man Massey had, they rushed to within a half mile of the town to plunder more. At the house of a Mr. Graham, a Mexican gave the alarm and some citizens gathered to respond to the raiders. As discussed in chapter 2, the pursuers did some damage, as when they returned to Frio City they reported losing sight of the raiders on the Leona River, although there were signs of blood on the trail.[13] Although warriors from the various tribes frequently received the blame for many atrocities which they had not committed, white men frequently paid the price for violating the eighth commandment. In mid-August, thieves stole some fifteen or twenty head of horses from various ranchers and then crossed into Mexico above Eagle Pass. A Mr. Sovereign gathered some armed friends and by riding hard the posse chased the rustlers almost forty miles deep into Mexico. Near the town of Zaragosa, Coahuila, they overtook the thieves. The three horse thieves—Americans—were no match for Sovereign and his party, and they were "sent to the happy hunting grounds" as the newspaper callously reported their violent demise. The dispatched horse thieves were identified as John Eastland, Rufus James, and one other, name unknown. Sovereign returned with the recovered horses.[14]

Occasionally the specific whereabouts of King Fisher during these turbulent times is next to impossible to determine. At times a report will suggest he was far from the Nueces Strip, causing us to wonder if someone else was using his name. In the Texas State Archives is a fascinating ledger entitled "Record of Criminals by Co[unty] Crimes, Description," which was the result of county sheriffs sending the names of wanted fugitives from their county to the Adjutant General. Occasionally the date of the crime is listed, as well as the date of indictment. The sheriff of Falls County, W. G. Etheridge, sent in a list of fugitives including the name of King Fisher, charged with "Assault to Murder" committed on September 10, 1874 and indicted September 22, 1874. A description is provided: "Light complexion, dark hair, 5 ft 7 or 8 inches tall, 24 or 25 years of age." The description doesn't fit John King Fisher exactly, but it could very well have been him. On the other hand, Marlin, the county seat of Falls County, is some 300 miles from Dimmit County, King Fisher's range. Although King Fisher could easily have joined a trail drive and stopped in Falls County during the return to Texas, conceivably some other character was using the catchy name of "King" Fisher.[15]

A few looked upon the land as an honest opportunity. In the late fall of 1874, a newspaper informed its readers how George Kerfoot Chinn, a Kentuckian who would join up with Captain Pat Dolan and Company F of the Frontier Battalion within a few years, was looking to purchase land to raise sheep. A later report stressed how healthy the country was for sheep raising, stating that the country about Eagle Pass was considered "to be the finest sheep grazing country in Texas, and the flocks are doing well. The sheep business seems to be fast superseding the cattle business, and experience has proved that it is much more profitable."[16] Chinn would be successful in locating his sheep ranch and later became a good friend of King Fisher.

Perhaps John King Fisher, who as yet at this time had no statewide reputation, kept informed of what was happening in Goliad County. It is doubtful that he ever considered going back to where he had spent some of his early years, but if he read the Galveston newspaper, which regularly carried news of many other counties, he certainly realized it was a different place than when he had lived there. According to one correspondent whose lengthy letter was printed in late November, new buildings were going up, while the old ones are kept in good repair. Everything in and around Goliad has a look of health, peace and prosperity. Every person seems to be perfectly satisfied with the past season. ... Money is more plentiful in Goliad at this time, than I have seen in any town west of here. Most of the stock men of this county, who have been to Kansas with cattle, have returned. They have realized good prices for the stock they drove there, and now they are settling up accounts, and they are putting a large amount of money in circulation.[17] The remainder read like a flyer prepared by the local Chamber of Commerce, if there had been such an institution there in 1874.

When the 24th District Court opened at Eagle Pass, seat of Maverick County, on December 7, 1874, among the grand jury members were none other than a young King Fisher, along with several of his friends: P. B. Vivian, Lafayette Vivian, John T. Vivian (his future father-in-law), and Charles Vivian. Only four indictments were handed out.[18] This claim by O. C. Fisher remains undated, but King Fisher would become familiar with the court system at Eagle Pass. And *El Paso del Aguila*, today Eagle Pass, would become very familiar with King Fisher and his associates.

The federal government had established Fort Duncan in 1846 at the start of the Mexican War, along with several other posts. After guarding the boundary and protecting settlers and travelers, the post was abandoned in 1859, mainly due to Juan Cortina's many raids in south Texas. It was held by Confederates during the war and then again garrisoned by federal troops afterwards. In 1870 a group of Black Seminoles were stationed there as scouts and guides. Today the old headquarters building serves as a museum.[19] Much is unknown regarding the settlement of Eagle Pass and its relationship to the buildings of Fort Duncan in the early 1870s, but apparently followers of King Fisher and he himself occasionally made little distinction between the military grounds and the town limits of Eagle Pass. Historian Ben E. Pingenot wrote that, "[f]ollowing the war years, bands of cattle thieves and fugitives led by John King Fisher dominated Eagle Pass through the 1870s, notwithstanding the multiple interventions of the Texas Rangers."[20] During the 1870s the population of Eagle Pass never exceeded one thousand and five hundred and was made up of Americans, Germans, and, principally, Mexicans.

The chief occupations of the working class were stock raising and mercantile business—and, of course, saloons. James Vivian, King's future uncle-in-law, owned the Old Blue Saloon, which King Fisher and his companions used as a hangout when visiting Eagle Pass. The town is on the east bank of the Rio Grande, and on the other side is the Mexican city of Piedras Negras.[21] The ever-changing political and military environment of this important point on the border would often send people scrambling for safety between these two towns.

Young and reckless cowboys like King Fisher were not the only ones who might suffer from the dangers of the wild country in the seventies. Even settlers with established ranches were in danger of attack by marauders. An unidentified band of Indians moving through Dimmit County came upon and attacked John T. Vivian on February 16, 1875 as he approached his home on the Pendencia. Vivian successfully fought off his attackers. He was lucky, as he was only slightly wounded instead of being killed and scalped. It was dangerous to be found alone in that country.

Most ranchers in south Texas realized they could not fight the *banditti* alone. They wanted United States troops to patrol the dangerous area and requested such aid from Adjutant General William Steele in Austin. Steele inquired of Secretary of War William Worth Belknap for the requested aid but received a negative reply. A news report quoted Steele's request of April 9, 1875 as follows:

> Calls from the Rio Grande border on the Executive of this State for protection from bands of robbers making incursions from foreign soil, have become so urgent that three companies of rangers have been sent to their assistance, making a force of six companies now in the service of the State for protection from incursions from beyond the jurisdiction of State authorities. This throws upon the State a burden that does not properly belong to it, but which you probably have no appropriation to cover. But it occurs to me that the expense might be lessened to the State if you would authorize the issuance of supplies from the military posts on the frontier line.[22]

Steele was not asking for additional manpower but simply "supplies," food for the men and forage for the animals. However, W. W. Belknap's reply was quick and brief: "I beg to acknowledge the receipt of your communication ... asking that the State troops serving on the Rio Grande be furnished with necessary rations, forage, ammunition and medical attendance by the military posts ... there is no authority in the war department to comply with your request."[23] *No authority.* So those ranchers and settlers suffering from raiders from within and without the state would have to deal with the problem on their own. The leading ranchers in the state were Mifflin Kenedy and Richard King who were suffering from stock thieves like everyone else. Captain King was not about to surrender to raiders and would survive on his own. He chose to ignore the soldiers at the far-flung military posts as well as General Belknap, believing he could protect himself and his property with his newly purchased weaponry. In April, he purchased four pieces of artillery, described as "brass, iron carriages. Two of them are twelve-pounders, rifled boat howitzers; two of them twelve-pounder howitzers, smooth bore. He will have on hand soon all the ammunition, etc., necessary for service." If anyone wondered where this artillery would be located, the reporter made it clear: "It is expected that he will take them to his rancho of Santa Gertrudes."[24]

That very month two droves of stolen cattle were crossed over into Mexico about fifty miles above Brownsville, Cameron County. The cattle bore the brand of not only Richard King (the "Running W") but also of ranchers Rabb, Hale, Parker, McAllen, and others. The three hundred head of cattle were driven by two parties of armed Mexicans: one a party of ten and the other, of twenty. In the same issue, the public learned that it was not only Richard King ready to defend his property, but also a Captain Foster who had arrived at Corpus Christi, bringing with him four boxes of arms and seven cases of ammunition.[25] Apparently, he was preparing to have his own little army to defend himself.

The situation was ripe for a bloody confrontation between ranchers and rustlers. Additional news from Brownsville reported that cattle stealing was going on, with droves "crossed into Mexico almost daily above here. The parties ... operate in the daytime and feel secure."[26]

The best news for those settlers living in the dangerous Nueces Strip was learning that Captain McNelly would soon be coming. In April 1875 it was rumored that McNelly was to raise a volunteer company to protect citizens along the border. The editor of the Brenham newspaper knew McNelly personally (McNelly's home plantation was at Burton, near Brenham) and the editor continued his report: "Mc. is a good commander and we promise all those anxious young men who wish to exhibit their patriotism, and are really spoiling for a fight to enlist under the Captain; they will undoubtedly get a chance to show their pluck if they but follow him. We have tried him and know whereof we speak."[27]

So, in 1875, the setting on the border was reputed to include organized rustlers from Mexico led by Juan Cortina, considered the chieftain of all the hundreds of thieves and protected by the Mexican authorities, facing the Texas Ranger Captain Leander H. McNelly with at most thirty men, whose orders were to quell the lawlessness. McNelly was certainly in the right place at the right time. Aware of the tuberculosis which would take his life sooner or later, he may have lived out a death wish on the border, treading where angels feared to go. And with his Civil War record unblemished, maintaining the respect of all while a captain of the Texas State Police, he had become a hero to most Texans, even those who walked the fine line between good and evil. One editor announced the rumor that McNelly was in the process of raising a "volunteer company" to operate against cattle thieves in the Nueces Strip.[28] This proved to be not a rumor but a fact. After enshrining his name in Texas glory on the deep southern border land, McNelly would focus his efforts on capturing others ... including John King Fisher. As mentioned, at this time Fisher was a youthful leader of men, ranching on the Pendencia and apparently not too curious or concerned about the background of the men who became his followers or took advantage of his hospitality. In some ways Captain McNelly was similar to Fisher, as they both were fearless, courageous, and reckless. In November of that year, McNelly had made the daring move of crossing the Rio Grande to recover cattle stolen from various ranchers, including Captain Richard King. This invasion of Mexico was considered an act of war by Mexican officials, but McNelly did force Mexican authorities to return a portion of the stolen cattle. Mexico could claim a pallid victory by returning only a pittance of the stolen cattle. However, McNelly could find satisfaction in having invaded Mexico, recovered some stolen cattle, and lived to tell about it.

With another new judge placed on the bench of the 24th District, the legal machinery was beginning to work against King Fisher. On May 3, 1875 Judge Edward Dougherty in Maverick County handed down an indictment charging Fisher and James Vivian, Fisher's future uncle-in-law, with having jointly committed an assault to murder against a man named George Washington, a Black Seminole scout working at Fort Clark.[29] The U.S. Army had discovered the Seminole scouts were excellent trackers and used them extensively to assist in dealing with renegades from northern Mexico and south Texas.[30] Despite the respect the scouts had earned from their military service, occasionally there were brawls between them and white civilians. The Seminole scouts and other black troopers stationed there were known to fire themselves up with whiskey and shoot off their pistols. "Especially was it lively after dark," commented one report, "when stragglers from the immortal Ninth Cavalry were allowed to come over from the fort, imbibe mean whisky and shoot off their pistols at pleasure, with no one to molest them or make them afraid."[31]

One such example of riotous behavior involved King Fisher and James Vivian. Few details of this brawl have been uncovered as to how this clash started, other than that it happened in Vivian's "Old Blue Saloon" in Eagle Pass. Fisher and Vivian were charged with assault to kill, the victim being Seminole scout George Washington. Judge W. A. Bonnet recalled the incident many years later. Washington ordered a drink and when asked to pay, "became insulted and someone began shooting. When it was all over King Fisher had a scalp wound and the Seminole was wounded in the stomach." This is how Judge Bonnet too briefly described the incident. Bonnet did not give a date for the clash, nor does he say Washington died from the wound, but noted that Fisher was indicted but came clear of the charge.[32] Sureties for Fisher were Doc White, C. N. Vivian, J. S. Vivian, and W. C. Bruton.[33]

John Creaton, an Eagle Pass resident, also wrote his memoirs years later. At one point he informs the reader that he was writing on March 17, 1931 and had begun writing in 1929, suggesting he had worked on his autobiography off and on over the course of several years. Acknowledging that the passage of time during those many years may have clouded his memory of the observed event, Creaton claims to have been a witness to the Fisher-Washington shooting, so we do not ignore his account.[34] He does not give a date for this incident but writes as if he was well acquainted with Fisher. Creaton was across the street from a saloon in Eagle Pass in which King Fisher and an unidentified Seminole scout were drinking. Apparently an argument began inside the saloon, and the scout exited in a hurry and "with a running jump and grabbing the horse's tail the scout mounted his horse from behind and then whirling the horse he struck at Fisher with his quirt, the only weapon he had. Fisher dodged the blow and shot and killed him."[35] Although Creaton claims to have been an eyewitness to the incident outside the saloon, he does not identify the scout who he claims Fisher killed, nor does he mention the saloon by name. He does comment that he never knew of the case going to trial.

Another source provides some additional information on the Washington incident. This is from an undated but lengthy article entitled "Centennial Recalls Mav.[erick] County History" and subtitled "Eagle Pass 100 Years Ago – Saloons – Society – and Revolution." This article gives the date as about Christmas, 1874, when King Fisher and some of his "gang had an encounter with some of the Seminole-Negro Scouts in the Blue Goose Saloon." There was a gun battle "in which Fisher narrowly escaped death from a bullet that creased his scalp." According to witnesses, Corporal George Washington "fled from the saloon with Fisher in hot pursuit. Washington grabbed his horse's tail and with a running jump mounted from behind. Quickly whirling his horse around, he struck at Fisher with his quirt, the only weapon he had. Fisher dodged the blow and fired his pistol into the scout's stomach." Although the author does not give an indication of how long Washington survived, the report closes the incident by explaining that he was taken to the post hospital where he eventually died "after lingering for months." No charges were ever brought against Fisher for this incident, reportedly.[36]

But the question remains: was Washington killed by King Fisher or merely wounded? Creaton may have witnessed the brawl but only assumed that Washington did not survive. Research by historian Larry G. Shaver discovered information Creaton did not know. Washington had enlisted as a private in August 1870 and served until May 1, 1873, when he was honorably discharged. He reenlisted on January 1, 1874 and was given the rank of corporal. His name appears on the bimonthly muster rolls during 1874 through October 31, but the name is missing from the December 31 listing.[37]

In March 1875, Lieutenant Alfred C. Markley conducted a census of all the Black Seminoles at Fort Duncan, and Washington is shown to be alive, but not necessarily well. The muster shows Washington, his wife Tina, and their six children, but by Washington's name Markley noted "in hospital, probably fatally wounded."[38] Another census taken on May 9 shows that Washington was still in the hospital, in which again the notation "very dangerous gunshot wound" appears.[39] District Court met on May 3, and the grand jury found an indictment against King Fisher and James Vivian for assault to murder George Washington. Both Fisher and Vivian made bond, paid for by W. T. Bruton and John H. Slaughter. Vivian was named, no doubt, because the incident happened in his saloon, but he was not vigorously prosecuted. When the court met in September King Fisher failed to appear and his $500 bond was forfeited. A *capias* for his arrest was issued and sent to both Goliad and Bexar Counties.[40] King Fisher now became a wanted fugitive. During the summer of 1875, George Washington expired, having lingered near death for those many months.

So, regarding the death of Washington, apparently caused by the gunshot wound inflicted by King Fisher during the course of a saloon brawl, what would a Maverick County jury determine? A report prepared by the prosecuting attorney provides the answer: Winchester Kelso, appointed to prosecute J.K. Fisher on behalf of the state, said that he would no longer prosecute for the following reasons: To wit: Because all the papers in the case including the indictment have been lost, misplaced or taken from the courthouse and cannot be found: that no data is obtainable with which to substitute an indictment and no witnesses can be found at present to obtain an indictment and the party alleged to have been assaulted has departed this life, and without his testimony no new indictment can be found, Wherefore it is ordered, adjudged and considered by the court that this cause be and is hereby dismissed.[41] Judge Kelso was no sickly judge who should not have been on the bench. Rather, he was a young and ambitious man who knew the area and the people. He was born in 1858 in DeWitt County, admitted to practice law and was elected county attorney of Maverick County before he was twenty-one years of age. His entire life was spent in the border counties, and early in his career he was recognized as an American authority on Mexican laws and judicial procedures.[42] He had been appointed by the governor to prosecute the case, as both the district attorney and the county attorney had been disqualified. It was fortunate for King Fisher, for one can only wonder what happened to those important legal papers. It is possible one of those papers was a death-bed statement made by Washington, giving a version of what had happened that would have worked against King Fisher. We will never know.

In June 1875, King Fisher entered the Bexar County jail for a different reason. Thirty-seven-year-old Deputy Sheriff Thomas Dashiell, accompanied by a citizen named Perrin, made the arrest based upon an affidavit provided by a young Hispanic man named Alejo Gonzales claiming Fisher had stolen cattle from him.[43] Raised in San Antonio, Gonzales was well known there. Texas newspaper editors of the time described Gonzales as "a bold, fearless man and [who] had plenty of the old Spanish grit" and as "a driving, energetic live businessman" currently operating "quite a large mercantile business in Piedras Negras."[44] Released under bond, King Fisher promptly forgot about his obligation to appear in court, left San Antonio, forfeited his bond, and never returned to answer the charge against him. The incident began a brew of bad blood between Gonzales and Fisher that would reach a climax one year later.

On June 25 Fisher was charged with another misdeed: illegally driving another man's two hundred head of cattle without written authorization and the livestock not having been inspected. He was ordered to report in person to the court on July 22. Fisher ignored the court order and failed to appear to answer this new charge as well.[45]

A curious item appeared in a San Antonio newspaper in late July of 1875, suggesting that perhaps editors during the approach of the country's centennial year were not above creating titillating news: "No doubt but six horse thieves, (among them King Fisher, recently released from our jail on bond) were hung near Hays [C]ounty, on one tree. The fact that the hanging was all on one tree, goes to show that tree planting should receive more attention than it does. Suppose there hadn't been any tree there? Horrible!"[46] One might suspect that the entire news item was a creation of someone in the *Herald* office. It is certain that King Fisher was not hung and doubtful that six horse thieves were hung together as, if true, there would have been reports in other journals. Further questions include: just where is "near Hays," as five counties surround it? Hays County is bordered on the north by Travis, on the east by Caldwell, on the south by Guadalupe, on the west by Comal, and on the northwest by Blanco. An irate mob may have lynched a man using the borrowed name of Fisher as his alias, but just one individual getting lynched was not always considered newsworthy.

The dangers of trying to exist in the Nueces Strip could not be minimized, and some brave and tough ranchers decided the benefits of living in this land did not outweigh the dangers. John Horton Slaughter, who gained some notoriety in Texas and New Mexico before locating in Arizona to become a highly successful rancher as well as highly respected lawman, was one. Living in Frio County in July of 1875, Slaughter decided to move on. The sale of his stock and holdings amounted to $215,000. He was not the only stockman looking to make his livelihood elsewhere: A. H. Nations sold out for $75,000; W. S. Hall sold out for $50,000. The countryside's physicality was changing as well. Ten years before, Frio County was considered "an open prairie," but now in mid-July 1875 that same land was "covered with a thick growth of mesquite timber and brush, rendering the handling of cattle very difficult."[47]

Under the heading "State News Kinney County," the *Galveston Daily News* of October 21 explained to its readers how, "From Fort Clark [south] to Eagle Pass, a distance of forty-five miles is one vast prairie, covered with mesquite grass, from which thousands of cattle feed." Years later in a brief review of John King Fisher's life a reporter told an obviously tall tale of how "[h]e owned thousands of head of cattle, and his neighbors told curious stories of the prolific nature of Fisher's branding iron that brought him calves faster than a thousand cows could produce them."[48] Though exaggerated, there is no doubt he could easily add to his own herd.

One of the most controversial events in the life of King Fisher occurred in the latter months of 1875. Reportedly on or about November 10, three Mexicans who worked for rancher Alexander Zimmerman claimed that three horses which were in E. A. Thompson's corral were actually their property, having been stolen. By chance King Fisher was there at the time, and he claimed that the horses in question belonged to him. A heated argument ensued and, in no time at all, gunfire punctuated the angry words. Fisher allegedly drew his pistol and commenced firing before the three men could react, killing all three. The trio of ill-fated Mexicans who worked for Alexander Zimmerman may have been Estanislado Nunez and his two sons. Nunez was a Mexican farm laborer who was about in his middle fifties when killed. In 1870, he and his family, wife Candelaria and their two sons, Pablo and Antonio, twenty-eight and twenty-five years of age respectively, lived in Cameron County, working as farm laborers.[49] It has not been verified that this is the right family, but a related incident may refer to Nunez and his sons. The *Galveston Daily News* accused King of murder, reporting how he "carried off horses, and was followed by an old man and his two sons. They found Fisher at his corral, claimed the horses peaceably, were invited to alight, and, when in the act of hitching their horses, he killed them all. Since then no one has followed stolen property."[50] It would not be until 1879 that Fisher would be indicted for this killing.

A similar version, although with different livestock involved, was related by Pancho Escuadro, who worked with King Fisher. He told his version of this killing to John Leakey, who later preserved it in his memoirs. As Escuadro recalled the incident, Fisher had several *vaqueros* working for him at branding time. It took place on the 7D Ranch, and the men working for King Fisher were not satisfied with the payment for their work, which amounted to a certain number of the cattle. King's explanation was not satisfactory to them:

King saw that they were planning to kill him, and though he apparently didn't notice it, he was watching just the same as he went on branding. Pancho was helping with the branding irons out to one side, one Mexican was working with King and three were sitting on the fence. King always wore his sixshooter [*sic*], and because the men had often seen the result of his aim, they were not anxious to start a battle. One of the three on the fence was also wearing a gun, and he was the one that King was keeping an eye on mostly. However, the one that was helping with the branding started an argument and suddenly put up a fight. King knocked him in the head with the branding iron. In a flash, the Mexican who was armed, jumped into the pen, his hand on his hip, but King was too quick for him; he killed him before he could draw his gun. Then he shot the two remaining on the fence and they fell off backwards. Pancho deplored the killing but he said nothing— just helped King dig the graves and bury the men. Later, Pancho put markers on their graves.[51]

Uvalde County Court Records show the case was still on the books as late as 1881. Cause No. 208 was called April 21, 1881, "Indictment for Murder" filed August 16, 1879. A jury of twelve men were chosen, with Celestin Pingenot foreman of the jury, "who having been duly empanelled and sworn according to law after hearing the indictment read and the plea of not guilty thereto entered by the defendant, the evidence, argument of Counsel and charge of the Court, retired to consider of their verdict and returned into open Court and delivered the following verdict to wit: 'We the Jury find the defendant, John King Fisher, not guilty.' C. Pingenot, Foreman."[52]

William Donovan, a neighbor of King Fisher, ranched a few miles below Eagle Pass. There were hard feelings between the two men for a reason now unknown. Donovan's ranch house burned down one night, but no one seemed to know what caused the fire or the purpose of the arson. Shortly thereafter, Donovan and his two adult sons began to find their cattle shot. Donovan suspected that King Fisher and his associates were responsible and, late in the year of 1875, decided to ride to Pendencia Creek to confront him.

On his way to Fisher's ranch, Donovan stopped to visit his friend Charles Sykes Brodbent, a former Pennsylvanian who had established a sheep ranch near Pendencia Creek. Donovan stayed the night and shared his suspicions with Brodbent, who urged him not to go. Brodbent had had a similar experience not long before. While tending sheep, he came upon King Fisher and some of his men soon after they had killed and butchered several of his sheep. Fisher offered to pay for the animals, however Brodbent graciously refused. Instead of making an issue out of the dead animals, he accepted an invitation to join them as they ate. He knew better than to confront King Fisher, but Donovan had other ideas. He dismissed Brodbent's advice not to go. Considered a brave man, Donovan foolishly determined to face King Fisher alone. Brodbent recalled that Donovan "had found a couple of their cattle that had been shot and believed it was done by the King Fisher outfit, and he thought he would ride down toward the Pendencia." Brodbent "told him it was dangerous to do so, especially alone. He said 'I'm not afraid of them. If they want to shoot me, they'll shoot me in the back.' I said 'well if they want to kill you they will shoot you in the back. There is no protection from a bushwhacker.'" And early the following morning, Donovan pointed his horse towards the Pendencia.[53]

Virginia-born Archelous L. Parrott worked as a traveling photographer and was engaged at this time to photograph King Fisher and his future wife, Sarah Vivian. Parrott had set up his portable gallery on Charles Vivian's ranch for this purpose. The date was December 27, 1875. As chance would have it, King Fisher and some of his men were at Parrott's tent following the taking of the photograph when Donovan rode up.[54] According to Parrott's later testimony, Donovan stepped down from his horse and approached Fisher in a friendly manner and asked if he was having his picture taken. King and Donovan went off a short distance and had a private conversation. When their talk ended and Donovan had left, King said to his men, "that damned old son-of-a-bitch is down here spying around." Then Fisher and several of his men rode after Donovan. With King Fisher were John Watson, Nicholas Reynolds, two brothers whose actual names may have been John and Pink Burns although they were also known as Smith.[55] They were not gone long, perhaps a half-hour or three-quarters of an hour. Later an unidentified Mexican approached Parrott's gallery and stated that he had found a dead man "up the road." The Fisher group then rode off.

A man named John Warner Canterbury was visiting that day and he and the Mexican rode off to find the body.[56] They found it and were able to identify it as William Donovan. Canterbury counted twelve bullet holes in the body, suggesting the party shot Donovan several times.[57]

Ironically another man later provided testimony regarding the Donovan killing: William T. Cavin, who on more than one occasion had infiltrated himself among outlaws while a ranger working for Hall. Cavin, the brother of J. E. "Ed" Cavin, later testified, placing the death of Donovan squarely on King Fisher:

> I had two conversations with J. King Fisher in regard to the murder of William Donovan. He showed me where he met Donovan and showed me the way he ran, then showed me where they got him down. I believe he said he was the hardest damned man he ever killed. Believe he said Johnny Walton [Watson] was with him, don't remember and one else. He said they killed him by shooting, he ran down the road from where he showed me about 50 or 100 yards as well as I can remember before he fell. ... I don't belong to the rangers now, am not on their muster roll, not in their service. [I] Became acquainted with King Fisher in July, 1876. [I] Had conversation with him as well as I can remember about 1st of September, 1876.[58]

King Fisher may have thought little of this incident at the time. Rather, during this Christmas season, he had thoughts of his fiancée, Sarah Vivian, on his mind.

# Chapter 4

# "Our Entire Frontier Is Infested with Outlaws"

**W**ith the new year of 1876 rapidly approaching, citizens of Texas may have thought of the country's first centennial, but those more pragmatic looked forward to the continuing presence of Captain McNelly in various south Texas counties. In Goliad County farmers were preparing the land for the coming crops; the editor of the *Guard* predicated that if the good weather held they would have their crops in by the twentieth of January. While men prepared the ground for seed a strange action occurred which must have caused some people to wonder what was happening. An old cannon dating from the Texas Revolution had lain on the courthouse square for several years, and Saturday night, the eighth of January, it "peeled forth again." It was not until the next morning that the editor of the *Guard* learned that the gallant officer, Captain McNelly, had passed through Goliad on his way to Austin to see the Governor with reference to the troubles on the Rio Grande. He does not state McNelly ordered the cannon to be fired, but possibly McNelly did liven up sleepy little Goliad. In spite of the cannon disturbing the entire town having "peeled forth," no damage was reported.[1]

Captain McNelly was not the only one who found it irresistible to ignore the use of the Texas Revolution cannon. Later that year to celebrate

Independence Day Joseph McDonald and "several other young men were firing salutes in Goliad, when McDonald met with the misfortune of having his right hand so badly torn by the accidental discharge of the cannon, that amputation was necessary." That was the fourth accident just that year involving the cannon.[2]

McNelly not only had seen the governor about the Rio Grande troubles but went on to Washington, D.C. with Colonel Uriah Lott and Judge McCampbell of Corpus Christi for the purpose of testifying before the committee investigating the border troubles. McNelly reported that among other outrages from 3,000 to 10,000 head of cattle every month had been stolen from Texas ranchers and had been driven across the river into Mexico since he went on duty in April 1875. One idea which was under consideration was to have the president declare martial law in that area south of the Nueces and north of the Rio Grande, the so-called Nueces Strip. This idea may have appeared reasonable on paper, but it never got beyond the consideration stage.[3]

McNelly's testimony before the Special Committee on Texas Border Troubles is fascinating and enlightening. "I am willing to take a great many chances," McNelly testified, "but I certainly would not live on a stock ranch west of the Nueces River, at any point from the mouth of the Devil's River to the mouth of the Rio Grande. ... My position, in command of a company of troops, I do not consider half so hazardous as that of those men living on ranches."[4] McNelly did not mention King Fisher by name as he had not yet had to deal with him. Perhaps Fisher, as well as McNelly, felt life on the Pendencia was hazardous as well.

Already citizens were becoming aware of the increasing lawlessness in the area. A correspondent expressed his concerns following the report of a disturbance at Fort Duncan. "The preservation of order is the keystone of the arch on which the social structure is reared," he began. What was the situation as he saw it? "Our entire frontier is infested with outlaws from other States, fugitives from justice, bands of horse-thieves and hard cases generally, who find in our but partially settled frontier counties that immunity from arrest, and an opportunity to practice their professions which is denied them elsewhere." The correspondent admitted that it was "exceedingly difficult" to break up the bands of outlaws and apparently some had encouraged mobs to deal with them. He explained that, "there is very little excuse for permitting mobs to take the execution of the law into their own hands, in the more thickly settled portions of the State." It appears the correspondent was stating mob law was permissible on the frontier, but not "in the more thickly settled portions" of Texas.[5]

On January 3, 1876 Maverick County Judge J. A. Ware issued a *capias* to arrest and detain King Fisher in order to guarantee his court appearance for the prior June misdemeanor charge of illegally driving cattle. Over the next nine months, a dozen warrants were issued for King's arrest. Besides Maverick County, he was sought in the following: Kinney, Blanco, Bexar, Goliad, Frio, Atascosa, Travis and Karnes. King was finally found and arrested in Maverick County. With sureties Lafayette and James Vivian, he again made bond.[6]

Also, in January rampant lawlessness increased along the boundary line of DeWitt, Karnes and Gonzales Counties. Twelve to fifteen young men, among them Alford Day, Warren Allen, two Callison boys—brothers, (Kallison, Kellison)—and a man named Sharp enjoyed endangering local citizens with their reckless conduct. They shot our lights and threatened people in the dead of night and took items from stores at gunpoint. Sharp finally murdered a man named Alfred Cone, with whom he had been feuding. Some area men even contemplated robbing the Goliad bank.[7]

In spite of Fisher being considered a gunfighter, he was primarily a rancher, only on a much smaller scale than Richard King or Mifflin Kenedy. As early as 1876, King Fisher recorded and maintained brands in Maverick County. The Vivian clan registered at least one dozen brands and the Bruton boys had a half-dozen.[8] Defacing the original brand, known as brand blotching, was a common ploy to increase one's herd. The letters "B" and "R" along with the numeral "8" were more effortlessly altered and the more brands registered to your name made it easier to blotch rustled stock.

One of the most valuable books dealing with Texas law-enforcement history is what became known as the "Ranger's Bible" which consisted of a listing of fugitives from justice, the list composed of names contributed by local sheriffs. Not every county was represented, but several names concern us here. The 1878 *List of Fugitives from Justice* includes Coryell County, adjacent to Lampasas County where the Fishers had once lived; the then Sheriff W. H. Belcher sent in a list of sixty-two names. King Fisher's name is among those wanted. His crime "Theft of a gelding" indicted in October 1872.[9] A previous sheriff was also listed, James M. Raby, charged with embezzlement. This is the single record placing Fisher in Coryell County, and one wonders if this is somehow related to the temporary theft of a horse from A. J. Turnbow of Williamson County. Between the two counties in question there is only a small segment of Bell County; perhaps Fisher's first brush with the law was in Coryell and not Williamson? It is doubtful that Fisher ever returned to Williamson County or Coryell County for that matter. The authorities in Coryell certainly did not expend energy or county funds to capture him. Whatever charges were on the books were apparently ignored by Williamson County officials.[10]

King Fisher had a most pleasing personality and easily made friends among the wealthy and the poor. In Eagle Pass there was a prominent Mexican family—Refugio and Maria Rita Teofila Alderete who had a son named Trinidad San Miguel. Trinidad was born on August 5, 1859 in Eagle Pass. The boy's father died on September 6, 1868 when Trinidad was but nine years old. No one recalled the date but on one occasion Trinidad's mother lost a Spanish pony which she had purchased across the river in Piedras Negras. For some reason she was especially fond of this pony, and believed the pony had been taken by some of King Fisher's men. Trinidad "took this matter up with King, described the horse, and asked him to help locate it." The very next day the pony was returned to the San Miguel household.[11] A slightly different version of this same incident was told in an interview with Trinidad San Miguel Jr. conducted by Frank L. Hobart. "Papa bought a grey horse and didn't brand him with the RA [Rita Alderete brand] because it was [the] wrong season [not the season to brand] … . And King Fisher's men got hold of that horse and Papa went to the Judge and says, 'Judge, King Fisher's men got one of my horses—a grey horse.' They said, 'Well, if you need a grey horse you better buy one—cause we can't do anything with those people.' Trinidad told King Fisher that one of his men had his horse. He (King Fisher) went to them. He says, 'Didn't I tell you not to take any RA brand?' He says, 'that horse hasn't got the RA brand.'"[12] The horse was returned; indeed, a tender side of King Fisher only a few got to see.

In early 1876, King Fisher was in Webb County where, according to the county sheriff, he stole a horse on February 8 and was indicted in April. This is the only reference to King's alleged "Theft of gelding" as it was listed in the *Fugitives from Justice*. Dario Gonzales was the sheriff then, elected February 15, 1876, and served until sometime in 1886. There is no indication to explain the length of time between the alleged theft and the indictment.[13]

On or about March 7, 1876 Lieutenant Colonel William R. Shafter reported to his superior General Edward O. C. Ord that at Fort Duncan a fight had broken out between citizens and soldiers against "a band of desperadoes." General Shafter telegraphed—the tone of which indicates his subject was well known—that late on the night of March 6th, King Fisher and two others entered the town of Eagle Pass, "charged about the streets" and fired some twenty shots into the house of Judge William Stone,[14] the Whiff saloon [Wipff?][15] and other houses, including the house of William Donovan, who was a victim of these desperadoes in December last. Judge Stone was a highly successful merchant of Eagle Pass with a wife and four children. This dangerous act is commonly known as "painting the town red" and in the reckless shooting a number of shots went into the post itself. The military could interpret that as an intentional act of endangerment, rather than accept it as indiscriminate firing by men "letting off steam." Colonel Shafter, intending to prevent any further mayhem and at the request of citizens, gathered twenty-five soldiers and entered Eagle Pass. Once there the imposing presence of the military's force prevented any further shooting, as not a single shot was fired. Shafter discovered that one of Fisher's men had been wounded whom he identified as Jack Watson *alias* Stone, but whose real name may have been John Walton. Shafter thought he was mortally wounded and placed him in the hands of the civil authorities. The colonel ended his communication with a prediction that Fisher would probably be in town again. Although one report stated that Judge Stone was the man Fisher's party was after, it is unlikely that if they were serious about killing Stone it could have been accomplished with the numbers they had. Perhaps it was merely intimidation. Judge Stone owned a large sheep ranch in the Pendencia area and may have been interrupting Fisher's suspect livestock activities.

During the same night H. C. Bradbury, a citizen of Frio County who was visiting the town, shot and killed an unidentified Mexican who was in the act of stealing his horse. Bradbury was arrested and placed in jail to await the action of the grand jury.[16] Colonel Shafter certainly had his hands full with dealing with the occasional celebratory visits of King Fisher and his men which terrified citizens, the isolated acts of attempted horse theft in the town itself, not to mention the potential raids from angry Kickapoo or Lipan Apache warriors.

Later that month Judge Stone found a message on a gravestone intended for him, stating that he and three other men "would rest in their graves in less than a year." The other three men were the two Donovan brothers—William and James, sons of William Donovan, and a man by the name of Andrew [Andres?] Porter.[17] Possibly Fisher's companion, "Jack Watson", was killed in retaliation for the death of William Donovan. Although Fisher wanted to leave the Donovan incident behind it did not go away. It would come back in early May, 1878 when he would be indicted for murder.

One of the most notorious of the Bruton boys, Charley Bruton, would later testify that Jack Watson bragged he had gunned-down William Donovan with two friends. When pressed as to who they were, Bruton remembered how Watson snapped saying it was "none of my business."[18] Certainly Donovan was reckless in going into King Fisher's territory by himself, angry at Fisher. Donovan's two sons were certainly aware of the group of men who fatally shot their father, but we have no definite record if they did anything to avenge their father's death. The shooting of Jack Watson, catching a bullet as he helped to shoot up Eagle Pass, may have been nothing more than bad luck.

Charles Sykes Brodbent, a native of Pennsylvania, lived in King Fisher's country raising sheep.[19] Allegedly King Fisher and some of his men killed a couple of his sheep for a meal. Brodbent refused payment, but graciously accepted the offer to join them. Here we become aware of the trouble between Fisher and Donovan, and although what caused the trouble was never made clear, it is apparent that there were hard feelings between the two men. Brodbent went on his way to tend his sheep. Curiously that night the Donovan ranch house burned. No one seemed to know anything about the cause or purpose of the arson. Shortly thereafter, Donovan rode into Brodbent's camp and spent the night. Donovan explained to Brodbent that he had found some of his cattle shot and that he suspected it was done by King Fisher or members of his gang. Brodbent advised him to let the matter drop, but Donovan was intent on going into the Pendencia and facing Fisher. How far Donovan got with his mission into the Pendencia is unknown, but after his departure from Brodbent he was never seen alive again. O. C. Fisher concluded that "Who was responsible for his death and under what circumstances he died became subjects of conjecture. Whether the King knew about it could never be determined. He had some dangerous characters in his outfit, and he was not always around when they did their dirty work."[20] The killing took place on December 27, 1875. There was eventually a trial, with Fisher being indicted for murder on May 2, 1878, in Maverick County. The case, number 379, was eventually transferred to Uvalde County on a change of venue, the change ordered by Judge Thomas M. Paschal.[21]

Although we generally think of King Fisher as being a Dimmit County rancher, by the mid-1870s people generally considered the town of Eagle Pass in neighboring Maverick County as his base. On December 27, 1875, Fisher, with several companions, visited Eagle Pass. One report stated they proceeded to get drunk and then rode up and down the streets shooting off their pistols indiscriminately. The townspeople of course scurried for shelter from the galloping horses and reckless shooting. Any loose dogs, or rats, or chickens wandering the streets became a target. No citizen was hit, which suggests the riders were not too drunk to be able to direct their shots harmlessly. One rider, perhaps King Fisher himself, stopped Judge William Stone on the street and "vilely abused" him. Indeed, as one headline proclaimed, King Fisher was "on the war path."[22]

Why was Judge Stone so "vilely abused"? Although we can't say for sure likely it was because Fisher had heard of the rumor that Judge Stone had offered a reward to anyone who would assassinate him. The rumor was false of course, but it had gained some credence. Rumor had it that William Rhett was the would-be assassin. In discussing lawlessness in Texas

Rhett spoke out against it, being interviewed by a New Orleans reporter. He denied the rumor "to the effect that Judge Stone, of Eagle Pass, offered him $2000 to assassinate King Fisher" claiming the rumor was without foundation, and that he wished, "in order that justice may be done to Judge Stone, to publicly contradict it."[23] A good denial was appropriate, but it suggests that someone may have thought Rhett was not above becoming a hired assassin. Little else has been learned about this individual William Rhett.

During this time rustling was on the rise. And along with increased rustling, mob action increased as well. On the night of April 3, an hour before midnight, a group of men numbering over forty, but certainly less than the estimated one hundred, entered the town of Goliad and found E. U. Brooking. They had come to deliver to him the message that the community would no longer tolerate his presence and they did not wish to hurt him, but he had three days to leave the country. In addition, Brooking's brother had to leave as well as some other men accompanying them which included a William Felix James, William Bruton, and Ady [Adolph?] Milde. The mob then left, having warned the undesirables what they had to do. It is suspected that the reporter erred in his identification of these men. Probably it was Upshur Brooking and William Bruton who were told to leave. The *Goliad Guard* reporter concluded by explaining the action was "caused by the loose manner in which these parties have been charged with handling cattle."[24] No further information has been located on this incident.

The members of the Brooking party who had been ordered to leave heeded those orders, but they may have had intentions to give reason to be remembered. Upon leaving Goliad a reporter managed to speak with a few citizens and learned what he already suspected: "Parties who left Goliad … report that there is every indication of a serious difficulty growing out of the stock troubles." Two of the men—David Williams and J. T. Southwell, both from Victoria County—reported being shot at by unknown parties. Two of the four shots fired hit their buggy. The pair believed it "extremely hazardous to proceed" and returned to Goliad.[25] Could the shots have been fired by Brooking or Bruton, resentful to being ordered out of the country? Other groups of stockmen took the initiative of recovering their own stolen cattle. Ranchers from DeWitt and Victoria Counties learned of the large number of cattle gathered in Goliad County. When discovering cattle with their brand the men drove them out and returned to their own range with the repossessed stock. Apparently, they had not involved any sheriff or deputies in this undertaking.

The men who had been ordered to leave the county did, but they did not stay away from their homes. Not long after, William Brooking, Andy Milde, Robert Lewis and "some few men of those that were ordered off from here, have returned, and say they will remain, and if they have violated the law they will abide by the actions of the courts."[26]

It was not only in Goliad County that vigilant committees were forming. A Deputy Collector of Internal Revenue who had visited Goliad felt it necessary to correspond with the *Galveston Daily News*, then the largest circulating journal in the state, that due to the dangerous conditions of the country it was no longer safe to travel alone. In addition to Goliad he had visited Bee and Live Oak Counties and learned that "a large number" of merchants intended to close out their businesses "on account of the unsettled state of the country. Every man I met was armed with a Henry rifle or six-shooter, and the country is in a feverish state at this time." Horse and cattle thieves "almost had control of the country of late, but the large cattle raisers have formed a vigilance committee and ordered quite a large number to leave Goliad and Live Oak [C]ounties." What if those ordered to leave failed to leave? The answer was simple: "should they refuse there will no doubt be war, as four persons have been killed in a few days." That last sentence suggests the war had already begun. The revenue collector ended his informative letter: "I was not molested in any way, but have come to the conclusion that it is not safe to make these trips alone."[27] Furthermore, a later report from an unidentified "representative" from the governor's office summarized the condition in Goliad County. Reportedly "lawlessness is as rampant as has ever been known. An organized band is spreading terror in the county. They have ordered off a number of citizens, who are in the brush organizing an opposition." The representative anticipated that soon there would be "regular and moderator organizations, as in former times in Eastern Texas. The present organization has good men in it, but others join in to have protection in acts of revenge. … Large bands had traversed the county, numbering from 80 to 150 armed men."[28] Events were taking place for a regular range war.

Perhaps things were much more peaceful in Dimmit County. King Fisher and his fiancée Sarah Vivian decided on a wedding day, and, according to O. C. Fisher, the pair were married on April 6, 1876 in Dimmit County. Grey White, a Justice of the Peace of the Pendencia, officiated, and "undoubtedly gave the union his warmest blessing."[29] Sarah was an attractive nineteen-year-old when she became Mrs. J. K. Fisher; King was considered equally attractive and was but a few years older. Rev. Bruce Roberts in his memoirs contradicted O. C. Fisher, writing that the marriage was on April 7. Interestingly, the Fisher Family Bible kept by Florence Fisher Kellogg states the date of the Fisher-Vivian marriage was April 7, 1876 "at Eagle Pass, TX by Grey White, Justice of Peace."[30] Roberts never knew King Fisher but did know his widow and three daughters well, having lived in Uvalde for many years. "The members of his family" Roberts wrote, "were among the first persons I came to know in Dimmit [C]ounty in 1898. I have known the family well and favorably through the fifty-one years, and for fifteen years we lived in adjoining blocks. From the first acquaintance, I have had a keen interest in the life and character and death of the husband and father. The family has from the first made it easy for us to talk about this, and I have felt free to ask regarding the home and inner life of the man."[31]

In May 1876 the area newspapers announced that government troops had strung 1,030 miles of telegraph wire. The word came from Denison in northeast Texas, announcing that the line from Denison, via Jacksboro, Concho, San Antonio and Eagle Pass, to Brownsville "was completed last night." This work now connected all frontier military posts and all the wires were in working order. This happened at the same time that the cattle trade was "beginning to liven up."[32]

In this dangerous area, only a few miles west of Pendencia Creek in Dimmit County, was another creek—Comanche Creek, but in southeastern Maverick County. Today the creek is dammed to form Comanche Lake west of Crystal City, Zavala County. There was a gun battle on Comanche Creek on May 29, 1876 and initial reports—although incorrect—identified Alejo Gonzales and three others killed and five more wounded.[33]

Charles Bruton had established his ranch on this Comanche Creek. It was about fifteen miles from the Rio Grande and thirty-five miles east of

Eagle Pass. It was not far from Fisher's ranch and he penned there the cattle he had acquired from Frank Porter. In late May fourteen horsemen rode up to Bruton's place from the south. They were from all appearances heavily armed Mexican *vaqueros*. On their arrival, they faced Bruton, Frank Claunch and his son George.[34] The leader, or at least the spokesman, was Alejo Gonzales. Gonzales asked if Bruton knew of any cattle in the vicinity. Bruton answered honestly, telling him that King Fisher had a penned herd some miles away. For an unexplained reason Gonzales became indignant and snarled that he would have the cattle or he "would follow them to hell." He and his men then wheeled their mounts and rode off in the direction of the cattle pens.

Claunch correctly interpreted Gonzales's anger as a definite threat against King Fisher and sent his son George—about nineteen years old— to King Fisher's camp to warn him of the dangerous armed body of men approaching to take the cattle. Then King went to Bruton's and they began to pursue Gonzales and his men. The Gonzales group discovered they were being followed, dismounted and drew their Winchester rifles, anticipating a fight. King did not choose to fight then, being vastly outnumbered. Instead he returned to his ranch and began to gather a handful of tough men to help. He soon had Frank Porter, Nick Reynolds and William C. Bruton, the older brother of Charles Bruton.

All concerned realized that a fight was imminent, but Fisher still chose not to begin the skirmish, the odds being so uneven. Instead of fighting, the quartet opened the pens and scattered the cattle in the dense brush in an effort to deny the *vaqueros* from taking them.

King returned to the Bruton place at 9:00 that evening—May 28, and sent word to neighboring ranchers to gather for a general meeting. By next morning at least a dozen men had answered the call. According to J. E. "Ed" Cavin[35] Fisher said he would do both—catch the cattle and kill the Mexicans. This was agreeable to all in the group.

While King held the meeting at Bruton's place, Gonzales and his *vaqueros* had gathered up as many of the scattered cattle as they could. They had now some two hundred head ... a lot more than they had earlier claimed had been stolen from them. The herd was a mixture of both Mexican and American brands. At daybreak, May 29, 1876, ten men at the Bruton ranch anticipated action. They were: King Fisher, Frank Porter, Nick Reynolds, William Bruton, John H. Culp, John Hudgins, J. E. "Ed" Cavin, Robert Lewis, Richard Horn and Augustine M. "Gus" Gildea.[36] Charles Bruton chose to remain at his ranch.

At 10 o'clock that morning the Texans caught up to where the cattle had been penned and found the *vaqueros* slowly driving the herd along Comanche Creek towards the Rio Grande. When those driving the cattle saw the Texans, they let the herd go on while they fell behind to meet their adversaries. Within one hundred yards of the cattle William C. Bruton dismounted and fired the opening shot with his Winchester. The *vaqueros* began to dismount to defend themselves but the Texans poured a murderous volley at them. Alejo Gonzales was hit three times and fell seriously wounded. A companion fell mortally wounded, later identified as Severino Flores. At least three others were hit; none of the Texans suffered wounds. Once the battle was over, the casualties were one Mexican dead and at least three wounded. The *vaqueros*, soundly defeated, fled south, leaving their dead companion where he fell and the cattle to roam at will.

The battle had taken place some fifty yards from Charles Bruton's cattle camp; he heard the shots but did not see the action. He later estimated about one hundred shots had been fired. Bruton rode to the site of the battle to see the results where he found the hat Alejo Gonzales had worn. Bruton also examined the body of Severino Flores, noting that he had been shot "through the head from ear to ear." Nick Reynolds bragged that he killed the Mexican. Later King Fisher would be charged with the killing of Severino Flores, but of course was not convicted.

The summary of the court testimony published in the *San Antonio Express* was provided by one whose *nom de plume* was "Western Texas." Were Alejo Gonzales and his men cattle thieves? It was acknowledged many of the cattle were marked with old Spanish brands and Fisher and his party were in the process of branding the cattle. The KP brands, reportedly owned by Fisher and Porter, were fresh and peeling on the cattle. Or were the *vaqueros* honest ranchers intending to recover their own property from the thieving *gringos* north of the Rio Bravo? No one today can say for sure. Both Gonzales and Fisher had on more than one occasion "thrown a long rope" and had driven cattle "from their accustomed range" as some court records euphemistically described plain cattle rustling. However, "Western Texas" defended King Fisher's actions pointing out how the Mexicans should have appealed to the courts and how Texas law justified homicide during the act of preventing the theft of one's property.[37]

The first news of any depth concerning this Comanche Creek Battle appeared in the *Galveston Daily News* of May 31, telegraphed from San Antonio. Errors continued. "Yesterday [May 29] Alejo Gonzales and eight of his hands followed cattle thieves near Eagle Pass. They came upon them, thirty in number, at Comanche Creek, thirty miles east of Eagle Pass, and engaged them in fighting from 9 a.m. to 4 p.m. The battle resulted in victory for the robbers; they killed Gonzales and four of his men. The other four escaped, and report five of the robbers killed."[38]

The *Express* of June 9 made the correction that Gonzales was not dead but was severely wounded. The *Galveston Daily News* in reporting news from Maverick County described him as "quite a young man, and raised in San Antonio."[39]

Attorney Trevanion Theodore Teel related shortly after the deaths of Ben Thompson and King Fisher in 1884, perhaps drawing attention again to the fact that he had been an attorney for Fisher, that Gonzales had followed a trail of stolen cattle which trail led to King Fisher's pasture. Fisher had ninety head of cattle there, with bills of sale from Mexican cattle thieves. Gonzales brazenly entered the Fisher pasture and rounded up the ninety head of cattle he claimed as his as well as a few others and started driving them back to Mexico. Not letting this go, Fisher supposedly rounded up some of his men and pursued Gonzales and the cattle. Fisher and his men reached them near Comanche Creek, and that is where the battle erupted.[40] So recalled T. T. Teel.

This Comanche Creek gunfight received little attention at the time, but it became part of the legendary aspect of King Fisher's life. Part of the legend-building process was accelerated by Napoleon Augustus Jennings who wrote of Fisher's "notorious gang of horse thieves, cattle thieves, and murderers."[41] Jennings does not claim to have heard of King Fisher before May 1876 when McNelly mustered him into his ranger troop. He became aware of the desperado just before arriving at the Fisher ranch on Pendencia Creek, which was as he recalled, "a little ranch there, and about forty or fifty of his followers were nearly always with him."[42] Jennings was part of the group ready to arrest King Fisher. If McNelly could locate King Fisher and arrest him it would be yet another feather in his cap.

According to fellow ranger George P. Durham when McNelly was ready to attack the Fisher ranch he did not know exactly where it was. For assistance in finding the ranch he went to Captain Levi English. English was naturally ready to help a fellow ranger, particularly since his general store had suffered occasionally from bandit raids. Captain McNelly "impressed into service a gangling young man, Drew Taylor, who was reported to know the shortest route to the Pendencia."[43] By chance, Taylor was aware that Fisher was at his ranch that same day; McNelly decided that day was the day to raid and arrest him, and reportedly Fisher had "considerable numbers of men" so he (McNelly) gathered about twenty-five rangers, leaving only "a corporal's guard at camp."[44] English had had an exciting life, not only as a Texas Ranger but also as a pioneer in the area. He is credited with founding the community of Carrizo Springs, donating land for the Mount Hope Cemetery as well as the Baptist Church and the first school of Carrizo Springs. Drew Kirksey Taylor became a Texas Ranger, and according to Durham, had done some work for A. L. Parrott, who had posed as an itinerant photographer while actually scouting the outlaw country.[45] Although the name of King Fisher may have proved terrifying to some settlers, English, Taylor and Parrott remained courageous.

Young ranger Jennings described how on June 3, 1876, McNelly and a small squad of his men did raid the Fisher Ranch and arrest King and others. He described with great excitement how McNelly, after dividing his command into two small groups "at a prearranged moment, all of us dashed for the house at full speed, six-shooters in hand. A fence was in our way, but the horses went over it like hunters after the hounds, and before Fisher and his men perceived us we were within a hundred yards of the place."[46]

Fisher and his men were relaxing when they "perceived" the oncoming galloping horsemen and thus were totally unprepared to resist. Most of them were playing poker when they realized men were galloping at them, and some of them entered the house. McNelly shouted to Fisher "You'll have to surrender or be killed!" Standing next to him was his lieutenant Frank Porter, whose real name was Burd Obenchain—according to Jennings. The men all surrendered, realizing that if they did not, they would be shot. They were "agreeably disappointed" in learning their captors were rangers—not "members of a vigilance committee." Jennings, obviously proud of playing a part in the capture, recorded the names of the desperadoes besides J. K. Fisher as Obenchain, Warren Allen, Bill Templeton, Will Wainwright, Jim Honeycutt, Wesley Bruton, Al Roberts and William Bruton.[47] Only Fisher had any degree of reputation. Ironically William R. Templeton had formerly served as a private in McNelly's ranger company. Allen had served as sheriff of Kinney County for a brief period back in 1874.[48]

Jennings further wrote: "A few weeks before we arrested them, King Fisher and Frank Porter, by themselves, stole a herd of cattle from six Mexican vaqueros who were driving the herd for its owner, near Eagle Pass. Fisher and Porter rode around the herd and killed every one of the six Mexicans."[49] This of course is a garbled reference to the Comanche Creek battle. Jennings added a macabre note, that the "vaqueros were all buried together, and I saw the place where they were buried. It was known as 'Frank Porter's Graveyard.'"[50] How much of Jennings's recollections were figments of his imagination and how much actual truth is at times difficult to say. Jennings was impressed with the appearance of King Fisher:

> He was the most perfect specimen of a frontier dandy and desperado that I ever saw. He was tall, beautifully proportioned, and exceedingly handsome. He wore the finest clothing procurable, but all of it was the picturesque, border, dime novel kind. His broad-brimmed white Mexican sombrero was perfectly ornamented with gold and silver lace and had a golden snake for a band. His fine buckskin Mexican short jacket was heavily embroidered with gold. His shirt was of the finest and thinnest linen and was worn open at the throat, with a silk handkerchief knotted loosely about the collar. A brilliant crimson silk sash was wound about his waist, and his legs were hidden by a wonderful pair of chaparejos [sic], or "chaps" as the cowboys called them—leather breeches to protect their legs while riding through the brush.[51]

This is the picture Jennings created for his readers and one may assume this was what Fisher wore when "dressed up" but certainly not while driving cattle or horses on the range. But Jennings adds more glamour to the picture.

> These *chaparejos* were made of the skin of a royal Bengal tiger and ornamented down the seams with gold and buckskin fringe. The tiger's skin had been procured by Fisher at a circus in northern Texas. He and some of his fellows had literally captured the circus, killed the tiger and skinned it, just because the desperado chief fancied he'd like to have a pair of tiger skin "chaps." His boots were of the finest high heeled variety, the kind all cowboys loved to wear. Hanging from his cartridge-filled belt were two ivory-handled, silver-plated six-shooters.[52] His spurs were of silver and ornamented with little silver bells.[53]

George Durham also provided an image of King Fisher: "He wore a *tres piedras sombrero* with a solid gold, coiled rattler, for a band and gold tasssels. His shirt was of the heavy, Mexico City silk, opened at the throat, and a silk, red bandana was knotted on his neck." Durham also recalled the weaponry— on either hip a pearl-handled pistol inlaid with gold designs. But the "leggins" struck Durham especially as they were made from the hide of a Bengal tiger:[54] "Where he had got it I can't imagine although I heard later that Ben Thompson killed one in a circus in north Texas and had the hide made into leggins for King. ... They was fit for a King and they was on a King."[55]

It is not believed that King Fisher and Ben Thompson ever met prior to the 1880s. It is doubtful that either man ever attended a circus in northern Texas. The arrest of King Fisher and men of his group resulted in not only attention to the name of King Fisher but additional glory to Captain McNelly. His name was at this point a household word due to his highly successful raid on the Palo Alto Prairie in which more than a dozen of Cortina's raiders were killed trying to escape across the Rio Grande with a herd of cattle stolen from the King Ranch. Later, in November of 1875, he and his small company of rangers had invaded Mexico to recover cattle stolen from Texas ranchers. This action nearly caused an international incident. Now, arresting King Fisher and his band, proved to be the most important arrest of 1876.

Initially the *Express* reported that the news from Eagle Pass telling of the arrest was "unusually interesting." Dario Gonzales, the Webb County sheriff, "attended McNelly, tendering his services to assist in the arrest."[56] San Antonio's *Herald* of the next day reported that Fisher and his men had given bail and had been released. The state of Texas was shocked by his immediate release from custody and newspapers across the state expressed the frustration felt by many citizens. The *Express* gave additional information a few days later. It was not good news either, commenting that the news from Eagle Pass "shows that region of country to be in a most revolting condition, socially, morally and politically. More than a passing censure should be directed to stop the outrages daily occurring there. If something is not soon done to return that country to peace and tranquility, and protect human life and the property of Texas citizens, the inhabitants will be forced to leave for sections where these rights and privileges can be obtained."[57]

Fellow McNelly ranger George Durham told of the arrest but added a great amount of conversation between the arresting rangers and the wanted men, all of which is "unusually interesting." The rangers searched the various out-buildings while McNelly took the main house. King Fisher answered McNelly's knock and demand to surrender and did so, neither one having drawn a pistol: "And right there, facing each other at not more than five paces, were by long odds the two best pistol fighters in Texas, before or since. I don't know, and didn't know at that time, whether King was his real name or his title. It could have been either. He was the nearest thing to my idea of a king I had ever seen."[58] Then Mrs. Fisher came out to inquire as to what was happening to her husband. McNelly is described as being nervous and frustrated as he had never had a prisoner surrender so easily before. After additional conversation, McNelly pointed out that he was taking her husband to jail in Eagle Pass. Most importantly he advised King and Mrs. Fisher that if her husband attempted to escape or if there was a rescue attempt, he would be shot. This piece of advice was unnecessary of course and doubtful that McNelly would mention it, this custom of *la ley de fuga*, or the law of flight. It had become a common excuse for murdering prisoners for years.[59]

George Durham and N.A. Jennings, both involved in this capture of King Fisher, left their accounts and provided conversation, pointing out that the *ley de fuga* was in force. Only Jennings, however, remarked on the attractiveness of Mrs. Fisher: "Before we started, Captain McNelly told us, in the hearing of the prisoners and of Fisher's wife—a pretty girl, with wonderfully fine, bold black eyes—that if any of our prisoners attempted to escape or if an attempt was made to rescue them, we were to kill them without warning or mercy."[60]

Captain McNelly happily telegraphed Steele the good news from Eagle Pass: "Have Arrested King Fisher and nine [*sic*, eight] of his gang and turned them over to Sheriff [.] will camp at Fort Ewell and scout country between here and Oakville until otherwise instructed. Country [is] in a most deplorable condition [as] all civil officers helpless."[61] Neither Jennings nor Durham made mention of the fact that King Fisher had in his possession between seven and eight hundred head of stolen cattle. McNelly took possession of them but after allowing the inspector to inspect the herd he had them turned loose as the citizens were afraid of what the Fisher party would do to them after they were released.[62] They were well aware that King Fisher himself had killed several men.

The Maverick County sheriff who at first accepted the King Fisher group was C. J. Cook, who had been appointed on April 18 of that year upon the death of Sheriff Manuel Van who passed in April. Cook was sheriff only until July 1877, as he absconded that year with $16,000 of State and county funds that he had collected. The *Statesman* of Austin reported he had "lit out" while the *Dallas Daily Herald* used the term "decamped"—either way he now became a hunted man. The common belief was that he was in Mexico.[63]

McNelly dutifully reported his accomplishment of arresting Fisher to Adjutant General Steele in Austin which in turn was reported in his annual report to the governor. There was no drama in his reporting: "June, 1876.— on 4th, arrested King Fisher and nine of his gang. On 6th, King Fisher and gang released, whilst Capt. McNelly was on his way with witnesses. Seven of the nine could have been indicted for murder in several cases. Had between six hundred and eight hundred head of stolen cattle and horses which were turned loose."[64] McNelly was not satisfied as he then left Eagle Pass to scout the country between there and Oakville, some three hundred miles if going through Carrizo Springs, searching for more desperadoes.[65]

An additional note that the newspapers of the day missed but Jennings reported is significant, that after McNelly and his men met Fisher after being released on bond, much to the captain's disgust, he gave King Fisher important advice. "If we ever come up here again, we'll come to kill ... and if you keep up your system of robbery and murder, you'll be hearing from us."[66] This warning reveals that underneath McNelly had a degree of admiration for King Fisher, which he perhaps did not recognize himself. Durham also recalled that McNelly gave Fisher the warning to change his ways, but again added considerable conversation. Fisher pointed out that he was not an outlaw but McNelly urged him to get out of the "outlaw business. The next time the Rangers come after you we just might leave you where we overhaul you—and you could make a better life for yourself. But it's up to you."[67]

Unfortunately, McNelly nor Jennings or Durham listed the names of the other rangers actually involved in the arrest of Fisher. Although both the latter were present and later wrote of the arrest, they chose to center on their own roles they played. But in addition to McNelly, Jennings and Durham, we know Lt. Lawrence B. Wright and A. L. Parrott were involved in the arrest.[68] As to how many others and who they were remain unknown. Interestingly, Durham was aware of Jennings's writing and commented: "This Jennings was taken up at Laredo as a field clerk to do the writing [of McNelly's scouting reports]. Later on he sure wrote. He sold stories on McNelly to a big magazine [*Saturday Evening Post*], and he put it in a book. The boy took it mostly out of his head, and it is pretty awful."[69]

It would be interesting to know what Jennings thought of Durham's writing, but Durham wrote much later than Jennings so there will never be a commentary. We can generally accept Jennings's writing as accurate, although writing of experiences thirty years or more later may have clouded his memory and we know that some of the events he described he was not personally involved in. But we accept the incident when he first met Billy Thompson, the reckless brother of Ben Thompson who would within a few years meet up with King Fisher. Jennings tells of his meeting up with Billy Thompson. It happened probably in 1874 or later but before Jennings had joined the rangers in 1876. He had gotten himself in some trouble in Nuevo Laredo with some Mexican gamblers and was about to be punished severely, he was fearful of being killed when an American—Thompson, interfered and saved his life. A few shots from Billy Thompson's pistol caused the mob to forget about killing Jennings. The pair then entered a saloon together and Jennings claimed he "took a drink of the vilest whiskey that ever passed my lips." This was his first meeting with Billy Thompson. At the time Thompson had a reward of $500 for his capture for his killing a sheriff in Ellsworth, Kansas.[70] Jennings later had the opportunity to repay Thompson for saving his life.

On this occasion Jennings and several other rangers were in Eagle Pass. Jennings describes how he and Ranger William W. McKinney went into Bruton's Saloon "to see if we could run across any of the desperadoes there." Within moments, who should walk in but King Fisher, not realizing any rangers were present. Slowly, Jennings and McKinney strode up to Fisher and stood on either side. Fisher then realized his situation and calmly "unbuckled his belt and gave up his two white-handled six-shooters without a murmur. Then we had the drinks and took him to our camp, and that night went with him and several of the Rangers to a *fandango*. Fisher, as usual, gave bail the next day and was released. He didn't mind being arrested very much; it was so very easy for him to get out of trouble again."[71] In the same barroom was Billy Thompson, unrecognized by Private McKinney but recognized by Jennings, who wisely advised him to "get back over into Mexico pretty quick [as] you are liable to be taken in." Jennings further added to this unusual incident: "Thompson thanked me and left the room. I was glad to see him take the hint so quickly, for although I truly felt I owed him a debt of gratitude, it went against my official conscience to connive at his escape."[72]

These incidents may have contributed to Durham's attitude towards Jennings. What we don't know is whether they were factual or something Jennings had created.

* * *

The *Express* had more to say about the lawless situation in the issue of June 10, headlining its article in bold and all upper-case letters: "The State on the Road to Ruin." The first line reinforced the pessimistic attitude of the journal: "As things now are, Texas seems, to use an irreverent slang phrase, to be 'going to the devil ahead of the regular mail.'" And it was western Texas which was suffering the most. "It is a melancholy fact. It is supposed that Fisher and his men constitute part of a large band of desperate men who have infested the country west of San Antonio for some months."[73] The editor concluded his "melancholy" report stating that with such desperadoes released on bond they would certainly remain. He did provide a solution. If Captain McNelly were to receive a troop of two hundred picked men to be "marched against them" the desperadoes would be dispersed. And what if this solution were to be ignored? "If not, they will rob the whole country west of Castroville, and almost depopulate it. Under present circumstances, none but men of nerve will settle between San Antonio and Eagle Pass. The Legislature must devise means to protect our frontier, and to have the laws executed."[74]

There were courageous men working west of San Antonio in spite of the *Express* editor's fears, and McNelly was not the only one. Men such as Levi English, Doc White, men of the Vivian clan and others would gradually prove that honoring the law was also an act of courage. And a few of the desperadoes of 1876, such as King Fisher, would someday be men to enforce the laws as well.

Many a Texas rancher was more optimistic and had faith in Captain McNelly. The captain had received some criticism for his irregular actions, such as crossing the Rio Grande and creating an international incident. McNelly felt enough pressure from his superiors that he had to provide assurances that his roguish behavior would not continue. To Adjutant General William Steele he wrote: "You may depend on my not doing anything that will not be justifiable legally, and I shall have a duly authorized civil officer accompany each of my squads."[75]

Always having a "duly authorized civil officer" riding alongside him and his rangers seems like a difficult proposition, as frequently he sent out several small squads scouting for desperadoes. The number of outlaws who gathered together were frequently called a mob, and the *Statesman* at least on this occasion had a recommendation: "We do not see how the disorderly swell mob of Texas is to be destroyed unless the Governor be invested with power to remove and appoint or suspend sheriffs" it began. And what to do? "If Governor Coke could send McNelly, clothed even temporarily with the functions of local supremacy, into a county rent by factions or overawed by highwaymen and jail breakers and stage coach robbers, the sheriffs would exert themselves much more vigorously in suppressing disorder and punishing crime."[76] There it was: send McNelly into the crime-ridden counties and give him free rein. He knew how to "vigorously" suppress disorder. It was an unspoken hearkening back to the Palo Alto prairie engagement.

Farther north in Austin, the politicians were gathering at a ratification meeting in front of the popular Raymond House. The *Statesman* reported there were between seven and eight hundred people in the crowd. A "colored band" provided "inspiring airs" to add to the dignity of the occasion. The first speaker was ex-Governor Elisha M. Pease who gave a "square-toed Republican speech." Ex-Governor E. J. Davis followed Pease, and then David Webster Flanagan spoke; he stated the purpose of the gathering was to ratify the nomination of Rutherford B. Hayes as President and William Wheeler as vice-president of the United States. Flanagan was followed by Honorable A. J. Evans who "went for the Democracy without gloves." What he said was perhaps more relevant to south Texas than to Austin, as he thundered that "there was no security for life and property, and that King Fisher, the desperado, had twenty counties under his control, and then dared the STATESMAN or any Democrat to deny his assertions, and referred to King Fisher's power." No one openly dared to deny his assertions ... but did anyone try and identify the *twenty counties*? Anyone unfamiliar with the conditions in south Texas would now realize that this man King Fisher, in mid-June 1876, had a reputation equivalent to an emperor. Although Evans did not say so in that many words, the empire Fisher "ruled" was the Nueces Strip. What Evans said was paraphrased, but to us today his remarks appear humorous. "He believed Democrats could out-steal Republicans" he said, and "that a party which had brought the country almost to the brink of ruin, could not and would not be entrusted to manage the government they had tried to destroy." Continuing on, no doubt to great applause, Evans "appealed to the young men to join their destinies with the progressive Republican party, and to cut loose from the opposition, which had disgraced itself with every catalogue of crime known to the statutes." He predicted Hayes and Wheeler "would be elected by an overwhelming majority."[77]

King Fisher was not in the crowd of hundreds in front of the Raymond House that day a politician accused him of having twenty Texas counties under his control, but we suspect he learned of the accusation. He was intelligent enough to be aware of what was happening politically beyond the Pendencia. Hayes and Wheeler did win the election of the centennial year, defeating Samuel Tilden, and Hayes served as President of the United States from 1877–1881. One of Hayes's first acts was to end Reconstruction by withdrawing Federal troops from those southern states still under occupation.

While King Fisher was on Comanche Creek fighting cattle rustlers, or perhaps stockmen from Mexico who intended to recover their own property, Captain McNelly was making plans to capture cattle thieves in "King Fisher's Territory." On May 31, he wrote from Laredo his intentions, although his communication did not mention King Fisher by name. "I am told that there are some twenty or twenty-five men out on the Nueces. I leave this morning to try & catch some of them. ... I will have hard work for the next three weeks at least. It will be necessary to break up the company in small Squads So as to make a vigorous pursuit after these people in case they escape me this time. We will have to Scout the country between Fort Clark & Oakville [. The] civil authorities don't pretend to take any consequences of any Kind of outrage."[78] Perhaps the civil authorities felt they should not risk their lives dealing with such people when McNelly and his men were willing to do it.

The arrest of King Fisher and members of his "gang" was certainly considered a blessing in some quarters. When Captain McNelly arrived in Austin to deliver prisoners he reported on the condition of affairs in south Texas. Much of the area of the Nueces Strip, between Castroville and Eagle Pass was "critical" as more than one hundred outlaws from different sections of the country had "invaded it and held the reins of power." The law was being trampled upon, civil officers were powerless, and Judge Dougherty did not "dare to sleep in his own house." McNelly reported that men under King Fisher took "property from citizens in daylight, and they dare not resist or attempt to recover it." This was certainly part of King Fisher's problem: men working under him brazenly stole; then word got to McNelly and he believed it, thus giving King Fisher a greater reputation as a thief than he truly deserved. An additional rumor was that Fisher's men had "inclosed [*sic*] pastures on the Nueces [R]iver, where they keep stolen stock until ready to drive. They go up the country by way of Devil's [R]iver and outside of the line of settlements to a market."[79]

During the night of June 14 McNelly's men captured two outlaws who had been jailed in Waco, McLennan County, but had escaped some years before. They would be delivered to authorities in Waco but not before a stop in Austin to jail them temporarily. The *Statesman* appreciated the importance of this arrest, and interjected some humor in the report. "Capt. McNelly and three of his men arrived on Sunday [June 18] with two men who claimed to be brothers and gave their names as Smith—a name no doubt familiar to some of the oldest settlers. The men were captured in Atascosa [C]ounty and they were charged with having operated with the Hardin gang and latterly with King Fisher. They are supposed to be two men who escaped from the Waco jail four or five years ago while under sentence to the penitentiary for assault with intent to kill, and their *alias* is believed to be Burns. Capt. McNelly says he made their arrest without having to fire a shot, and, that the thieves and robbers that are now operating on the frontier have rendezvous posts from twenty-five to fifty miles apart."[80] This is the only known reference to the Smith/Burns brothers being with Hardin.[81] Pink Burns, according to Kinney County Sheriff L. C. Crowell, had stolen a horse in his county and was indicted in September 1875, reporting "Theft of gelding". Burns was still wanted when captured, although McNelly may have been unaware of the previous charge of horse theft.[82]

The *Galveston Daily News* of June 28, 1876 published an encouraging report about rural Maverick County. The editor stated, "The sheep business of this county is large. East of Eagle Pass lie the ranchos, of Pendencia, Comanche and Carrizo, which are principally cattle ranchos of Messrs. Whaley, Vivian, Gibson, Grey, White, Busby, Hamilton and others." Judge William Stone, "one of the largest sheep owners in Southwestern Texas" was prominent among many other sheep men of the region. Twenty miles northeast were the Finley [*sic*, Fenley] ranchos, "comprising both sheep and cattle. ... Messrs. Tarpe, and widow San Miguel, [Trinidad's mother]" and others, "have also flourishing ranches in the same neighborhood." Providing protection from

"Indian raids and thieving Mexicans" in this vicinity was Fort Duncan, "located just south of the town of Eagle Pass, being only separated from the town by a small creek." Conspicuous by omission, unlike previous reports by the *News*, nothing was mentioned about King Fisher's rancho on Pendencia Creek.[83] One week earlier the *News* had claimed, "Citizens in that section say they have not suffered half the anguish from Indians and Mexican forays that Fisher caused them."[84]

Curiously, the name of King Fisher was gaining notoriety as far away as St. Louis, Missouri. The source of the article is unknown, as it appeared in the *St. Louis Republican* as an item of interest, with no explanatory headline. Other articles on the same page were headlined "The Mormon Propaganda", "What the South Wants", and "Reformed by the Lash", suggesting the editor needed material to fill the columns. The article is worth repeating in full as it reveals the writer's efforts at acceptable word play as well as underscoring the growing reputation of King Fisher. It later appeared in a San Antonio newspaper:

KING FISHER is the suggestive name of the chief of a band of robbers who have long been the terror of the people of the western border of Texas. The king fishes for plunder and generally succeeds well in the catch. But he was threatened with bad luck recently. Capt. McNelly, commander of the Texas State Guards, had been looking for him, and succeeded in "corralling" and capturing the king and seven of his men at Eagle Pass on the Rio Grande. The prisoners were turned over to the civil authorities to be dealt with according to law. The king sent word to a number of the "best citizens" of the country that he wanted bondsmen to go bail for him. The aforesaid "best citizens" responded with alacrity to the request, the robbers were carried before a judicial tribunal and held to answer, the bonds being fixed at five hundred dollars in each case. The "best citizens" signed the bonds and King Fisher and his merry men rode away. The prospects for extirpating brigandage on the Texas border are not brilliant. It is due to say on behalf of the "best citizens" that they excused themselves on the ground of their mortal dread of the king in case they refused to sign for him and his band.[85]

While lawless depredations were daily occurring in the Nueces Strip, as well as most other parts of Texas, the legislature debated bills which hopefully would reduce the lawlessness. The intimidation of citizens swelled stories of how even the rangers were no longer a match for so many outlaws. One tale again brought King Fisher's name into the limelight. Hon. C. L. Wurzbach "alluded to a rumor" which had appeared in the *San Antonio Express* that *seven* of McNelly's rangers had been killed in a fight with King Fisher and his men. This of course was totally untrue, but Wurzbach indicated he would telegraph to the editor for verification or else a denial of it happening.[86] It was a Mr. W. W. Lawhon of Pleasanton who learned that McNelly had a fight with King Fisher's "brigade of desperadoes" about ten miles above Fort Ewell, La Salle County, and seven of McNelly's men were killed.[87] Captain McNelly scoffed at the report. In truth during McNelly's years as a leader during the State Police period as well as a Texas Ranger, he lost only one man in action and that was during the battle on the Palo Alto Prairie Battleground in 1875. Reporting that McNelly had lost seven of his men was only a canard.

John King Fisher was free and with his wife Sarah was living again on the Pendencia. The Cavin brothers, J. E., called Ed, and William lived double lives. They rode with desperadoes like the men King Fisher worked with but were often informants to the Texas Rangers. Ed was with King and the others at the Comanche Creek cattle fight, while William "became acquainted with King Fisher" a couple of months later "in July 1876." William Cavin later testified how on or "about September 1st, 1876," Fisher took him to the place where Donovan was killed. Cavin stated, "I had two conversations with J. King Fisher in regard to the murder of William Donovan. He showed me where he met Donovan and showed me the way he ran, then showed me where they got him down. I believe he said he was the hardest damned man he ever killed." Cavin only recalled King naming "Johnny Walton [Jack Watson] as being with him." King described how they shot Donovan, yet he still "ran 50 or 100 yards ... before he fell."[88]

Although no comment from King Fisher was published, he certainly learned of it. The new law which both houses of the legislature had passed would have, "it is reasonable to assume" according to the *Galveston Daily News*, "an immediate moral effect of a very beneficial sort." That was not enough to assure the readers of the *News*. "The news of the event will not be relished by the desperadoes, whose audacity has hitherto known no limit, and will inspire a feeling of some security for life and property in communities which have been overrun and distracted by lawless bands. Cheers are in order for the men who are enlisting in this force for the protection of society against its worst foe in this State." And there was no doubt as to who that "worst foe" was: "By the time they have shown what they can do for the King Fishers and their followers in one or two instances, the improved order of things, which we expect to see inaugurated at once, will be an assured fact, marking a new era in the affairs of Texas."[89]

On August 13, correspondent "M" of the *Inter Ocean*, a Chicago newspaper, wrote to his editor of having met King Fisher. How or why this happened he does not explain but his impression of Fisher was memorable. Back in Austin he described his experience, beginning that "A few days ago, for the first time, I had the rather doubtful honor of seeing and conversing with the notorious desperado, King Fisher, and I must say that I was surprised and disappointed." Apparently, he had been in south Texas when he met Fisher, "the notorious desperado", rather than in Austin, but why both "surprised and disappointed"? He told of having read about the "notorious cattle thief and murderer" and had developed a mental picture of the man; he "naturally expected to see a ferocious looking man, with his character stamped upon his countenance." But he was surprised: "On the contrary, I found him to be little more than a boy, with a tolerably good face and pleasing manners. He is the last man I would take for the desperado who has defied the law and terrorized over a great portion of Western Texas." King Fisher, correspondent M informs us, "does not even wear the usually indispensable sombrero with a snake [skin] around it, but dresses and acts like any other civilized being. … During his stay in town he has dispensed with the six-shooter." It is apparent that this reporter presented a picture of the man which greatly differs from many other writers. In appearance he seemed "little more than a boy" and his wearing apparel was not unlike others of his age. There was no red sash around his waist or bells on his spurs. Perhaps the Chicago visitor was in the town of Eagle Pass, or Carrizo Springs? Possibly San Antonio? Curiously M stressed the political aspect of this visit with King Fisher: "Fisher is of course a good Democrat and having almost supreme control of elections

by intimidation and violence, he is very useful to his party, and consequently will never be punished for his many fearful crimes. Such men as
Fisher and his gang compose one-half of the Democratic party in Texas,
and even Governor Coke and the Legislature dare not take any steps to
put a stop to the reign of terror now existing in this State."[90] One might
wonder if correspondent M was aware of the political meeting in front of
the Raymond House in July.

When correspondent M was considering his thoughts for the *Inter-
Ocean* readers he was unaware of the bank robbery in Goliad. On Tuesday,
the 15th of August, eight masked men rode up to the back door of the Goliad
Bank and dismounted. Two brothers, Edward and Henry A. Seeligson,
owned and operated the sole bank of the county. There was but one man
inside, cashier Mitchell, and the leader ordered him to open the safe. Mitchell
bravely informed the robbers that he could not open the safe as it was impossible to do so without the other key held by a partner, and that person was
not in. The robbers did manage to find $300 in the teller's drawer and then
left town yelling and shooting off their pistols in a dusty gallop.[91] Strangely,
as the robbers left with six-shooters blazing, Goliad resident William
Brooking[92] and one or two others fired back. One report states that the others
firing at the fleeing bank robbers included the notorious Bill Taylor and Bob
Holt.[93] Apparently, no one was hit by flying bullets, probably because the
men shooting did not intend to hit the bandits. Several were recognized even
though they wore masks to hide their identity; the identity was probably made
by recognizing the horses they rode. On Wednesday the 16th, the day after
the robbery, some thirty-five men rode into town, surrounded the Case Hotel,
had the women and children removed, and then "seized Andy Milde, of the
Brooking party, disarmed him, tied him to a horse, and the party rode off
with him, taking the Clinton road."[94] This bit of news came from Goliad on
the 23rd, and even without saying one suspects that the thirty men believed
what the correspondent wrote: "Intentions unknown, but something desperate
will take place. These thirty men were good citizens."[95] The "good citizens"
determined that certain parties who "continued lurking 'round and satisfied
with their booty" should absent themselves from the community. Good citizens
organized themselves into a vigilante company and sought the undesirables.

One rumor reached the *Goliad Guard* that Adolph Milde had been arrested and was found hanging at what was known as the "Lone Tree Water Hole."[96] Historian Victor M. Rose, editor of the *Victoria Advocate*, in his history of the Sutton-Taylor Feud, wrote that Milde, "who, refusing to leave the country in conforming to the edict of expatriation, was forcibly taken from the Case Hotel, in Goliad, in the daytime." The body was found floating in the Guadalupe River near the town of Victoria. Rose wrote that his lifeless body "told in eloquent though mute terms the terrible fate that had befallen him."[97] One suspects that whatever his final fate, whether hanged and then his body tossed in the river, or simply shot to death before being tossed in the river, Milde lost his life by action of the Goliad vigilantes.

A view opposing that of correspondent M regarding King Fisher appeared in the same Chicago newspaper less than a week later. In this issue a lengthy article appeared headlined "Affairs in Texas" and included an eye-catching paragraph describing "A Reign of Terror." It described how cattle thieves were traveling around Texas in bands stealing cattle by the hundreds and murdering anyone who opposed them. They openly defied the authorities, even announcing to some citizens to leave the country or else be killed. One of them was singled out: "King Fisher, the most notorious thief, murderer, and desperado of the lot, was arrested by Captain McNally [*sic*] (of Mexican frontier notoriety), and lodged in prison. After McNally left, Fisher applied for a writ of habeas corpus, and with his whole gang went into the court room and forced the Judge into releasing him on bail, which, of course, is a virtual ending of the prosecution. Fisher will not appear, and the bail cannot be collected." The article continued explaining how a few days before Fisher was in San Antonio and was the center of attraction. "He was escorted round by the Chief of Police, several Aldermen, and other prominent citizens of Democratic proclivities, and was the lion of the day. Yet this man is known to have murdered nine men individually [and] will probably be the next Democratic nominee for Governor, or for Congress."[98] Assuming the incident of Fisher being "escorted" around San Antonio did take place, we must believe that correspondent M was an observer of the incident. But we have found no additional reports of the unusual situation, and who were the police and alderman who escorted "the lion of the day" around San Antonio?

On occasion King was blamed for acts of rustling based on the notion that he simply had the ability to rustle and his reputation would justify the accusation. Citizens of Frio County were the subject of a raid in September. Based on absolutely no evidence, the reporter began by saying that the "party who committed the depredations here are supposed by many of our citizens to be members of King Fisher's clan, if, indeed, they were not commanded by King Fisher in person." Several weeks before thieves had driven off about fifty head of horses. In this latest raid they " 'got away' with twenty-five or thirty head of good horses." Some brave Frio County citizens organized a posse and began a pursuit. At Capt. Jim Speed's ranch this same group stole five more head. Here they awakened two men; one of whom fired his revolver which brought about an immediate response from the thieves. They fired back some fifty or sixty rifle shots before leaving the scene. The Frio County posse apparently had no success in capturing the thieves or recovering the stolen horses.[99]

Further demonstrating hard feelings between Judge William Stone and King Fisher, gossip of how Stone wanted Fisher dead reached the newspapers. In discussing lawlessness in Texas, William Rhett naturally spoke out against it, being interviewed by a reporter for the *New Orleans Republican*. His interview was published on September 3, 1876. In it Rhett firmly denied the rumor "to the effect that Judge Stone of Eagle Pass, offered him $2000 to assassinate King Fisher" claiming the rumor was without foundation, and that he wished, "in order that justice may be done to Justice Stone, to publicly contradict it."[100] If King learned of the denial, it was not enough to calm him because his bitterness against the judge continued. It does suggest that Rhett was a man some felt was not above becoming an assassin for hire. Little else has been learned about this individual William Rhett.

King Fisher may have considered himself extremely fortunate that he was not with his men when Sergeant John B. Armstrong[101] made a raid at Espantosa Lake in Dimmit County. Armstrong's version of the killings reveals the workings of a Texas Ranger in the wild in the 1870s. In his report he explained that he was unable to reach Carrizo Springs until the night of September 30th due to heavy rains. The same heavy rains aided the rangers by denying the sound of their approach to the unsuspecting outlaws. At Carrizo Springs Armstrong had learned that "a party of desperadoes" was encamped on the shore of Lake Espantosa, ten miles northeast, and that another party would pass the night at the Pendencia, whether this meant the community or somewhere on the creek is not clear. Armstrong sent Corporal M. H. Williams and ten men with some concerned citizens to the Pendencia while he with the balance headed for Lake Espantosa. Armstrong hoped to find King Fisher there.

> I arrived within sight of the camp about twelve o'clock p.m., where we dismounted and proceeded on foot, leaving two men to guard the horses and a desperado whom I had captured on [the] way. I discovered their camp on the bank, directly in front of us, and advanced slowly to within twenty yards of them, when two of them commenced firing on us with their six-shooters. We responded promptly, and a lively little fight ensued, resulting in the deaths of three of them, and the wounding of another in five places.

Armstrong identified the three dead as John Martin, Jim Roberts, and George Muller; the wounded man was Jim McAllister, "who had but lately joined the party." The rangers with Armstrong were George Durham, N. A. Jennings, George W. Boyd and A. L. Parrott. The so-called desperado who had been captured "on the way"—Noley Key, attempted to escape from the two rangers left to guard him and was shot to death. The rangers left to guard Key were Thomas Netteville Devine and Thomas J. Evans; they employed *la ley de fuga* to prevent his escape. During this same night Armstrong learned that nearby was a "bad Mexican at Whaley's ranch," eight miles distant, and sent three men to arrest him. The Mexican refused to surrender peacefully, resisted "desperately" and the three men "were obliged to kill him in self defense." Five desperate men were killed by the rangers that night while resisting arrest. Although citizens who had suffered at the hands of cattle and horse thieves welcomed the news of Armstrong's accomplishments, some considered his action nothing more than blood-thirsty murder, their badge giving them the "authority" to kill fearlessly.

Following the gunfight Armstrong took his squad to the ranch of E. A. "Bud" Thompson, hoping to find Alford Day and the Callison brothers there, suspects in the recent Goliad bank robbery. The rangers did recover fifty head of stolen horses and twenty-two yoke of oxen which had been taken from Mexicans on the Rio Grande. They did not find Day or the Callisons, which was a disappointment, and a further disappointment was their learning that King Fisher had left this group about a week before with a large drove of cattle. Frank Porter was supposed to be accompanying Fisher.[102]

Strangely enough the rumor of McNelly losing seven of his men to outlaws again surfaced, the rumor somehow continued to live. As late as October the hoax appeared in the state's leading journal, the *Galveston Daily News*. Not only seven of McNelly's men had been killed, but also the town of Oakville had been burned. The editors of the *News* investigated and learned that the statement of seven of McNelly's men being killed had appeared in a letter from Oakville, dated October 17th "briefly stating alleged facts of the killing ... and the burning of the place by robbers. The extraordinary nature of the story suggested at once a suspicion that it was a hoax, but it was related in such a manner (apparently from a very illiterate source and in broken English, as if from some person of foreign birth) as to cause some anxiety and lead to investigation. We are glad to find our first suspicion sustained."[103]

In early November, Lieutenant Hall sent in a report to Adjutant General Steele regarding his efforts in solving the August Goliad Bank robbery. He had arrested Frank Callison, who then made a full confession as to who else was involved. He named his brother Thomas Callison, William T. Cavin, James T. Trimble, Lark Ferguson [later to become notorious as Pete Spence], Alford Day, John Green, and a freedman identified as Thomas Jasper as those "who were engaged in the attack" on the bank.[104] Freedman Thomas Jasper may be the real name of Bob Holt who also shot at the fleeing bank robbers, but intentionally missing. An article in the *Goliad Guard* stated that he "was young in years but old in crime. He is the same kinky-headed gent who was with Wm. Brooking and Bill Taylor on the memorable day the Goliad bank robbery took place, and pretended to be firing at the robbers as they left."[105] ... On November 15, he reported that Frank Callison had turned state's evidence, now naming four others as aiding and abetting the bank robbers: King Fisher, Bill Taylor, Dock Cornett and William H. Brooking, the man who allegedly shot at the fleeing bank robbers as they galloped out of Goliad.[106] It is difficult to accept Fisher, Taylor or Cornett as aiding and abetting the bank robbers. Fisher and Taylor had enough troubles with the law without knowingly helping anyone intending to rob a bank. Had William Brooking and the others purposely missed hitting the seven men as they made their escape from Goliad? It would appear so.

Strangely a modern historian chose to place King Fisher, Bill Taylor and William Brooking as the leaders of the gang which robbed the bank, quite contrary to what the court record said. Dr. James M. Smallwood wrote in his revisionist book *The Feud That Wasn't* the following: "Their leaders were Billy Taylor, King Fisher, and William Brookings [*sic*], all three wanted for crimes ranging from murder to horse and cattle theft. Both Captain McNelly and Lt. Lee Hall began scouting the area for the highwaymen."[107] Suddenly King Fisher arose from aiding and abetting the Goliad Bank robbers to becoming one of the leaders, a claim with no evidence whatsoever.

The name of King Fisher has never been linked as a killer of men on the scale of John Wesley Hardin or the bragging of the wanton murderer "Bloody Bill" Longley. If he had lived a few years more or a decade or two longer he may have been inclined to write his life story as Hardin did, and Ben Thompson, the future city marshal of Austin through his attorney Walton did, and to a lesser degree Longley in letters to the Giddings newspaper. If King Fisher had provided history with an account of his exciting life, it certainly would have provided historians with answers to the many unanswerable questions.

In far off Austin, Texas, over two hundred miles north, on Christmas Day, 1876, the well-known gunfighter-gambler Ben Thompson was forced into a face-to-face shootout with a saloon owner named Mark Wilson, when Wilson cut loose with a shotgun but missed Thompson. Five seconds later Wilson was dead on the floor with multiple gunshot wounds and his bartender severely wounded. Ben Thompson was never a rough and tumble cowboy like King Fisher, however similar to Fisher the newspapers accused him of many crimes he did not commit. In some ways the two men were equals, but in many ways their lives were very different. Both ran with bad company, were equals in the handling of a six-shooter and yet were happily married men enjoying their families. One called the capital city of Texas home, while one lived virtually on horseback in the *chaparral*. At this point, at the end of the Centennial year of 1876, the two men probably had yet to meet, however their lives would eventually cross in a tragic and unforgettable way in less than a decade.

# Chapter 5

# "A Sort of Prince Among Bandits"

**N**ewspaper editors have always had a singular way with words, and those of the Southwest were no exception. An item from the *Corpus Christi Gazette* provides an excellent example, touching on the frequent conflict between ranchers and pointing out that "Mexican raiders have been quiet just as long as consistent with their revolutionary ideas and the disturbed condition of the frontier. With the success of the revolutionists in Mexico the desire among the Cortinanois on this bank of the Rio Grande to return to their native land develops itself, and as evidence of their loyalty to the principles inculcated by their bandit leaders, they naturally wish to carry back with them a liberal supply of booty." In this editor's mind, "booty" certainly consisted of cattle and horses stolen from Texas ranchers.

*Gazette* readers then learned how a group of raiders descended upon a village known as Piedras Pintas, some fifteen miles southwest of San Diego in Duval County. A young boy who was tending stock learned of their approach and warned some brave citizens, who then provided the raiders with "a warm reception." As the raiders entered the little town, shouting for Cortina, "an effective fire was opened upon them" and three of the bandits fell to the ground dead. The remaining surprised Cortinistas gave up on accomplishing anything but "beating an inglorious retreat." A combined force of brave men from San Diego and Piedras Pintas were in pursuit at last report.[1]

Although we generally think of King Fisher being a Dimmit County rancher, by the mid-1870s people generally considered the town of Eagle Pass in neighboring Maverick County as his base. Fisher, with several companions, during the first week of January 1877 visited Eagle Pass and they proceeded to get drunk. They then rode up and down the street shooting their pistols indiscriminately. Occasionally the *San Antonio Express* began its reporting of violence in an almost jovial tone, claiming the news source was "a party from Eagle Pass, the frontier city" and no doubt it was. The newspaper's source said that any loose dogs, or rats, or chickens wandering the streets became a target. The townspeople of course scurried for shelter from the galloping horses and reckless shooting. No citizen was hit, which suggests the riders were not too drunk to be able to direct their shots harmlessly. After detailing the recklessness of Fisher and his men the report became serious. One rider, perhaps Fisher himself, singled out Judge William Stone and stopped him on the street. The rumor of the judge's attempt to hire an assassin certainly irked Fisher and he took the opportunity to "vilely abuse" the judge. King Fisher indeed, as one headline proclaimed, was "on the warpath." [2]

The editor pointed out that Fisher had no less than nine indictments against him for murder, some of which he did not deny having committed. His middle name of King seemed applicable, as he considered the law no more than "a song"—a fact which was a disgrace to the State of Texas. This attitude placed "a premium on murders ... and bodes but evil wherever it is allowed." The editor continued with his solution to the frontier problem, stating that crime cannot be abolished unless "it is actively discountenanced, not only by the law, but by the masses of the people themselves." To this editor's view, the way of "half-condoning unlawful deeds, that is so generally prevalent in frontier counties, breeds more crime than any other cause existing." What should be done was clear: arrest King Fisher and his men, try them in a courtroom, and if convicted then make them suffer the punishment of the law. This appeal was for proper judicial action, not an appeal for vigilantism. If the citizens of Maverick County could not perform this action then it should be the special duty of the State Rangers, or so believed the editor of the *Express*.[3] The man certainly knew of Captain McNelly's earlier success on the border, and now unknowingly he provided a foreshadowing of the great success of the rangers in his statement of what he thought should be done.

The subject of lawlessness and what to do about it was a constant subject for legislators as well as newspaper editors. The *Castroville Era*, the leading journal of Medina County, had this to say about those who disrespected the law: "Mexicans are not the only cause of trouble upon our borders. Desperadoes and horse-thieves hold high carnival all along the line and openly defy the officers of the law." In this case the *Era's* editor offered no solution to the problem.[4]

In mid-February a report from Maverick County to the *Galveston Daily News* stressed the need for immigrants. The principle town in the county, Eagle Pass, boasted a population of over eighteen hundred citizens. The report told of "several settlements scattered over the county," with Pendencia being the largest, yet having only forty families. "At present," the reporter noted, "there is a feeling of uncertainty as regards stock, growing out of Mexicans raids, but with the arrangement for future protection, both by the general and State governments, there will come a better condition." In spite of such concerns about stock thefts, the reporter concluded by stating, "There is no more healthy country."[5]

The arrival of Lieutenant Lee Hall wasn't announced in local newspapers, but citizens quickly learned of his presence. By making arrests the rangers proved their efficiency and people became less worried about what had become known as "King Fisher's Territory." In February and March 1877, Hall and Sergeant Armstrong both were kept busy scouting and making arrests in McMullen, Karnes, DeWitt, Gonzales, Goliad, Atascosa, Bee, Live Oak, San Patricio, Nueces, and Refugio Counties. On February 11 Hall stopped Charles Bruton at Fort Clark and cut out thirty-nine uninspected cattle from the herd he was driving. Sergeant Armstrong telegraphed the good news to Adj. Gen. William Steele, further informing him that King Fisher was back on the Pendencia and was "gathering a crowd around him again."[6] But Armstrong was aware also that it would be difficult to get witnesses to testify against Fisher.[7] Making arrests was relatively easy; the more difficult task was getting attorneys and juries to bring murderers and thieves to justice. The press seemingly could not give praise enough to Hall and his rangers. The *Goliad Guard* underscored his effectiveness, which notice in turn was printed in the *Galveston Daily News*: "Lieut. Hall and his men, whose headquarters are here, are rendering signal service in many of the western counties in disturbing the movements of parties engaged in unlawful hide transactions. They are also picking up rascals of all grades."[8]

Lieutenant Hall was becoming more and more the key figure in combating lawlessness in south Texas, only because McNelly's physical condition prevented him from being in the field. His tuberculosis, or "white death" as the disease was frequently identified in the nineteenth century, was worsening and it would claim his life in September of 1877. Hall was the right man in the right place to replace McNelly. Jesse Lee Hall was a young man from North Carolina who had extensive experience as a lawman in northern Grayson County, Texas.[9] By early 1877 he was continuing the work McNelly had to abandon.

About this time someone stole horses from Nicolas Sanchez. King Fisher was suspected of the theft, which allegedly occurred on February 17, 1877. The horses were found near Fisher's camp on Chicon Creek near Laredo. The court records state that Fisher did "unlawfully, feloniously and fraudulently steal, take and carry away 27 head of animals from the possession of Nicholas Sanchez." Denacio Sanchez and Roberto Sanchez were named as witnesses. This was listed as Indictment 229, while Indictment 228 included the theft of two geldings from Nicholas Sanchez. Indictment 242 stated Fisher was charged with the theft of seventeen geldings. Sanchez was a successful horse herder: the 1870 Non-Population Schedule of Webb County (Agriculture census) shows 100 head of horses, among other possessions.[10] T. T. Teel defended Fisher and, not surprisingly, he was found not guilty.[11]

In March, in the area south and west of San Antonio, came "a wail of mourning on account of the depredations of horse thieves." The lack of adequate funding for Captain McNelly's company reduced the number of men he had under his command. Because of this, thievery became rampant, except where his few men were visible. On Sunday, March 25, 1877, rancher Steve Gould lost three horses and a mare only eight miles south of the city.

Many of his neighbors had also lost horses due to thieves. No redress of their grievances could happen unless there was a large force of rangers in that dangerous area ready to track down the thieves, and hopefully recover the stolen property. The *Daily Express*, referencing the reduction of McNelly's force, stated the feelings of the ranchers best: "his old command reduced so as to almost destroy its effectiveness, no matter how efficient its commander, or how vigilant and energetic its members, horse thieves have had matters pretty much their own way, save in the immediate neighborhood of where the Rangers are known to be."[12]

At times it seemed that the greatest crimes were, first, the theft of good horses and, to a lesser degree, the theft of cattle—not the crime of murder. There was a danger in committing either crime, of course. A report from Laredo to the San Antonio *Daily Express* on the fate of King Fisher stated that "no definite information regarding the reported killing" could be determined, and initially the belief was that he had been killed during an escape attempt. About mid-March, Fisher and three others were arrested near Laredo and jailed there, and Fisher was charged with possession of stolen cattle. The unidentified individual from the Rio Grande making the report could provide no definite information, only the rumor that King Fisher had been killed while attempting to escape. Rumor also stated that a group of people in Laredo had made an unsuccessful attempt to lynch Fisher, but that the presence of the military, which had been called in to assist the civil authorities, prevented that from happening. This was what the *Daily Express* of San Antonio reported, which then appeared in the *Galveston Daily News* of March 20, 1877. Further, in Webb County "the most bitter hatred exists against King Fisher," and citizens would not provide him bond. One wonders if the difficulty King Fisher had had with the Sanchez family's horses may have been the cause of this ineffectual attempt to lynch Fisher. In contrast, many citizens of neighboring Maverick County were eager to provide bond. The *Daily Express* could only report the rumors and make a conclusion: "King is evidently in a 'bad fix,' and if all reports are true, his reign upon the border is nearing its end."[13] By mid-April, the *Daily Express* could continue with its reporting on the fate of Fisher, obviously pleased that he continued to be such a worthy news item: "King Fisher's bonds have been placed at $5,000, and so far he has failed to give them; neither can he secure attorney, it is said. A motion for a change of venue will be made in his case."[14]

The news from the Nueces Strip was frequently confusing. Somehow King Fisher and an unidentified Mexican had a disagreement over some trivial matter. Apparently, the Mexican believed King Fisher was intent on killing him and fled across the Rio Grande. The unidentified Mexican, described as an "outlaw and desperado ... returned to Eagle Pass a short time ago, thinking he would be safe as long as King Fisher was in jail." King Fisher had perhaps forgotten all about the incident, but on or about the eleventh of April 1877, the Mexican again got into a quarrel, this time with a saloon-keeper named John Smith. He drew his revolver and shot Smith "dead in his tracks." Bystanders saw the injustice of the Mexican's action, and reacted immediately, not waiting for a lengthy trial. The body of the murderer of John Smith "was pierced with thirty bullets fired by a crowd of bystanders."[15]

Not long after this incident, a band of Indians, numbering between sixty and seventy, crossed the Rio Grande between Eagle Pass and New Town, going as far south as Castroville. Then they split up into smaller war parties. Rangers and U.S. troops under Colonel William Shafter struck their trail and followed them nearly to the Rio Grande without engaging them. Efforts at engaging marauders sometimes failed, as in this case due to heavy rains causing the trail to disappear.[16] Although these actions may not have concerned King Fisher directly, they show how dangerous this territory was. Besides, even reporting rumors which may not have been true could result in increased sales of newspapers. Apparently the use of Fisher's name was newsworthy, whether reporting as a rumor or a fact. The danger on the border was always present, just as the innocent saloon-keeper Smith and the man who killed him learned. Traveling alone or even with a group could be extremely hazardous.

The recent September 1876 gunfight on the shore of Lake Espantosa brought attention to the name of Sergeant Armstrong. He was not one to rest on his laurels, as on May 11, 1877 he arrived in Laredo with two prisoners and then made more arrests. On the night of Sunday, May 13, Lieutenant

Hall arrived in Eagle Pass with warrants for the arrest of Williams, the partner of Joe Horner in a recent stage robbery. Hall and Armstrong crossed over the river and arrested Williams on the streets of Piedras Negras, Mexico.[17] They also arrested John Murray and several other fugitives. The telegram from Eagle Pass to the *Galveston Daily News* said that, even with the proper requisition, the arrest and delivery back into Texas was accomplished "after considerable talk and diplomacy"—which meant perhaps the exchange of money. Judge Thomas M. Paschal played an unspecified part during the diplomatic negotiations. As of May 14, Hall and Armstrong had made sixteen arrests.[18] Hall's monthly return lists the number of arrests made in Maverick County and Piedras Negras in May 1877: J. B. Kirkpatrick, *alias* Dorn, J. T. Jones, *alias* Williams, John Murray, William Bruton, Robert Lewis, King Fisher, Jim Burditt, C. H. Thayer, F. J. West, E. H. Parkerson, one Terry, A. Reagan, Wesley Bruton, Andres Porter, two others identified only as Flores and Rodregan.[19] Hall additionally noted to which jail each prisoner was delivered.

Surprisingly, Charles Vivian, King's uncle-in-law, was foreman of the Grand Jury hearing case number 172—the State of Texas v. John King Fisher. The charge was the killing of William Donovan on December 27, 1875. W. C. Bruton was indicted for assault to murder on May 18, 1877. Judge Paschal issued a change of venue to Uvalde County, stating: "There are influences existing in Maverick county in favor of said defendant."[20] Unfortunately, he did not elaborate on what the favorable influences were. T. T. Teel was Fisher's lead attorney.

Judge Thomas Moore Paschal, along with four commissioners, wrote a letter to Governor Richard Hubbard on May 15 advising that when District Court adjourned there would probably be some dangerous prisoners left in the local jail, which would require the employment of additional guards, an expense which the county could ill afford. He hoped that additional rangers could be sent to Eagle Pass. And there was more: "We also wish to express the confidence we feel in Lieut. Hall and his company and to testify the obliga-tion that we feel under to them for the assistance that they have given us, and are still affording. Their presence having inspired our officers and the people generally with confidence, and we feel that the county indictments found by the Grand Jury now in session, and the three arrests made, are largely due to their presence and valuable assistance."[21] The three arrests referred to were Williams, Jim Burditt and of course King Fisher, the latter described as "the most renowned cattle and horse thief and independent bandit on the north side of the Rio Grande."[22] The same bit of news was printed in the Brenham newspaper, which gave King Fisher a different title, calling him "a sort of a king among cattle and horse thieves–a sort of prince among bandits; and said to be one of the worst men north of the Rio Grande."[23] The Brenham editor always carried news of what McNelly and Hall accomplished, due to considering McNelly their hometown boy, although he was from the neighboring village of Burton.

Lee Hall's monthly return listing the company's activities during May merely recorded the arrests made, miles traveled on scouts, and other pertinent information. The entry for May 15 reveals nothing of the excitement which certainly must have accompanied something so special as the arrest of King Fisher: "King Fisher, murder & theft, arrested in Maverick Co. Escorted to Medina Co." This entry was followed with two others: "Jim Burditt, murder, arrested in Maverick Co. Escorted to Austin" and "C. H. Thayer, embezzlement, arrested in Maverick Co. Escorted to Austin."[24]

There was indeed an explanation as to how Lieutenant Hall was so successful in arresting fugitives: "The direct and unmistakable cause of the restoration of the confidence of the law-abiding people and the present supremacy of the law, is the presence of Lieutenant Hall. As soon as a capias is made out it is handed to his boys and 'they take them just as they come to them.' A member of the command has been sworn in as deputy sheriff and the court is virtually run by the company."[25] Hall had significant experience with courts and how the law worked, because he had been Sergeant-at-Arms in Austin back in 1875.

The work of Lieutenant Hall in Maverick County and Piedras Negras was similar to the work of Major John B. Jones in Kimble County in April: arresting everyone in the county who could not give a good accounting of their presence. Major Jones and other Frontier Battalion company commanders arrested over thirty men in what came to be known as the "Kimble County Roundup."[26] In Hall's case, it amounted to the "Maverick

County Roundup." An interesting brief biography of Jones appeared in a Texas newspaper in September 1877. Ranger Mervyn Bathurst Davis, identifying his contributions as "Mervyn," wrote:

> Major Jones has met and defeated the Indians in fifteen battles. Several times he has fought hand to hand with the savages, and on all occasions he has proved himself a soldier and hero. Impervious to the extremes of cold or heat, able to endure the tortures of hunger and thirst, a Bedouin in the saddle, he leads his wild Rangers through the gloom of midnight, along the forest trails, and the wolf and the owl fly from his path, but the red fingered murderer he drags into light to toil in chains or dangle at a rope's end as justice decrees. ... One by one the desperadoes are being captured and handed over to justice by these sun-browned, cartridge-girdled riders, captured or sent to that place whence they return no more to trouble.[27]

What Private Davis wrote about Major Jones could easily apply to the red-haired Ranger Lee Hall. However, whether King Fisher would be considered a "sun-browned, cartridge-girdled rider" if captured by Major Jones is a very different question.

Lieutenant Hall, on May 21 with his "gallant company," passed through Uvalde *en route* from Eagle Pass to Castroville, having in charge ten desperadoes captured on the frontier.[28] King Fisher was the best known, although he had not intentionally created the image of being the number one desperado of the Nueces Strip. The other who received considerable attention was Williams, the partner of stage robber Joe Horner. These ten prisoners would be placed in the Castroville jail for safekeeping, but not for long, as they would be delivered to the county where they were wanted.

In addition Medina County deputy sheriff Stevens delivered Frank Ankrum to the Bexar County jail on a charge of murder "said to have been committed seven years ago. The extreme youthfulness, the good standing and quiet behavior of Mr. Ankrum tends to make it appear that he is maliciously prosecuted."[29] Ankrum, identified in the press as a jailor at Castroville, was accused of killing his stepfather in 1870 "on the Medina." The Grand Jury found ten or twelve indictments against various individuals but none against Frank Ankrum, resulteing in Ankrum's immediate release. He now was able to return to Castroville. Perhaps he had been "maliciously persecuted."[30] On December 10, 1877, while Ankrum was working as a deputy constable for Medina County, a body of a man was found on Chicon Creek some thirty miles southwest of San Antonio.[31] Ankrum held an inquest on the body and found that he had been both hanged and shot: "One shot was through the head and another passed through the ankle. He had been dead several days." No papers were found to identify him.[32] At this point Frank Ankrum seemed to be in good standing in the community of Castroville. But we shall see that Frank Ankrum was headed for prison, and there is evidence that King Fisher was in part the cause.

At some point Fisher—the most intellectual of the group, perhaps— spoke for the prisoners and requested the *Castroville Era* to give their thanks to Lieutenant Hall and his men and to Sheriff Ferdinand Niggli and his deputies "for the kind and courteous treatment received at their hands."[33] The *Era* said that none of the officers involved had ever allowed a prisoner to escape and that they were always kind and humane to them. The *Era* awarded great praise to the men and services of the Frontier Battalion.[34]

Citizens in Bexar and Medina Counties by mid-1877 were so intrigued with King Fisher that they may have forgotten about the notorious Juan Cortina and his raiding on Texas ranches. A correspondent contributing to the San Antonio *Daily Express* who identified himself only as "Malleus" may have witnessed the rangers transporting the prisoners through Medina County on their way to the Bexar County jail. Malleus composed an interesting letter on May 31 giving the readers an interesting question on which to ponder.[35]

Malleus begins by stating that he presumed "the Rio Grande people feel somewhat relieved since the arrest and imprisonment of King Fisher but how long will they feel good?" He points out that with Fisher in prison and Cortina "released from duress, of the two, which is to be dreaded the most?" He raises the question to the people living on the Rio Grande: "is King Fisher not some protection against marauding bands of Mexicans on the Rio Grande, and had they rather Fisher would live, and to a certain extent be free from their Mexican bandits, or would they rather Cortina have existence and be in continual dread of him or some of his emissaries?" Here Malleus points out that the Mexican marauders are afraid of King Fisher, and "I expect it is well they are; but Fisher says he has never injured a white man. Can Cortina say as much?" Malleus then states his belief, which was suspected of King several years before: "I believe he was in a measure *a protector* [emphasis added] to them against the Mexican marauders."

Malleus then provides an interesting comparison of the two men. Cortina "is of low birth ... entirely unlettered he has cultivated the coarser passions until he is incapable of doing justice to any man, especially an American." In contrast, King Fisher is "a young man about 27 years old, has a family living on the Rio Grande ... he is possessed of rather an intelligent look, and is capable of being corrected. He is beyond a doubt incapable of committing as dark deeds as Juan Cortina has committed." Malleus is in favor of considering King Fisher judiciously. He is accused of crimes, but that question should be established in the proper court, "and the penalty fixed as the law directs."

Now the further question stands as to why there was, as Malleus put it, such "an accumulation of desperate men" on the Rio Grande.[36] The cattle business in West Texas had "almost ceased." The large cattlemen had fenced in pastures and "scores" of cowboys were now out of employment. These young men were out of work and knew no other business, such as farming. They soon fell into "bad company and bad habits." The United States government continued to endeavor to establish peace and good order on the Rio Grande, but to no effect: "as long as the U.S. government continues its leniency to Mexico, so long will the Rio Grande trouble be in existence. Young men who would make good citizens under a different state of affairs will, as the rule is now, make desperadoes." Malleus does end his letter with a solution: "Let the American Eagle flap her wings over Mexico ... obliterate the line of demarcation between Mexico and the United States. Let them both be under the same rule; then, my word for it, civilization will advance to the Pacific coast, and there will be no more border troubles, unless it be with some other nation. If any one can find a better solution, let me hear from him."[37] In brief, Malleus argued to let "manifest destiny" move forward to the Pacific as a "natural" course.

When Hall and his prisoners reached San Antonio, the press announced his arrival, stating he had brought with him "a Superb Gang of Scoundrels." Various correspondents had kept the *Daily Express* informed of Hall's actions while he operated in the area of Eagle Pass during the previous weeks.[38] Near the end of May, Hall had distributed most of the thirty-three prisoners he had captured "to the places where their presence is desired."[39] Two of the group Hall left at Castroville—King Fisher and Andres Porter— and the remaining eight were to be placed in the Bexar County jail or taken to the Travis County jail in Austin. At this time, Fisher had six indictments against him for cattle stealing and one for murder, or so reported the *Daily Express*. As discussed in previous chapters, rancher William Donavan had been murdered, and circumstantial evidence pointed to King Fisher's complicity, if he was not the actual triggerman. Porter was also indicted for murder. In addition to listing the names and alleged crimes of these prisoners, the *Daily Express* praised the work of the rangers: "In the zealous discharge of his duties, Lieut. Hall crossed over into Mexico and secured the arrest of a number of the above outlaws who, being ignorant of extradition treaties, felt themselves secure on that side. Too much praise cannot be awarded to officers like Lieutenants Hall and Armstrong, who have accomplished so much for the public good at such great risk to themselves. Criminals are fast finding out that 'the way of the transgressor is hard' in Texas, and are disposed to migrate to the Black Hills."[40]

With the news of these arrests, the attitude of many ranchers in Maverick County changed. The district court was in session and, for the first time since the county was organized years ago on September 4, 1871, grand jurors were performing their duty "fully and impartially."[41] Correspondent "Ourdab," who contributed this insightful message to the *Galveston Daily News*, pointed out that the District Judge and District Attorney were "strenuous and zealous in their duties" and many citizens were waking up to the necessity of "putting forth all energies to make a clean sweep of the desperado element which has so long terrorized this community." Ourdab stated that the reason for this "unprecedented animation on the part of the citizens" was that Lieutenant Hall and his "gallant boys" provided the moral support. Hall and his detachment had arrived only a few days before and they had already made numerous arrests, including the most notorious—King Fisher, "our de facto ruler." Ourdab continued, explaining that Fisher had been "dethroned, and now lies in jail under an indictment for murder in the first degree, which deed, though committed two years since on the person of a well-known and law-abiding citizen, has escaped the notice of four grand juries."[42] This was a strong statement, and Ourdab certainly was aware that, if his true identity were made known, he could become a target for any number of these desperadoes. While Ourdab wrote these brave lines, the justice system was working: King Fisher was no longer in the Eagle Pass jail but was being delivered to the more secure jail in Castroville.

Ferdinand Niggli was the Medina County sheriff when King Fisher and the others were delivered to his jail. Born in Switzerland about 1849, he now was in his first term as sheriff, elected on February 15, 1876. He would serve until June 1882 when he resigned. He certainly had earned the respect of Medina County citizens and the respect of the jail's prisoners as well.[43]

Lieutenant Hall was eminently successful as a Texas Ranger. Seemingly he had no difficulty in arresting wanted men and delivering them to the county authorities who wanted them. Austin's *Weekly Democratic Statesman*, at the end of May pointed out that Hall was "distributing his prisoners over the several counties in which they are indicted." At the time he had about thirty in the Travis County jail. Elsewhere in the same issue, the editor pointed out, perhaps only half in jest, that the county jail had become "almost a branch of the penitentiary. It now contains seventy-five prisoners, about half of whom have been brought here from other counties for safe keeping."[44]

State support for the Texas Rangers and Hall's company of rangers in particular was frequently an issue with the legislature. Funding men and mounts was not an easy task, and typically many counties of east Texas felt that the expense should be borne by the counties which needed extra protection, which were generally in west Texas. When the Frontier Battalion was created in mid-1874, each of the six companies had seventy-five men, but now they were frequently reduced to fifteen or less. In June 1877, it became common knowledge that Captain Hall's command was to be greatly reduced or even disbanded entirely. Now counties were advised to take up a fund to support the company. If that were to happen, then *maybe* the state would reimburse the counties. A concerned citizen composed a lengthy letter to the *Galveston Daily News* in early June indicating that it was "pretty generally understood" that Hall's company would be disbanded by June 15 if the people did not take up a fund sufficient to keep them in the field. "Nym Myrtle," as he signed himself, expressed his outrage: "Nothing is more discouraging to the West Texan than the thought that he is compelled to pay toward the support of a Legislature that squabbles away valuable time, makes vicious laws, ignores the vital interests of his section, and leaves him to the mercy of thieving Mexicans and murderous desperadoes." To Nym Myrtle there was only one solution to the state's problem: strengthen the existing ranger force. He explained that "the sheriffs of most of the western counties are timid and incompetent—not fit to handle prisoners and arrest desperadoes of King Fisher's stripe."[45] This individual was writing his letter to the editors of the *News* from Rockport on the fifth of June, and he was certainly aware of the stealing of horses and cattle and the brand blotching, as well as other crimes.

Why Nym Myrtle identified King Fisher as a symbol of the lawless men that would soon have free rein if Hall's command was legislated out of service is open to speculation, as there were certainly worse men than Fisher acting in the Nueces Strip and coastal areas. Perhaps with John Wesley Hardin out of the state and Bill Longley in prison, John King Fisher had become the most noted desperado in Texas. Some Texans considered King Fisher in some manner a special breed among men. A writer in Dallas expressed clearly that thought, and added his appreciation of what the governor was attempting to accomplish: "There are more distinguished desperadoes in Texas to-day than in any of the western states, from the simple fact that since the war until very recently there has been no organized or promising action to meet them. King Fisher and John Wesley Hardin are fine examples of these original cusses, and a hundred lesser suns revolve around these great luminaries of crime. Governor Hubbard is doing a great service in his faithful support of the frontier forces."[46]

On the fourth of July, a writer in San Antonio reinforced the notion that Fisher was the King of Outlaws and commented on the thievery of the two nations:

> [h]ere in San Antonio everybody knows that the Texans steal as much in Mexico as the Mexicans do in Texas. The thieves are principally Mexicans who live on this side of the Rio Grande, but they have no lack of a fair sprinkling of American thieves. For instance, King Fisher, the most dangerous of Texas desperadoes, is the dread of all citizens beyond the Rio Grande. The Mexicans have driven their cattle into the interior of Mexico, but their distance does not insure their safety, for the Texas thieves bring vast herds of horses and mules to San Antonio, and none of the so-called owners can show a bill of sale.

But no solution was offered to resolve the problem.[47]

King Fisher was still lodged in the Castroville jail in mid-July. He was to be delivered to Uvalde to be tried on a writ of *habeas corpus*. Somehow Judge Thomas M. Paschal learned of a possible rescue attempt by friends of Fisher— not just a few, but a group numbering forty. Fisher was to leave Castroville on July 11, in the charge of twelve of Lieutenant Hall's men. At least one report stated that there would be rangers of Captain Pat Dolan's company to assist in getting the prisoner safely to Uvalde.[48] That Hall would place twelve of his men in charge of one prisoner underscores the importance of Fisher at this time. The dozen rangers had received instructions that if a rescue attempt was made, they were to shoot him "attempting to escape." Hall informed Fisher of this brutal fact of life, reminiscent of McNelly's message to him the year before after the arrest, and reportedly Fisher "quietly remarked that he was willing to take the chance of being shot." The *Daily Express* concluded its "exciting report" that if such a rescue attempt was made, then "we may expect to hear of some bloody work."[49] This bit of "exciting" news appeared not only in the San Antonio *Daily Express* but also in the *Daily Democrat* of New Orleans and perhaps other newspapers as well.[50]

There was no rescue attempt. The forty friends of King Fisher remembered the custom of shooting prisoners attempting to escape and wisely reconsidered. At Uvalde the trial of Fisher ordered on the writ of *habeas corpus* had to be granted a continuation, because one of his needed witnesses was not present.[51] Not only was the case continued, but it was transferred to Castroville. Fisher was now doubly watched, not only by the Medina County authorities but also by Lieutenant Hall's rangers. In spite of the careful watch, he and other prisoners made an "ineffectual attempt to escape" the night of July 26, which failed.[52] It was big news that the State had now produced a new witness to testify against Fisher. This new witness in essence testified that he had been with King Fisher after the defendant had killed Donovan and that Fisher had shown him where the killing had taken place. This unidentified witness also testified that Fisher had told him that Donovan was "the hardest d—d man he had ever killed." The witness was the ranger informant, William T. Cavin. This evidence from one who was supposedly an ally of Fisher was "widely at variance with the common tenor of previous testimony, and produced a ripple of sensation." Fisher, through his counsel, merely stated that that particular witness lied. The District Attorney, John C. Sullivan, stated that he would continue to prosecute Fisher for all he was worth.[53] Although the testimony in this case had not been found, Fisher was still to stand trial under the writ of *habeas corpus*, charged "for the murder of one Donovan," with "considerable interest" was taken in the matter.[54]

If we can believe the press, King Fisher attempted an escape on August 5, with help from the inside. Medina County jailer Frank Ankrum had been accused of providing tools to King Fisher that he could use in making his escape attempt, in exchange for $500 Fisher was to give him. It was earlier reported that Ankrum was delivered to the Bexar County jail. If this was true, he apparently had been discharged, as he was back working as a jailer in July and August. Ankrum provided the tools with which Fisher removed the lock from his cell door. But the plan failed because Fisher was taken to the Bexar County jail. It was another prisoner who had "squealed": Jasper Merritt. Merritt revealed the plot before the grand jury because Ankrum had mistreated him. Sheriff Niggli received the warrant for Ankrum's arrest and placed him in jail.[55]

Later in August Fisher wrote from cell number four to the *Castroville Era*, complaining "that the citizens of that place do not send fruits, late papers and magazines to the prisoners, as well regulated communities do."

The editor commented that the letter was "unique in its way" but added that the letter was "about as original as those of Bill Longley."[56]

Nothing was completed during July and August, but the jail became overcrowded, in part due to the effectiveness of Hall's rangers in arresting wanted men. Sheriff Niggli and deputy August Hornung delivered Fisher, William Bruton, Robert Lewis, and Nicholas Reynolds to the Bexar County jail, known as the "Bat Cave."[57] Fisher's case dealt with the murder of William Donovan, while the other three were charged with being implicated in the murderous assault of Alejo Gonzales on May 29, 1876 during the Comanche Creek gun battle. After a hearing before Judge Thomas Paschal, the prisoners were denied bail.[58]

The Bat Cave was an uncomfortable place even on the best of days. It had been built back in 1850 along with the new courthouse on the northwest corner of Military Plaza. The jail's only entrance was through the ground floor of the courthouse, and it was surrounded on three sides by walls. The jail was a four-cell affair and was generally overcrowded, but the worst may have been that there were bats living there, hence the nickname. By the time King Fisher was incarcerated in it, there was concern from some citizens of San Antonio regarding the conditions in which prisoners were held. One concerned citizen wrote to the *San Antonio Light* asking if the city should not "remove the bad impression, both at home and abroad, relative to the condition of the city calaboose?" It was known not only as the "Bat Cave" but also the "Vermin Quarry," as well as the "Rat Cave," as occasionally rats would make it their habitation as well. This concerned citizen didn't complain about the jail's food or treatment of prisoners but only that the "cave" itself was "a blighting disgrace."[59] On some occasions the press referred to the facility as the "Black Hole of San Antonio," a reference to the notorious jail of Calcutta.[60]

Fortunately, a *Daily Express* reporter was allowed to visit the Bexar County jail to report on the condition of the facility and interview its most noted prisoner, King Fisher himself. This unidentified reporter first acknowledged the courtesy of Deputy Sheriff Thomas P. McCall[61] and jailor William Lyons. The visit was in the afternoon of September 3 just before the evening meal. The reporter appreciated the "excellent opportunity of conversing with the prisoners and gaining an insight into the general management of the prison which seems to be excellent, all things considered." He noted that the building was much too small, considering the number of prisoners, and the ventilation was poor and the enclosure was cramped. However, the prison and grounds were perfectly clean, and the prisoners were "cleanly and in excellent spirits not withstanding their confinement. Floors of the cells were as bright and clean as a country farm house in the days when carpets were less used than now; and the stench usually considered inseparable from a Texas jail, was not noticeable." In case the readers wondered about the food, the reporter informed them that meals were served twice a day, in the morning at 8:00 a.m. and again at 4:00 p.m. The food appeared wholesome and in sufficient quantity. The prison was clearly and consistently guarded, and there were no irons on the prisoners. The exception of course was that if a prisoner chose to rebel against prison authorities he would be shackled. Then came the most important part of the reporter's visit, a conversation with King Fisher and his associates: Nicholas Reynolds, Robert Lewis, and William Bruton.

The reporter described Fisher's slender build and dark hair and eyes and how Fisher reminded him of "an easy, jolly kind of country youth, such as one often finds around the camp-fires of a wagon train—possessing more than the ordinary intelligence of the class alluded to, not so rough as to be repulsive, neither particularly refined in manners or conversation." Fisher stated that he expected to give bond in the amount of $25,000 in a few days and then be set at liberty. He also indicated he understood he would be arrested on another charge for "the killing of some fellow he had never seen or heard of." He suspected the arrest was because one of the State Rangers held some personal ill will against him, and further, Fisher complained of the rough manner in which his name had been handled by the newspapers, saying they had even charged him with being a horse thief. He then with "exceeding earnestness" remarked: "they ought not to accuse me of that, for I never stole a horse in my life and everybody that knows me knows that."

Fisher, the reporter judged, was in his mid-twenties. The other prisoners associated with King Fisher—Lewis, Reynolds, and Bruton—were likewise "all comparatively young men and though impatient to regain their liberty seem cheerful."[62] These three received a small amount of publicity when they arrived at the Bexar County jail. Ranger Parrott, of Hall's command, arrived about August 9 with Nick Reynolds, who was charged with being implicated with King Fisher in the Donovan killing. Captain McNelly arrived about the same time with Charles Bruton and Bob Lewis, also charged with murder. "The three prisoners captured by Hall's men are here in prison. A perfect war against the lawless is raging," commented the *Daily Express* correspondent, identified only as "C. B. O." An important additional bit of information as to how the McNelly-Hall rangers were able to be as successful as they were is provided in C. B. O.'s conclusion: "In their scout the party which 'took in' Charles Bruton and Bob Lewis rode seventy miles in less than twelve hours, which killed McNelly's horse and badly injured the other animals ridden. McNelly lost his horse on the road returning, two miles from Eagle Pass, and footed this distance to reach the town. His loss is about $125, which the States should make good."[63]

The *Daily Express* reporter was not the only member of the journalistic trade who was interested in King Fisher. A reporter from the *Pleasanton Journal* had "quite an interesting interview" with the noted prisoner while on a visit to San Antonio during the latter part of September. This reporter also noted Fisher was about twenty-five and of dark complexion and medium stature, "with a well knit frame, and has a very pleasing countenance; in all, he is quite a handsome and somewhat polished man." Fisher, it was pointed out, had numerous friends, "among them some of the largest and most influential stock men of Western Texas, who will strain every nerve to bring about his acquittal."[64]

Prisoners, at least not King Fisher, did not have to depend on jail food for their meals. Some years later Joseph C. Foster, professional gambler of San Antonio's Vaudeville Theatre, admitted to befriending Fisher while he was incarcerated in the Bat Cave, adding that they were "warm friends. When he was in jail here in Bexar county, I fed him and furnished him with everything he wanted for his personal comfort at my own expense." One only wonders why Foster was so inclined to provide Fisher with such creature comforts.[65] They must have become acquainted in some past incident of which we have no knowledge.

The Goliad Bank robbery had not been forgotten. Frank Callison had accused King Fisher of aiding and abetting in the robbery, but no charges were ever made against him. Callison was considered the instigator, and he paid a steep price for his involvement. In late October, James Lincoln, the capable Goliad County sheriff, was observed delivering his prisoner to Huntsville, Callison, having been sentenced to serve nine years in Huntsville, along with Eli Brown, sentenced to serve time for horse and ox stealing. Bill Taylor, also accused along with Fisher of aiding and abetting the robbers, had his case of murdering Gabriel Slaughter in 1874 continued. He was sent to the secure jail at Galveston for safekeeping.[66] Judge Henry Clay Pleasants appointed Messrs. Swann, of Beeville, and Wells, of Rockport, to defend prisoner Frank Callison. Although dealing with bank robbers and slayers of men was serious business, occasionally the press could report humor among the counselors. During some private conversation with their client, they took him outside, when he said, "Gentlemen, all I want you to do is to get the case continued. Before next court comes on I know where I can get hold of five or six hundred dollars, and then I will employ a *good* lawyer." Clearly, these gentlemen were of the opinion that, by the time he served his nine years, he would have sense enough to know a good lawyer when he saw one.[67]

By reputation, in Texas in the 1870s, the most notorious Texas bad man was John Wesley Hardin. He had killed numerous men but had left the state due to the vigilante actions against his friends and family members after his killing a deputy sheriff in 1874. Although out of the state, Hardin had not been forgotten. The Texas Rangers in general and one of Captain McNelly's men in particular remembered him well. John B. Armstrong was the man who had accidentally shot himself and could no longer even ride a horse, but he could focus on trying to find out where John Wesley Hardin was hiding out. Armstrong combined forces with Jack Duncan, a detective from Dallas, and the pair eventually located Hardin in far off Pensacola, Florida. The Texans, with several Florida law officers and civilians, managed to capture Hardin and deliver him safely back to the Travis County jail in August of 1877. One might think that, with Hardin behind bars in Austin and Longley await- ing the hangman's noose in Giddings, John King Fisher's star would have risen dramatically. But this was not the case. Although the name of King

Fisher was familiar to most honest citizens and lawmen over the state, he had not attained the recognition of Hardin or Longley, and he never would. Fame would have to wait. As his star ascended, Fisher chose to abide by the law rather than break it.

King Fisher was not the biggest news of 1877. The biggest news of the summer took place in August when Sergeant Armstrong delivered John Wesley Hardin safely to the Travis County jail. Besides the incarceration of Hardin, there were other major desperadoes of the Southwest no longer on the loose. The *Daily Democratic Statesman* recognized the significance of this and provided an editorial which reflected what the state troops had accomplished. Headlined "CASTING OUT OF DEVILS— HOW TEXAS DOES IT," all in uppercase and bold letters, suggesting that the state was setting the example for other states to follow in dealing with the criminal element. If King Fisher was able to read this issue, he may have felt a sense of regret that he now was on the wrong side of the law-and-order coin:

> Murderers and thieves have suffered fearfully of late in Texas. Two notorious scoundrels, Ringgold [John Ringo] and [George] Gladden are imprisoned or dead. King Fisher is incarcerated or has been released on bail remaining under the surveillance of the State troops. Scott Cooley was arrested and died in a spasm of rage and chagrin. Bill Longley sweats and swears in the Giddings jail. Ham White, the famous stage coach robber, makes cigars for life in the West Virginia penitentiary. Jim Taylor, of the Taylor gang of desperadoes, was killed while resisting arrest at San Saba last Thursday. … Bill Thompson, well known in this city, is now in the Ellsworth city jail, charged with killing the sheriff of Ellsworth, Kansas. Wesley Hardin, cousin of the Taylors, the most reckless murderer ever known in Texas, was committed to our jail yesterday. He has killed, so the story goes, twenty-five or thirty white men besides Mexicans and negroes.[68]

The editorial continued with a review of various lynching bees, not only in Texas but in other states. Although there were a few errors in his writing, editor John Cardwell made his point: the State Rangers, whether led by McNelly, Hall, or Major Jones, had accomplished a great deal in reducing the lawlessness within the borders of the state. John Ringo would leave Texas and go on to greater fame in Arizona, and George Gladden would remain in prison in Huntsville, Texas, not West Virginia, until 1884 when he was pardoned. He then went to Arizona. Scott Cooley, an important figure in the Mason County "Hoo Doo War" alongside Ringo and Gladden, died in agony, perhaps by poison, in June of 1876. Bill Thompson, brother of the more notorious Ben, was captured by State Troops, stood his trial in Ellsworth, Kansas, and was acquitted of the killing of Sheriff C. B. Whitney.

One may wonder if King Fisher ever thought the rangers were focusing their attention on him more than he deserved. He may never have stated that feeling, but if he had it would not be surprising. After all, correspondent "Ourdab" on May 17, 1877 wrote that the court in Maverick County was "virtually run by the company" of Lee Hall. Years later one of McNelly's most trusted men, George P. Durham, stated what was perhaps obvious, or at least what he perceived to be true: "With Captain [McNelly] on his sick bed in San Antonio, Lee Hall took command; and Lee thought to make a reputation he had to do something to King Fisher. He kept sending over details to arrest King." Durham continued: "Well, damn it, we didn't have any case on King. He stood trial on that Daugherty [*sic*, Donovan] killing and come clear. They proved that the two men was sworn enemies; that they met on the prairie and it was a swap-out; and King won."[69]

King may have occasionally felt the rangers were harassing him due solely to his reputation when there were others much worse in actuality than he. He probably didn't ponder these questions much, as there were more important things on his mind. On October 31, 1877 King and Sarah welcomed their first child, Florence Fredonia, to the world. She would live well into the modern age, death not claiming her until June 9, 1952.

John King Fisher circa early 1880s. Photographer unknown. *Courtesy of Lawrence E. Vivian and Larry G. Shaver Collections.*

Ovie Clark Fisher, author of the first biography of King Fisher. *Courtesy of the Larry G. Shaver Collection.*

Grey "Doc" White with wife and family in 1891. As Dimmit County Justice of the Peace, White performed the marriage ceremony of his friend King Fisher to fiancée Sarah Vivian. *From left*: Sophia A. and Wade A. standing in front of mother Louisa Jane; Oliver L. standing in front of father Grey; Benjamin C. and Ira L. on fence; Walter G., far right. *Courtesy of Thomas C. Bicknell.*

Charles B. Bruton and wife Eliza Agnes Cornett Bruton in the mid- to late 1880s. *Photographer unknown. Courtesy of Lynn Cornett.*

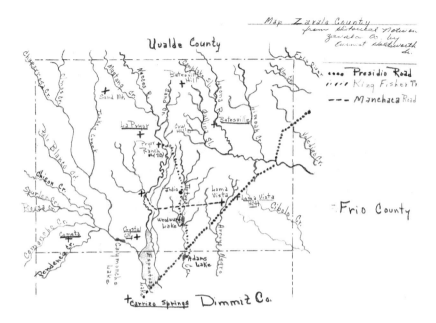

King Fisher (*left*) with good friend John H. Culp in 1873 in Goliad County, Texas. The Western History Collection, University of Oklahoma Libraries, #2153.

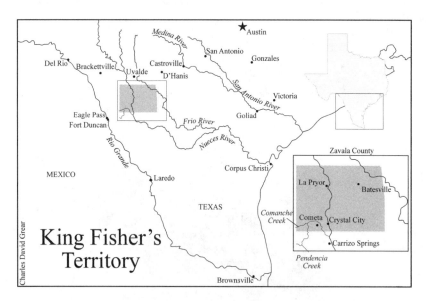

Map of the Nueces Strip. At one time King Fisher was described in a speech by A. J. Evans as being in charge of twenty counties in south Texas, as if he were a "robber baron" (*Austin Daily Democratic Statesman*, June 27, 1876). *Map courtesy of Charles David Grear.*

King Fisher and fiancée Sarah Vivian in their usual attire. Image by ranger-photographer A. L. Parrott on December 27, 1875 shortly before the William Donovan killing. *Courtesy of Ernesto Dovalina and Larry G. Shaver.*

L. H. McNelly. Image made by Inglis in Montreal, Canada in 1872.
This shows McNelly as a Captain in the Texas State Police during his
pursuit of absconding Adjutant General James Davidson. *Courtesy of
the Albert and Ethel Herzstein Library, San Jacinto Museum of History,
La Porte, Texas.*

Trinidad San Miguel (*seated*) of Eagle Pass, Texas and Piedras Negras, Mexico. From a photograph made circa 1873 by Maximilian T. Jesse. *Courtesy of the Frank L. Hobart Collection, El Progreso Memorial Library, Uvalde, Texas.*

A young A. M. "Gus" Gildea, one-time deputy sheriff of Kinney County, Texas, as he appeared in 1875. Cabinet card image credited to "Lewis, 203 W. Commerce Street, San Antonio, Texas." *Courtesy of the Cecilia G. Stirman and Chuck Parsons Collections.*

The John H. Culp Family. *Standing, back row from left*: John Marion Culp, Julia Culp, Marion John Sawyers, Maggie Culp, George Wesley Culp, Lona, and Susan. *Front, from left*: Alfred Alonzo Culp, Beulla Culp, John Henry Culp, Madora Culp, and Ellen Bruton Culp holding Ida Culp. Image made in 1901 at the Culp home in Roswell, New Mexico Territory. Ellen Bruton Culp was the sister of Charles, Wesley, and William Bruton, friends and associates of John King Fisher. *Courtesy of Patricia L. Skinner and the Larry G. Shaver Collection.*

Napoleon Augustus Jennings, Texas Ranger, columnist, and author of *A Texas Ranger*. Although written in a near-fictionalized style, Jennings' memoir provides considerable information about King Fisher and the times in which he lived. This engraving appeared in the July 9, 1899 issue of the *Salt Lake Tribune*, Salt Lake City, Utah.

PURIFYING THE BORDERS.

THE TEXAS RANGERS RAIDING A HEADQUARTERS OF HORSE THIEVES, CATTLE-RUSTLERS AND "BAD" MEN.

An artist's depiction showing the capture of King Fisher and his gang by Captain McNelly and Texas Rangers. This originally appeared in the New York publication, *Life*, on December 19, 1901. Fisher is represented in the lower right-hand corner wearing a white hat and in the act of drawing a pistol. Note the sign above the doorway, "King Fisher His [*sic*] Shack" and the ranger identified as "Field Secretary Jennings" taking notes and having rolls of paper in his saddle bags. *Courtesy of the Larry G. Shaver Collection.*

John Barklay Armstrong, who engaged members of King Fisher's "gang" at Espantosa Lake, with fatal results. *Courtesy of the Chuck Parsons Collection.*

Jesse Lee Hall. The earliest known image of this man, who replaced the ailing Captain McNelly and gained fame as a Texas Ranger, later serving in the Philippine Islands during the Philippine Insurrection. The original image is a mere .5" × 1" and is held by a 2.75" × 1.75" gutta percha frame of flora design. *Courtesy of the Kurt House Collection.*

Judge Thomas Moore Paschal. Paschal had once served as King Fisher's defense attorney. Fisher faced Paschal the judge numerous times during his career but was never convicted of a crime. *Courtesy of the Frank L. Hobart Collection, El Progreso Memorial Library, Uvalde, Texas.*

The old "Bat Cave" jail in San Antonio which housed King Fisher at one time. Between 1879 and 1890, the building was used as a recorder's court, police headquarters, and city jail. *Courtesy of the Frank L. Hobart Collection, El Progreso Memorial Library, Uvalde, Texas.*

Florence Fisher at the age of three years. *Courtesy of the Larry G. Shaver Collection.*

Old fortified San Miguel Rancho, twenty miles above Eagle Pass, Texas, built in 1860. *On the ground*: Trinidad San Miguel, personal friend of King Fisher (*far right*) and Judge Bonnet (*far left*). *Courtesy of the Frank L. Hobart Collection, El Progreso Memorial Library, Uvalde, Texas.*

Jane Lewis Maury Maverick and husband Albert Maverick. Mrs. Maverick innocently enjoyed a pleasant conversation about home life and children with King Fisher, and she was surprised to learn later that he was a notorious rustler. *Courtesy of Thomas C. Bicknell.*

A view of Eagle Pass during Fisher's lifetime, focusing on a typical stagecoach of the era. *Courtesy of the Frank L. Hobart Collection, El Progreso Memorial Library, Uvalde, Texas.*

Owen Clinton Pope, who influenced King Fisher to change his ways and follow the "King's Highway." *Abilene Photograph Collection at Hardin-Simmons University Library, Abilene, TX.*

This adobe building once housed the famous and very tough "Sunset Saloon" and livery stable, owned and operated by King Fisher and Balis A. Bates, located on Adams Street in Eagle Pass, Texas. *Courtesy of the Frank L. Hobart Collection, El Progreso Memorial Library, Uvalde, Texas.*

City Marshal Ben Thompson as the quintessential gambler, photographed by H. R. Marks. *Courtesy of the Austin History Center, CO # 2525.*

The marker at the grave of P. L. Fisher, King Fisher's only son, born November 25, 1881 and died January 2, 1882. The cemetery is located in southwestern Zavala County. *Courtesy of the Larry G. Shaver Collection.*

Trevanion Theodore Teel, noted southwestern attorney who defended King Fisher numerous times. *Courtesy of the William A. Mills Collection.*

Both John and Thomas Hannahan are believed to be buried among these graves but without certain identification. John Hannahan was killed by King Fisher while resisting arrest. *Courtesy of the Frank L. Hobart Collection, El Progreso Memorial Library, Uvalde, Texas.*

William H. Simms. As proprietor of the Vaudeville Theatre, he witnessed the killing of Jack Harris by Ben Thompson and later participated in the assassination of King Fisher and Ben Thompson. *Courtesy of the Kurt House Collection.*

John Benton Boatright, the sheriff of Uvalde County who chose King Fisher as one of his deputies. Fisher was acting sheriff when assassinated. Image credited to Holley of San Francisco, 1891. *Courtesy of the Larry G. Shaver Collection.*

Ben Thompson's brother Billy was in San Antonio the night Ben was killed but was prevented by Officer Shardein from getting involved. *Courtesy of Thomas C. Bicknell.*

The actress Miss Ada Gray, immensely popular during the 1880s, was the first woman to star in the extremely popular play *East Lynn* in the United States. Her first stage appearance was as Juliet to John Wilkes Booth's Romeo, according to the New York Times of August 29, 1902. Ben Thompson and King Fisher attended her performance the night of March 11, 1884. *Courtesy of Thomas C. Bicknell.*

# The Vaudeville Theatre,

## W. H. SIMMS, General Manager.

## Sumptuous Repast for March 10, 11, 12

# ASSASSINATION

### Or, The Night Owls of Alamo Plaza.

Ready Bob,     }
Tim Timidity, }          Outlaws.          { Charlie Frye
                                           { Ed Sylvester

### Other characters by the company.

The Vaudeville Theatre's playbill for March 11, 1884. Note the title of the final entertainment for the evening: "ASSASSINATION." *Courtesy of San Antonio* Light, *March 11, 1884.*

San Antonio's "Den of Infamy," the Vaudeville Theatre. *Courtesy of the Kurt House Collection.*

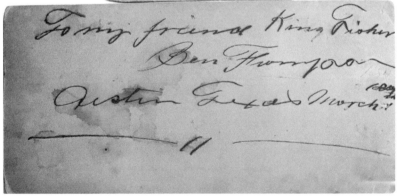

Former Austin City Marshal Ben Thompson. As a token of friendship, he inscribed this photograph to King Fisher on March 11, 1884. Photograph was taken from Fisher's body; note the bloodstains. *Courtesy of the Robert G. McCubbin Collection.*

BEN THOMPSON'S FINAL EXIT.

THE LAST ACT OF A FIERCE AND DESPERATE CAREER, AS PERFORMED IN A SAN ANTONIO, TEXAS, TEMPLE OF THE WILD AND UNTRAM-MELED DRAMA.

Dramatic but highly inaccurate engraving depicting the death of Ben Thompson and King Fisher. Despite numerous errors, it realistically expresses the confusion during the shooting. Note the men "escaping" over the railing with one of the "drink girls" in the background. None of the figures are identified, but the man shooting at left is perhaps meant to be Simms, Coy, or Foster. Thompson is at right facing the shooter, while a figure perhaps intended as King Fisher is represented further back, despite that Fisher never drew his pistol. This appeared in the March 20, 1884 issue of the *National Police Gazette* of New York. *Courtesy of Thomas C. Bicknell.*

The pistol King Fisher wore the night he was killed, which remained in the scabbard: a .45 Colt revolver, serial number 84630. *Courtesy of the Lawrence E. Vivian and Larry G. Shaver Collections.*

San Antonio City Marshal Philip Shardein (*top*) closed the Vaudeville
after the shooting—to all except authorities and newspaper reporters.
The repaired Shardein grave marker (*below*), destroyed by a storm.
*Courtesy of the Kurt House Collection.*

The San Antonio undertaking firm was called to the Vaudeville Theatre to remove and care for the remains of King Fisher and Ben Thompson. Notice how Carter & Mullaly give "special attention to forwarding bodies." The two gunfighters were placed on trains and returned to their respective homes in Uvalde and Austin. *Courtesy of Thomas C. Bicknell.*

Original coffin of King Fisher, exhumed in 1954. *Courtesy of the Lawrence E. Vivian and Larry G. Shaver Collections.*

The final resting place of John King Fisher in Pioneer Rest Cemetery, Uvalde, Texas. *Courtesy of the Chuck Parsons Collection.*

The women of King Fisher's life. *Back row from left*: daughter Florence Fisher, wife Sarah "Sallie" Vivian Fisher, and daughter Eugenia; *front from left*: Margurite and cousin Roxie Ware, daughter of Sarah Fisher's sister. *Courtesy of the Lawrence E. Vivian and Larry G. Shaver Collections.*

Sarah Vivian Fisher in her later years. *Courtesy of the Larry G. Shaver Collection.*

King Fisher's widow with their daughters. *From left:* daughter Florence Fisher Kellogg, Jane O'Neal Vivian Fisher holding grandson Pat Gardner, Maurine K. Gardner, and Sarah Vivian Fisher holding Paul Gardner. *Courtesy of Paul Gardner and the Larry G. Shaver Collection.*

The alleged Winchester rifle once owned by King Fisher. *Courtesy of the Frank L. Hobart Collection, El Progreso Memorial Library, Uvalde, Texas.*

The Uvalde High School Graduating Class of 1895. *Left, second row:* Florence Fisher, King Fisher's oldest daughter wearing polka-dot dress. She later taught school and was a strict church member. *Courtesy of the Frank L. Hobart Collection, El Progreso Memorial Library, Uvalde, Texas.*

# Chapter 6

# Escape from the Rangers

Inaccurate reporting in the media is not new. A century and a half ago, "yellow journalism" was a commonly used term, and the gunfighters and desperadoes of the Wild West were not exempt from such sensationalism. A reporter identified only by his initials "E. S. E." issued a lengthy telegraphic report from Galveston, Texas on December 27, 1877 to the New York *World*. Nine days later it appeared on page two of his paper, bringing exciting news of the top desperadoes of Texas: Bill Longley, Ben Thompson, Wes Hardin, and King Fisher. E. S. E. could hardly contain his excitement as he rode the stage from Austin to San Antonio, not safely inside but on top with the driver, "where we were kept dodging and ducking to escape being scraped off by the limbs of the trees," all the while listening to the driver's experience of being robbed by no less than the group of bandits led by Jesse James.

As they rode, the reporter was "gratified to note the moral improvement made during the past twenty years." This "moral improvement," he wrote, was due not only to the work of Governor Hubbard, but also to "the effective surveillance of Captain Hall's mounted police and the rapid settlement of the State." To assure the reader that Hubbard and Hall had not completely pacified Texas, E. S. E. pointed out that several "outlaws and desperadoes are still at large, but the worst characters are in jail, either awaiting sentence or undergoing punishment."

The stagecoach journey ended at San Antonio, where the riders entrained to continue on to Galveston in order to pay a visit to its jail. Here the reporter met William P. Longley, "one of the most prepossessing of men." Longley, during his ten-year career, had killed no less than thirty-six men, or so the reporter claimed. Probably in an effort to lengthen his article, the reporter discusses the earlier stops in his travels. After reviewing Longley's career, he next gave attention to Ben Thompson of Austin, who "belongs to a different type altogether." E. S. E. wrote as if he had interviewed Thompson, explaining: "There is nothing of the coward in his make-up, and he generally gives his opponent the first shot never firing until self-defense demands it. Ben is one of the handsomest and best-dressed men in Austin, with a foot and hand as small as a lady's and a geniality and courtesy of manner which would lead any one to set him down as the most inoffensive of men."

E. S. E. could not avoid discussing John Wesley Hardin, with whom he *had* conversed while visiting the Austin jail. Hardin was "another mild-mannered desperado who is now lying under a twenty-five years' sentence, with the proverbial appeal in the background." A lengthy summary of Hardin's career allowed the reporter to give hyperbole to his account, pointing out that the rewards for Hardin in the aggregate amounted to $20,000. In reality the most money offered for Hardin's capture—dead or alive—was $4,000.

Regarding the other shootists, E. S. E.'s prose would contribute to the legends: Some days ago J. K. Fisher was lodged in jail to await his trial for murder. He is known along the border as Kingfisher, and is considered fully the equal of Longley and Hardin in cold blooded atrocity. He, too, is less than thirty years of age, and when first sent to the penitentiary was pardoned on account of his extreme youth. The prosecuting attorney, who was the means of securing his conviction, states that going to the Rio Grande he established himself at Laredo, where he became the leader of an organized band numbering fully a hundred men. They terrified the authorities, and made it a rule to kill all witnesses, so that if any of the gang were captured it was a difficult thing to establish their guilt.

E. S. E. continued by describing how Captain Hall and his rangers "swooped down upon these scoundrels some six months ago" and had fifty of the so-called Fisher gang in custody at once. "Kingfisher," according to E. S. E., "is under indictment for killing four persons, and will undoubtedly be convicted by some of his own men who have been induced to turn state's evidence." One of the witnesses to King Fisher's thievery was a Maverick County official, name not given. E. S. E. continued giving evidence of just how evil supposedly Fisher was: "This officer was found by the roadside a few days after with twenty-five bullets in his body. Kingfisher was also concerned in the Goliad Bank robbery of 1873, where the money secured was less than $300." The intended lesson was obvious.

Although this New York *World* article is of great interest, it has numerous errors of fact. The Goliad Bank robbery was not in 1873, for example, and the reward for Hardin was not $20,000. Curiously, E. S. E. knew about Fisher being pardoned for other crimes seven years before his visit to Texas. Was the fact that Fisher had spent time in Huntsville as a youth common knowledge at the time? Being aware of Fisher's time in Huntsville seems rather unlikely, since he was unaware that it was Captain McNelly who captured King Fisher "some six months ago." Significantly, this article placed Fisher at the same level as Hardin and Longley in wickedness.[1]

On the other hand, perhaps the early experiences of King Fisher *were* well-known. Judge William Andrew Bonnet arrived in Eagle Pass in 1878 as a boy and describes Fisher as "very well known around here, for not standing any foolishness."[2] Although E. S. E. portrayed Fisher as a heartless murderer, Bonnet knew him differently. In Bonnet's innocence he once asked Fisher how many men he had killed, which would have shocked Bonnet's mother if she had been present. Fisher answered that his victims numbered seven, to which Bonnet answered that he thought the number was more than that. "Oh, I don't count Mexicans" was Fisher's casual reply to the boy. Bonnet wrote his memoirs many years later, having had time to reflect on the characters he had met during his lifetime. "Please do not think from what I have said that King Fisher was a bad man, as men were here then," he wrote. "There were many like him, only worse. And it took men like this to make the frontier fit for us to live in today. At that time I worked in a store, and just across the street at a saloon a fight started, and King Fisher came over where I was. I asked what was the matter and he said there was a fight. 'I thought you liked a fight?' He said, 'I never fight unless I have to.' This probably was true."[3] Regarding this point, an interesting article about Bonnet appeared in the *Marshall Messenger* in July of 1926, headlined: "This Is Fisher's Road; Take Other." Within the article itself the famous order is given correctly: "This is King Fisher's road; take the other." Judge Bonnet was born April 15, 1867, so when he arrived in Eagle Pass he was about eleven years of age. Through the years and after some reflection on Fisher's career, he had developed a very different opinion of the man than that held by E. S. E.

According to Bonnet, King Fisher had a Mexican "retainer" known as "Pest House Pete," and after King Fisher was killed Pete told Judge Bonnet how Fisher had killed three Mexicans on the bank of the Nueces River and ordered "Pest House Pete" to cross the river on horseback and drag the bodies to him. On another occasion Fisher killed a Mexican across the border and Pete again crossed the river and returned with the body. Pete declared he was never able to understand Fisher's reason for this action.[4]

Former defense attorney for King Fisher, Thomas M. Paschal, Judge of the Twenty-Fourth District, had the dubious honor of listening to King Fisher's appeal for bail. For an unspecified reason, this was to be done at D'Hanis, a small village in Medina County. The judge appeared in order to hear the application on a writ of *habeas corpus*, but "[o]wing to some negligence or mistake the witnesses were not in attendance, and the hearing was not held."[5] A later report suggested how the community was "somewhat in doubt" regarding any *habeas corpus* trial of Fisher, which later took place in Judge Paschal's chambers. From what the reporter could learn, "great sympathy" was felt for King Fisher.[6]

Fisher may have been losing weight, and his tanned countenance may have faded due to his long confinement, but his thoughts must have been active about escaping. It is unknown which of the prisoners in the Castroville jail began planning their rush for liberty, but by mid-February the escape plan was set in motion. John T. Fogg, the keeper of a livery stable in Castroville, somehow discovered news of the intended escape and shared his information with the editors of San Antonio's *Daily Herald*. According to Fogg, several escape attempts had recently been made, but additional guards were not placed in or around the jail. On the night of February 16, 1878, a party of horsemen with extra mounts had ridden up to the jail, but Sheriff Ferdinand Niggli managed to scare them off.[7] Whether they had wanted one specific prisoner or a general jail delivery remains unknown.

What *is* known is that after dark on Sunday, February 17, 1878 four of the prisoners succeeded in cutting through their cell bars and entered the jailor's room. There they armed themselves with a shotgun and a pistol and thus were prepared to fight back against anyone bold enough to challenge their action for liberty. Although, as we believe, King Fisher may have planned their movements, but it was Jasper Merritt who would suffer the most. He had been convicted of stealing a horse and was sentenced to a term of five years in Huntsville. Denied bail, he was incarcerated while waiting for the result of his appeal. Somehow the sheriff learned of the escape plot and arrived at the jail to see the prisoners outside of their cells but still within the building. Merritt was about to scale the outside wall when Sheriff Niggli appeared. He immediately recognized what was in progress, drew his pistol, and fired twice at Merritt. One shot took effect in the ribs and the other in his back, passing under his kidneys, or, as the *Herald* reported, the sheriff "shot him through the bowels." This sound of gunfire frightened the other three prisoners who, realizing the break had failed, tossed their weapons down and ran to their cells. Neither Fisher nor the others exhibited any boldness in their action to escape, leaving Merritt, dangerously wounded, to whatever fate would befall him.[8] A few days later, rumor had it that Merritt had died from his wounds.[9]

Sheriff Niggli regretted having to shoot prisoner Merritt, but no one believed he could have acted otherwise. Correspondent Fogg expressed his opinion in summing up his report: "Taken in any light therefore the shooting was clearly justifiable."[10] To add further concern—for the sheriff by now was getting used to the reality of strangers wanting to take prisoners from his jail, as well as prisoners wanting to escape—by the time he had King Fisher in the Bexar County jail, he knew he had to replace a horse. After he placed his mounts in the Braden stables on Market Street, one of them showed signs of sickness. Within ten minutes the horse collapsed and died. This was unusual, as the horse had not been driven hard. They finally determined the horse had collapsed from bots, a stomach infection due to botflies not unusual to horses.

Sheriff Niggli may have had his suspicions about how the prisoners managed to get out of their cells. Whatever detective skills he had developed through the years proved to be beneficial, as he arrested a Castroville constable who had helped Fisher and the others with the escape plan. The constable was Frank Ankrum, who, as mentioned previously, had been found not guilty of the murder of his stepfather some years before. He now was apparently working as a trusted employee in the jail, but he betrayed Niggli's trust, for which he received a sentence of five years in the Huntsville penitentiary. By late April, Niggli with Ankrum and another prisoner, Dionicio Garcia, were on the road to Huntsville.[11] Sheriff Niggli safely delivered the pair, but they did not serve out their terms. Prisoner Ankrum, number 6686, was placed in stocks in August of 1879 after attempting to get prisoners to go on strike. He escaped on September 30, 1881.[12] Where he hid out his remaining years is unknown. Prisoner Dionicio Garcia, number 8569, escaped May 6, 1880. Presumably he returned home to Mexico.[13]

In our view, Niggli may have placed additional guards on his jail while he delivered prisoners to Huntsville in April. Perhaps he felt confident that the "Bat Cave" was more secure. And the prisoners may have done some serious thinking, having failed in their escape attempt. Fisher and the others must have considered keeping quiet as much as possible. Fisher was not only the best-looking desperado, but indications are that he was above average in intelligence. Finding a good attorney was a necessity, and this realization of the need to work within the system is expressed in the press of the day. Nor had the *Goliad Guard* forgotten their former resident, noting that in May there were five murder counts "against the notorious villain" and that he would be released from jail upon furnishing a $40,000 bond. In addition to the murder counts, he had "a large list of crimes of lesser note," or so reported the *Guard*.[14]

On May 13, 1878, Maverick County witnessed the opening of the spring term of District Court. Attorney T. T. Teel was there to represent

King Fisher. Among the Grand Jurors summoned were Lafayette Vivian and James Vivian, but James was excused. Four men who had been summoned failed to appear, leaving only five jurors. Somehow the trial was allowed to continue, but on the following day the judge became angry due to the lack of seating arrangements in the courtroom. The judge made his feelings known and gave an order for the Commissioners Court to furnish the District Court with sufficient chairs so the court's business could take place. As if this was not bad enough, the district attorney informed the court that the indictments and all other pertinent papers in thirty-one pending cases could not be found. The missing cases included seven against King Fisher, five of them for murder. Upon this announcement, the courtroom exploded in an uproar. The judge ordered that the district attorney have substitution papers presented. On the fourteenth, the District Attorney represented to the Court that he had procured a certified copy of the original indictments and prayed that the certified copy be substituted in lieu of the original indictment. King Fisher, by May 20, made bond in six of the cases: one for $5,000; three for $2,500 each; and two for $1,200. Prominent ranchers signed the bail bonds: George W. Whaley, Benjamin C. Flowers, C. L. Fielder, José Angel Oliva, Francisco Zertouche, and Lafayette and Charles Vivian.[15] King Fisher was now out on bail, probably meeting with his attorneys as well as focusing on his family and ranching.

It had only been a week earlier that the murder case against Fisher, charging him with killing an "aged Mexican" named Estanislado, was transferred to Uvalde County on a change of venue. Why was this done? According to the court documents, "In this case, it appearing to the Court, that no Attorney can be had in this County to prosecute this cause in behalf of the State, and therefore no trial can be held and it appearing to the Court that the Attorneys of Defendant and the State by A. M. Oliphant, who represents the State only for the change of Venue" apply to the Venue of Uvalde County. Estanislado had been an employee of rancher Alexander Zimmerman. King Fisher pled not guilty to the charge.[16] The killing allegedly occurred on November 10, 1875, and King was indicted November 19, 1877. Now he would be tried in 1879. Were the wheels of justice finally grinding against King Fisher? Were the bonds that allowed Fisher to go free worth the paper they were written on? A shocking item in an Austin newspaper stated that the bond given by King Fisher was "not worth a second hand chew of tobacco."[17] According to another report, the bonds were "amply sufficient, unquestionable and according to law."[18]

A comment on Fisher's ability in handling a six-shooter combined with his supposed occasional bloodthirstiness was reported later in the popular *Texas Siftings* newspaper edited by Alexander E. Sweet. In the "General Comment" column, the editor had this to say of Fisher: "King Fisher was a remarkably handy man with a pistol. On one occasion he discovered three Mexicans in the act of taking cattle out of his pen. One of the Mexicans had a pistol, and on Fisher remonstrating, the Mexican fired and wounded him. King Fisher wrenched the pistol from the Mexican, and killed all three of them with it."[19] This may be a belated reference to the alleged killing of two of Zimmerman's herders. Sweet did not clarify just when the supposed incident happened.

While the wheels of justice ground slowly in Maverick County, violence in the form of "terrible, outrageous murders" was taking place in Webb, Duval, and various other counties. These atrocities were not by King Fisher's men but "by Mexicans in the garb of Indians." The report was first sent to Congressman Gustav Schleicher from a "prominent citizen of Corpus Christi" who claimed to have lived in the counties of San Patricio, Live Oak, and Nueces for thirty years. The letter described how some twenty-five men and fifteen children from seven to fourteen years old had been slaughtered by these raiders. The raiders had been on a horse-stealing raid and, in addition to stealing between five- and six-hundred head of horses, they attacked the settlers. Apparently some of the men and women had been able to hide in the brush to escape the slaughter. This report appeared in the Galveston newspaper. The writer could only conclude that the United States government should demand of Mexico that the raiders be surrendered, and if they were not, then troops should be sent over to "take the whole country."[20]

Albert and Jane L. Maury Maverick were two young people who wanted a place to build their ranch and raise a family. They finally found it on the Medina River between Bandera and Medina City, today a small community known simply as Medina. The Mavericks began their family there, and in 1928 Mrs. Maverick wrote of her adventures as a young woman living on the ranch. She had taken note of the forms of amusements of cowboys and travelers and of life in general. The year of 1878 may have been the most memorable. Of the "celebrated people" to visit them, she recalled King Fisher "at the height of his career." She remembered Fisher "arrived late one evening with a lot of cowboys and a good-sized bunch of cattle. Someone explained that he wished to sleep in the house for fear of being killed in the night by one of his various enemies. That night he was careful when he sat at the supper table not to be a target for a gun, but as Rose Kalka, a little Polish girl happened to touch him while handing around the butter cakes, he jumped like his time had come.[21] He slept in a small room on the gallery." Mrs. Maverick was still somewhat gullible at this time, and she had heard tales of King Fisher's life and believed them: "Someone had told me of his many wild experiences, how he said that he had killed twenty-seven men, one for each year of his life. After all was quiet, I spent a very restless time—and one time when he got up to get a drink of water from the bucket, I held my baby very tight thinking we would die together. I didn't realize that he was a man killer and not a baby killer." To Mrs. Maverick's "inexperienced eye," King Fisher "was a very innocent looking cowboy, tall and thin and dark. He and I had a very pleasant conversation about his wife and babies before I knew who he was."[22] Mrs. Maverick placed her memoir as having taken place in 1878, but if King Fisher talked of his wife and babies it had to have been in early 1880, as King's second daughter was born in December 1879. But whenever this visit of King Fisher occurred, it shows clearly that the man could be a regular gentleman.

The question of lawlessness was always a concern, and in January, 1879 the *Galveston Daily News* provided two lengthy articles dealing with the subject: one from Eagle Pass written by "A. M. O."; the second, continuing in the same column and provided by an Austin citizen, signed only as "Lex." The identity of Lex remains a mystery, but A. M. O. was A. M. Oliphant, a forty-year-old lawyer who had served in the Confederate Army and was now a practicing attorney in Eagle Pass.[23] His letter, dated January 18, was headlined: "Frontier Protection." It opened: "It is with surprise and deep regret that we have noticed what seems a well authenticated opinion, expressed through the public press, that Governor [Oran Milo] Roberts is not well inclined towards frontier protection." A. M. O. then points out that if frontier protection is withdrawn, then Roberts's lack of concern "will simply be a shameful recusancy of a public duty." He reminds the readers that, only a few years before, "the better part of the community were wholly at the mercy of the desperado element." There were over one hundred "loose characters" in Maverick County who had "drifted" from Goliad and DeWitt Counties and else-where and who "subsisted by plundering workingmen." Local police were inadequate to deal with these "loose characters" and, until Captain McNelly and Lieutenant Hall arrived, "no one dared to appeal to the law by making a complaint."

Oliphant pointed out how the situation had changed: "But the 'Hoodoos' as the gallant Hall and his rangers were called, came."[24] Their action broke up the outlaw organizations and "[a] feeling of security exists, and hopes of future prosperity, such as have not been felt for years, now pervade the public mind." He concluded finally that Maverick County, without the strong arm of rangers like McNelly and Hall, would again become a refuge for "the drift of the refuse of society flowing in upon and concentrating among us from abroad. The lonely uninhabited parts of our country furnish a suitable rendez-vous for the refugee criminals of eastern Texas, who find a subsistence in our flocks and herds scattered upon the prairie."[25]

The communication from A. M. O. demanded not only the strong arm of local law enforcement but help from the state. Lex's contribution imme-diately followed that of A. M. O. and was headlined: "Enforcement of the Law."[26] Lex began his essay by arguing that, with the legislature now in session, it was time to "rivet" the attention of the legislators upon the "imper-ative necessity of a faithful execution of the laws." The legislature must look "immediately toward the suppression and punishment of crime is the thing which the condition of society demands." In other words, laws on the books are necessary, but without "executive force" the laws become powerless and the result is "the abominable policy of mob law." Lex reminds the read-ers that within the boundaries of the state of Texas "mobs can almost at all times and occasions overrule the power of the sheriff and his posse. Let but a few desperate men conspire together, and the arm of the law is completely paralyzed." Lex continues driving home his concerns. The average citizen cannot stand up to "the physical power of the desperado and the professional robber." How could he be prepared "to perform the perilous duties of the detective and the gendarme to buckle on his armor, mount his steed and at the risk of his life grapple with the fierce criminal, over take him in or out of the state, and bring him to justice?" Officers, juries, and witnesses are intimidated he explained, "dreading revenge and assassination; then public trials become a mockery and a farce, and mob law in its most terrible apparition … raises the bloody flag … strikes death-blows at the innocent as well as the guilty, and substitutes riot, anarchy and murder for law and good order." In these circumstances, men like King Fisher, John Wesley Hardin, Sam Bass, and other less famous individuals "defy the civil authorities, and robbery, murder and jail deliveries are the order of the day!"

Obviously, the name of King Fisher was uppermost in Lex's mind. Hardin was already locked securely within the walls of the state penitentiary at Huntsville, and Sam Bass—stage, train, and bank robber that he was— was dead and buried in Round Rock and also, strangely, well on the road to becoming a Texas folk hero. Lex was aware of the numerous charges against King Fisher and anticipated that by 1880 he would be free of all indictments. According to Lex, "executive force" must be in the form of state troops: a few good detectives under the command of the governor and the adjutant general, with headquarters in Austin, ready to be dispatched "to any section of the state where emergency requires."[27]

Before long, a somewhat curious item appeared in Austin's *Daily Democratic Statesman* without any type of sourcing given, intending to show Fisher as a completely reformed man. Although no date is given, it must have happened in early June of 1879. The article began by describing Fisher as "the desperado of former years" and continued by identifying him as "a quiet, placable, industrious rancher." But somehow Fisher "began to feel the devil getting the better of him a few days ago and rather than have any trouble or shoot anybody else he shot himself through the thigh and is now lying up to cool off. He may be a priest yet." The final sarcastic comment is less than clear: "There's nothing like self-punishment and 'mortification of the spirit,' if you don't have to submit to amputation."[28] Evidently, the editor of the *Statesman* knew that no lengthy explanation of King Fisher's reputation was needed. Presumably he left any ranching duties to his cowboys until his limb completely healed. Strangely enough, Texas Rangers accidentally shooting themselves with their own pistols was not unheard of. Two of Hall's men, Sgt. John B. Armstrong and Sgt. O. S. Watson, both accidentally wounded themselves with their pistols, so King Fisher was not an exception to the rule. If, now with an injured leg, he felt the need to travel, he probably used a buggy or a stagecoach.

The number of newspapers that reported the accident is impossible to determine, but Fisher first read of it in the *San Antonio Express*. The tone of the article in question regarding his self-inflicted wound bothered King, especially when the press misrepresented him. The following item may be the one which Fisher read and which caused him to respond: "King Fisher, who a few years ago received so much attention and won such notoriety as a desperate man, recently met with a very painful accident at his home on the Carizo [*sic*]. A revolver he was handling exploded, the ball passing through one of his legs. King, it is said, is now one of the best citizens on the frontier, having changed his adventurous life and settled down to hard work."[29]

He felt the need to respond to the errors of the *Express* and on June 26 prepared a lengthy letter to the editor which was published in full. King explained that while driving cattle up to the ranch of Parker and Ladd he "happened" to come across the paper which, to his mind, contained an article about him which was totally false. He stated that he did not live on the [Carrizo] but on the Nueces, seventy miles below Uvalde. Secondly, and perhaps most importantly, "my revolver did not go off while I was fooling with it, as the person who wrote that article would have known had he been better acquainted with me. I am not in the habit of playing with such things." To Fisher the incident was "such a small matter" and "so far from the true statement of the case" that he felt it "no more than right in me to restate it in the way it took place." Here, according to Fisher, is how the accident happened: "I laid my revolver down previously to going out hunting,

and somebody picked it up and didn't put it back as they found it. Not thinking anything was wrong, I got on my horse and started after a cow, but in
chasing her my hat came off and I threw myself back in the saddle to catch
it, when my revolver struck the saddle and went off, the ball passing through
the fleshy part of the leg." That clarified the self-inflicted wound, but King
Fisher wanted to make one more point: "As for being a desperado" he wrote,
"all I can say is that I have never killed a man unless it was in self-defense
or in defense of my property, and I have very little respect for anyone who
would not do the same, especially in certain parts of the state where there are
so many horse thieves, etc."[30] Interesting that King Fisher, touted as the King
of Desperadoes in some circles, would express the concern about those many
horse thieves "in certain parts of the state."

The use of stagecoaches to travel and transport mail and valuables was
still popular but, with the increase of the railroad, gradually becoming a
thing of the past. One robbery which may later have had an effect on King
Fisher happened in July of 1879. A special telegram from Uvalde reported
that the Eagle Pass and San Antonio stage had been robbed on July 11 near
Turkey Creek. There were but two passengers on the stage, a J. F. Giles and
a Mr. Cohen. Giles had been able to hide his money, but Cohen admitted to
losing $1.50. Giles was able to give a detailed account of the robbery to the
*San Antonio Express* reporter. This robbery received considerable attention,
and the general consensus was that the robbers were amateurs.[31]

In September 1879, Fisher was to appear in court in Laredo, and three
men of Lieutenant Thomas L. Oglesby's detachment, a trio selected by
Capt. Lee Hall, were tasked to deliver him safely to authorities in Laredo.
That the prisoner was not an ordinary felon but required special consideration is obvious in that three men were given the duty: Corporal George
H. Allen and two others who were not identified in the record. Some eight
miles from Laredo, Fisher saw an opportunity to escape and took it. He was
at this point taking a great risk, as one might expect the rangers to shoot at
the escaping prisoner, for, if challenged, they would be able to say that *la ley
de fuga* justified them in shooting him. Lieutenant Thomas L. Oglesby, who
had the responsibility of reporting on what happened to his superior, wrote
this in his report: "Corporal Allen left camp with two men for the purpose

of delivering to jail at Laredo King Fisher. Fisher made his escape eight miles from Laredo on the evening of the 3rd." This was reported in the *Castroville Quill* and later in the *Galveston Daily News*. Fisher was gaining greater notoriety due to the press.[32]

But King Fisher knew better than to run far. The simple strategy of stampeding the pack mules had created enough confusion for him to make his escape, but he soon decided that surrendering would be the wiser course of action. The *Galveston Daily News* gave him page-one attention in bold uppercase letters: "KING FISHER SURRENDERED." It would appear that the noted desperado John King Fisher, now all of twenty-five years of age and having a wife to care for, was seriously considering a change in his lifestyle. He couldn't forget the advice that Captain McNelly had given him: to change his ways. After giving the matter some thought, he composed a letter justifying his actions, which appeared in the *Castroville Quill* and other newspapers. That King Fisher letter, if the original still exists, would be worth many thousands of dollars but apparently has not survived. Numerous other newspapers reported of it, the *Gonzales Inquirer* for one:

> King Fisher, the noted west Texas outlaw, writes to the Quill his excuse for escaping from the rangers while being taken to Laredo. He says that opinion runs so strongly against him in that place that if taken there the Mexicans would mob and kill him. Furthermore, on the same day he was to be in Laredo he was wanted in Uvalde to answer a more serious charge than that preferred in Laredo, and that he immediately went to Uvalde, where he is willing to be tried as he does not fear the law, but only mobs.

The editor of the *Inquirer* did not simply report this interesting bit of news, but also commented: "Well, we hope he will have a first class chance to test the claims of the law upon him."[33] Officers Hall and Oglesby may have had to give serious thought as to the effectiveness of Corporal Allen. The Monthly Return merely states that Fisher had escaped *en route* to Laredo with no further details. It is likely that the three were given extra guard duty.

Fisher did not "immediately" go to Uvalde, but he was there by mid-October, present in court on the fifteenth, forty-three days after the escape.[34]

Ranger George Durham, who was in a position to know, wrote years later about how Fisher managed to escape from the rangers knowing that *la ley de fuga* could end his life. Durham wrote that somewhere along the river to Laredo "he stompeded the pack animals; and when Allen and his two men run for them, King dived his mule into the river and crossed to Mexico." Durham also wrote that there was "another big scare piece in the newspapers about this escape, and I was damn glad. Because King was a better man than Allen." What Durham considered a "big scare piece" in the press has not been located, but Durham obviously had a low opinion of Corporal Allen for an unspecified reason, certainly more than just King Fisher's escape.[35]

What King Fisher did once he had escaped from the rangers is uncertain. Mob law had not been eradicated from Texas by any means, and Fisher had reason to be fearful of a vigilante group forming when he was unable to defend himself. There had been plenty of vigilante action in south Texas during and following the end of the Civil War, not only against Anglos but against Blacks and Mexicans as well, and King Fisher was certainly aware of it. In addition to caring for his own livelihood, as 1879 was nearing an end he had his family to think about. His wife Sarah Elizabeth—generally referred to as "Sallie," was busy keeping house and raising their daughter Florence, now two years old. Adding to his responsibilities as a husband, father, and rancher facing criminal charges, there would soon be another mouth to feed. In December 1879, Sarah gave birth to another daughter, Eugenie or "Minnie." King Fisher must have thought seriously about changing his lifestyle.

In June 1880, John R. Baylor conducted the census for Zavala County. He identified the stock raiser as "J. K. Fisher," a 25-year-old white male and a native Texan. His family was composed of Sarah, four years younger, who "Keeps House"; and the two little girls, Fredonia, three, and Eugenia, six months. William Stidham, a 22-year-old white man, boarded there and was listed simply as a laborer.[36] Certainly the noted frontiersman Baylor realized the notoriety of those he enumerated. This may have been the first time the two noted men met. Earlier he had visited his friend John H. Culp and the Culp family. The census only provides the essential information which the government required on its form.

A year later King Fisher was again in the news, and this time he received the most positive publicity possible. In the form of a letter to the editors of the San Antonio *Daily Express*, one E. A. Carothers took exception with a telegram from Austin appearing in the April 7, 1881 issue in response to an article headlined "King Fisher on the Warpath—King Fisher is on the Nueces near Carrizo and is causing trouble."[37] Carothers states he had left Carrizo "late last Saturday evening," which would have been April 2, and that, if there had been any trouble, he would have heard about it. He went on to say that Fisher was home at his ranch on the Nueces River, some thirty-five miles above Carrizo, with his wife and two little girls, "and is one of the most industrious and law abiding citizens in that part of the country, in proof of which, at the recent attempt at the organization of Zavalla county he was the almost unanimous choice of the citizens for the position of sheriff of the county." Carothers claimed to have visited repeatedly at the Fisher ranch and, with Dr. M. A. Taylor of Austin, "spent the night there a couple of weeks ago, and was most hospitably entertained by Mr. Fisher and his estimable lady. On this occasion I offered King a toddy, which he declined, and which elicited the fact that he had not drunk a drop of liquor in several years." Carothers was obviously impressed with his host and was aware of the reputation King Fisher had acquired only a few years before. The well-traveled man stressed that there "has been a great deal of exaggeration about the state of affairs in that part of the frontier, and King Fisher has been made the scape-goat for the deviltry of others, and for many things that never occurred, and I suspect your special correspondents' 'trouble' will be found to belong to one or other of these classes."[38]

# Chapter 7

# On the King's Highway

**W**ith two infants King Fisher must have felt proud, understanding to some degree the miracle of birth and also realizing the responsibilities involved in raising them to be healthy, both physically and emotionally. He certainly understood, perhaps with the suggestions of his wife Sallie, that the former days of freely riding the range, gathering loose stock, and occasionally painting the town red were now things of the past. Indeed, Captain McNelly had made it abundantly clear that a change in his lifestyle was necessary, lest he spend long years in prison or dangle at the end of a rope. As historians we can look back at his life and career and see a radical change in the man's behavior, although we cannot pinpoint just when the change happened or state unequivocally what caused it. The result however is clear: sometime during the late seventies, the man's attitude was altered from what it had been.

We consider John King Fisher as one of the most famous, or notorious, of the gunfighters in Texas's violent history. John Wesley Hardin left his autobiography for posterity; Ben Thompson left a record of his deeds with Attorney William M. Walton; "Bloody Bill" Longley left a number of letters, some of which survived to leave us with a brief autobiographical sketch of his life. These gunmen left enough clues for later historians to research and complete their biography. So far as we know, King Fisher never attempted to establish how he wanted history to remember him. Perhaps if he had lived another decade or two, he would have considered leaving his version of the important actions of his life. He left a few bits of information, but those few pieces of writing leave us with little around which to construct his life.

It is ironic that much of what we know about Fisher is thanks to several individuals who faced him with pistols drawn. In 1876, he faced Captain McNelly, the tubercular ranger described as "one of the greatest law-enforcement officers that Texas ever knew," but we can only make inferences from McNelly's official reports. McNelly "did not hesitate to let others know of his appreciation of this man who had gone in wrong ways."[1] Much of the information available about King Fisher was offered by Napoleon Augustus Jennings and George Preston Durham, two young men who served under Captain McNelly in the mid-1870s and who years later wrote about their experiences as Texas Rangers. Not surprisingly, both thought highly of King Fisher. Durham especially considered King Fisher a man of much nobler character than some of the rangers who served alongside him.

Rev. Bruce Roberts left for posterity reminiscences of his years preaching the Gospel in south Texas. Although he never knew King Fisher personally, he became acquainted with his family and produced a valuable sketch of the husband and father, avoiding the temptation of narrating the adventures of Fisher but rather focusing on what aspects of society cause us to even consider remembering the man. To Roberts, he was "a character that demands interpretation; for after sixty-six years [in 1950] since the tragic death of young King Fisher, he lives in the thinking and questioning and conversation of thousands. His name is still spoken from platform and pulpit, and some of the latest books have given more space to his career than was given in any book of half a century ago." To Roberts, the man had many virtues but was maligned by some and misrepresented by others. Yet there were two elements which "entered largely into his reputation, viz. misunderstanding and hero worship."[2]

Roberts cites as an example of the misunderstanding the purpose of the now-famous road sign also mentioned in previous chapters, which allegedly said: "King Fisher's Road—Take the Other." Roberts observes that many writers believed that the sign represented a "robber secure in his dominion of crime, into which dominion no man must set foot under penalty of being shot." Roberts cites Judge W. A. Bonnet of Eagle Pass, "a man of recognized fairness in all judgements" for an explanation of the road sign. King Fisher "had built on his unfenced range some pens just off the road. The road to the pens soon became a plainer way than the through road, and travelers wanting to follow the 'main road' would find themselves at these pens, with no road leading past."[3] The sign therefore was put up at the fork in the road to prevent travelers wasting time and energy by taking the dead end. Fisher may not have realized that to some the wording of the sign suggested arrogance and unfriendliness. If he had known this, Judge Bonnet suggested that Fisher would have chosen an alternate wording to clarify the intention: "Come By" rather than "Take the Other."[4]

Not surprisingly, the newspaper serial version differs in small ways from the published book. Durham recalled meeting a man from Karnes County who described Fisher as "jefe of the Eagle Pass section and all the upper reaches of the Nueces. That he dealt principally with wet horses, or horses brought across the river [stolen]; that he didn't raid on this side; that he raided the raiders and sold his stock in San Antonio. He said King Fisher had five hundred men under him and that he was more than double poison. Him and Captain McNelly was bound to lock horns it looked like." Further, the Karnes County citizen said, he had seen a sign outside Eagle Pass where the trails forked. The sign read: "This is King Fisher's Road. Take the Other!" Supposedly Fisher had a little empire "locked up in the palm of his hand. That no one could come in or go out without King's permission."[5]

In regards to hero worship in the case of King Fisher, Roberts viewed King Fisher as one of the most colorful characters in the Nueces Strip during his day, arguing that there may not have been "at any time one of more magnetism." Both lawmen and desperadoes admired Fisher. Roberts records that, after Fisher became McNelly's prisoner and surrendered his two pistols, he said: "Nice work, Captain." McNelly "beamed in admiration as the two men shook hands."[6] As yet no other evidence of this compliment has been found, but it may have happened. Stranger things have occurred in history, and it is unfortunate that King Fisher's contemporaries and later historians have not been more vocal about this meeting between the reformed outlaw and the lawman.

Rev. Bruce Roberts was not the only preacher who was impressed with the legacy of King Fisher, although he had never met the man. In 1882 the Rio Grande Baptist Association met at Carrizo Springs, beginning on July 14. Representatives from the faith, or "Messengers," were there from the counties of Dimmit, Zavala, Uvalde, Edwards, Bandera, Medina, Atascosa, McMullen, Frio, La Salle, and Webb. The Superintendent of State Missions, Dr. Owen Clinton Pope, was also there.[7] This was an important event, as it was the second annual meeting of the Association and the first time Super-intendent Pope had visited that part of Texas. Consequently, Carrizo Springs was filled with its own citizens as well as many from area villages. One of those interested individuals was King Fisher. The theme of Dr. Pope's message was the danger of drifting: drifting off the path of righteousness, associating with bad company, and drifting into lawlessness, all of which ultimately would lead to destruction. After the message there was what would become the traditional dinner on the grounds. Naturally, many in attendance wondered why King Fisher was present if perhaps something Dr. Pope said had offended the man.

After dinner, Fisher drew Dr. Pope aside and spoke privately. What Fisher said to Dr. Pope "made a profound impression of [sic] the listener, as it did when passed on to me later. Dr. Pope seemed to hold the little conver-sation in a kind of sacred confidence." In essence, Fisher wanted to bear testimony to the truth of what Dr. Pope had said that day:

> I know how easy it is in drifting, but still I had [a] pretty good idea of what I wanted to be. Then I drifted into bad company, and there didn't seem to be anything much to hold me back from doing wrong. Some of the older people seemed to like me, but it seems they didn't know how to tell me how to go straight. Of course they thought I wouldn't pay any attention to anything they'd say, but I wish they'd tried me out a little more.

In the main, Captain McNelly's advice was strongest:

> But Captain McNelly gave me some mighty good talk. I've heard that he always carried a little Bible with him. Anyway, it seemed like Captain was on the right road. It made me think of a preacher I heard once talking about being on the King's highway. I remembered that I said to myself, "King, it would be a lot better for you, if you could be on the King's highway." I never saw the Captain any more. He had a cough at that time that sounded bad to me, and sure enough in a little more than a year he was gone. I have wished that I had when we were together that time talked with him about his road, but being a prisoner—you know—well, I didn't.

Fisher told Dr. Pope that he remembered the talk Captain McNelly had given him and that he would remember his talk as well: "I am trying to shape things up to where I can travel a different road." The following year Rev. Roberts and Dr. Pope met again at the Rio Grande Association session, although King Fisher was not there. Roberts could advise Dr. Pope that all indictments against Fisher had been dropped and he was now serving as deputy sheriff of Uvalde County, not only a free man but a changed man.[8] In this year of 1883 with the indictments against King Fisher a thing of the past, Rev. Roberts and Dr. Pope may indeed have realized that the former outlaw, now turned lawman, was on a different highway, and perhaps this was due to King Fisher himself wanting to follow the true King's Highway, having formerly taken the other.

Although the memoirs of such distinguished gentlemen as Rev. Roberts and Dr. Pope are valuable to the historian, their lack of providing dates of such events is frustrating. Contemporary newspaper accounts as well as legal documents provide a much clearer picture of what was happening. A letter from E. A. Carothers which appeared in the *San Antonio Daily Express* of April 8, 1881 proves valuable as it reveals that, as mentioned in chapter 6, the citizens of Zavala County thought seriously of making King Fisher their sheriff, proving they had a great deal of trust in the man. A recent headline, also mentioned in previous chapters, about King Fisher being "on the warpath" was denied by Carothers and his companion Dr. M. A. Taylor in their letter. Indeed, they described King Fisher as "an honest and law abiding citizen."[9]

The notion of King Fisher being a changed man was reinforced in the Austin *Statesman* on April 15, 1881. A simple sentence stated: "King Fisher, the once noted desperado, is living quietly on a farm on the Nueces, attending to his own business, and taking no more scalps."[10] Austin citizens who may have missed the notice in the daily edition could read it in the weekly issue of April 21. Coincidentally, the two cases charging Fisher with the alleged killing of two Mexicans (Estanislado and Pancho, employees of Alexander Zimmerman) were to be heard on April 21, having been shifted from Maverick County to Uvalde County. The sheriff visited the Frio County home of Zimmerman several times but could never find him there. Zimmerman was supposed to be a star witness for the state. In April 1881, Judge T. M. Paschal directed the jury that the alleged murder of an elderly Mexican known only as Estanislado could not be proven. Since the State had failed to prove that there had been a murder, the jury was further directed to return a verdict of "Not Guilty."[11]

The county seat town of Uvalde must have been an exciting place during those days of April 1881. Not only was the Fisher trial uppermost in the minds of many, but on the nineteenth a "terrible shooting affray took place at Pipeco's camp yard ... in which General Baylor and his son and Mr. Gilchrist and his two sons were the principal actors." All were residents of the Nueces Canyon, and "the shooting occurred over a difficulty arising from an old feud of some years standing." According to other sources, the family feuding with the Baylors was actually named Gilcrease, and threats had been exchanged for some time. Apparently, on the nineteenth of April, when Baylor and his son Henry entered the yard to look after their horses, the Gilcreases began shooting at them. The result of the Baylor response was that the elder Gilcrease was dead, one son was fatally wounded, and the other son "escaped from the deadly scene with a skin full of holes." Young Henry W. Baylor was wounded in the arm. Baylor Sr. was acquitted of the killing of the Gilcreases.[12]

King Fisher, fortunately, had not been involved in this feud, despite that he and the Baylors had established a friendship. John R. Baylor had developed a considerable reputation as a fighting man, and this friendship perhaps helped Fisher in dealing with his legal charges. He reported to the court in Eagle Pass, and on May 16 the District Attorney was compelled to drop the charges due to insufficient evidence. Baylor may have accompanied Fisher.[13]

King Fisher may have avoided another charge of rustling if he had been at his ranch in early summer. A Pendencia character identified as Dick Woods, well-known throughout western Texas, was arrested by the rangers and delivered to Eagle Pass in June. He gave bond and returned home by the 26 of June. Then the sheriff of Dimmit County arrested him on yet another charge and, while delivering him to Carrizo, a group of vigilantes liberated Woods and shot him to death. Remarkably, although mob law in some counties seemed almost acceptable, apparently this was the only example of it in Dimmit County. Commented the reporter: "The organization of a vigilance committee, heretofore unknown in this section, is probably due to the laws' notorious uncertainty and delay."[14]

King Fisher may have been in the most dangerous situation of his life. He faced six charges of horse theft. He demanded to be tried and, with the assistance of John Robert Baylor, he was acquitted. The date was July 14, 1881. Similar to the indictments for murder, the cause charging King Fisher with fatally shooting William Donovan proved too weak and the prosecution therefore failed to receive a conviction. During his years as a rancher in the Nueces Strip, he had been indicted twenty-one times, had faced a jury six times, and in each case had been acquitted or had charges dropped for lack of evidence.[15]

He was now a free man and his future only looked bright. He could go home to his wife and daughters. During his time in Eagle Pass, King Fisher had an interest in the Sunset Saloon, which, according to the oldest daughter Florence, he decided to sell. He commented "that it was certainly no credit to the two daughters for it to be known that their father was in the saloon business."[16]

Being unencumbered with legal concerns may have been like a fresh breeze to Fisher and his family in July 1881. Perhaps he was unaware that, due to his notoriety, others claimed his name and gained recognition. In neighboring New Mexico Territory, the *Las Vegas Gazette* printed a lengthy article describing how cowboys there enjoyed shooting recklessly on the main streets, "alarming everybody at night by the discharge of their revolvers." One was identified as King Fisher, who allegedly had stolen the horse of mail coach driver Charlie Hamilton. This King Fisher denied being a horse thief but, since he was in "a tight fix" with the law in pursuit, he "couldn't be very particular." As he rode off, he explained to Hamilton: "I ain't no horse thief, but I have taken horses under such circumstances." He promised that the horse would be returned in three days, and said he was going to join the more famous outlaw "Billy the Kid" on the Staked Plains.[17] It wasn't the first time someone had used the name of King Fisher outside of the Nueces Strip. If this man did join up with the notorious outlaw, he lost his new companion the night of July 14, because that is when Sheriff Pat Garrett finally caught up with the fugitive, ending the reign of New Mexico's most famous outlaw.

The question must be asked: could King Fisher and Billy the Kid have had any communication as to possibly joining forces? It seems unlikely, since from Eagle Pass to Lincoln, New Mexico Territory is over five hundred miles across, similar in distance from Eagle Pass to Dallas—both long hard rides. Certainly the two were aware of each other's names, but it is unknown whether either had been interested in joining with the other. We know that King Fisher was comfortable in the Nueces Strip, but it is less than clear what would tempt him to travel as far west as the Staked Plains. One item in a Las Vegas, New Mexico newspaper is intriguing in this regard. It purports to come from a gentleman "recently arrived" from Fort Clark, Kinney County, who reports that King Fisher, "the famous old frontiersman," had met with a serious accident: "While returning to his ranch in Maverick [C]ounty, his steed became unmanageable, and ran away, throwing him with great violence against a musquet [*sic*, mesquite] tree injuring his thigh so that he will be more or less crippled for life." But we should not worry for the injured man, the gentleman from Kinney County assures us, as King Fisher "is well-fixed ... in worldly posses-sions, having numberless horses and cattle, to support him in the declin-ing years of his life." Strangely perhaps, whoever composed the original was aware that King Fisher was known in Maverick County and well-fixed with livestock and so would not face becoming a pauper. But he described

King Fisher as a "famous old frontiersman" whose eventful life "covers a period of forty-six years"—which definitely eliminates the King Fisher then of Uvalde County.[18] Possibly by coincidence, Billy the Kid's companion Tom O. Folliard, who was from Uvalde County, and possibly he and the Kid had discussed former times when evading capture, and thus the Kid and King Fisher were aware of each other. Garrett managed to kill not only the Kid but two of his companions, Tom O. Folliard and Charles Bowdre. Garrett was no McNelly to warn anyone of his dangerous ways. Perhaps all we can conclude from these various contemporary sources is that the name of King Fisher had a certain ring to it so that others could easily confiscate it for their own use.

As late as December 1881, the name of King Fisher was often seen in the press within and outside the borders of Texas. A journal in far-off Fort Wayne, Indiana printed an article about desperadoes and "cow-boys" of western Texas. A reporter asked the question as to who was "the greatest desperado" and in reply was told: "There were a number. Billy the Kid, Tom Bois and his crowd, Curly-headed Joe and King Fisher, who I think, was the worst of the lot." This King Fisher "would think nothing of driving off a herd of two or three thousand head of cattle, overpowering those who had them in charge, and hustling them off to market for sale." Certainly readers who believed that a single "cow-boy" could drive off that large a herd and control it to market were ignorant of the cattle business.[19] The average herd ranged from between 1,500 to 2,500 head and, generally, ten men were required to drive that large a herd.

By the 1880s driving cattle to northern markets had become a thing of the past for John King Fisher. The charges of murder and rustling were behind him. He had to focus his energies and attention on his wife and daughters and his ranching interests. Whether moving elsewhere to raise their daughters was his decision alone or one made with his wife, he chose the town of Uvalde in Uvalde County. King had been there before, and he may have found it attractive at that time: one of his rustling cases had been held there and the case was continued.[20] In preparation for this relocation, Fisher maintained awareness of Uvalde happenings by reading the newspapers. In early March the "Sunset" railway was running regular trains "as far west as Uvalde."[21] That same month ground was broken for a new jail. Difficulties between residents and visitors took place, of course. For example, in May a quarrel erupted between two men in front of the Uvalde Hotel. A man named Christian Schroeder, only recently arrived from Germany, was the unlucky victim. The quarrel involved Tom Weymiller and some Germans employed on the construction of the new jail. Weymiller was stabbed in the quarrel and, while seeking medical assistance, resolved to shoot the first "Dutchman" he saw. At the hotel he met Schroeder, determined he was somehow involved, and shot him, even though Schroeder was blameless. Weymiller was arrested and charged.[22] Uvalde was becoming a busy place, in part due to District Court being held there, as civil and criminal dockets brought in witnesses and numerous attorneys. Even with a new jail, prisoners managed to escape. On the morning of April 23, two prisoners managed to break out of jail, having sawed through the bolt which secured the inner door.[23] Occasionally, lighter news was reported concerning the future home of the Fishers. In early June, a Uvalde resident wrote a letter to Ben Thompson, City Marshal of Austin, asking him "if he knew where he could purchase a breast or body plate, or whether he (Thompson) would sell his," as there was a rumor that Thompson wore such a thing, which he didn't. Thompson saw some humor in the situation and responded that, instead of acquiring a breast plate, he should "get into a strong rock house when danger approached."[24] In September full reports from all the precincts gave a majority of fourteen votes favoring prohibition: "The citizens of Uvalde … assert their determination to enforce the law, while the saloonist says he will sell liquor."[25]

King Fisher purchased a home in Uvalde at 128 Mesquite Street, although the date of purchase is unknown. On November 25, 1881, another child entered the world, but the baby did not survive and passed less than two months later on January 2, 1882. The baby, named Paul L., King's only son, was buried in the old Vivian Cemetery, also known as the Pendencia Creek Cemetery.[26] The burial ground, not far from the ghost town of Cometa, holds at least seventeen graves, but time and the elements have done their natural damage so that the wording on half of the stones is now illegible.[27] We can only imagine the feelings of the Fisher family. Mother Sarah especially must have been hurting almost beyond reason. Her emotions must have ranged the gamut, with the joy of her husband being free of all criminal charges and moving to the county seat of Uvalde County near San Antonio and yet the loss of her baby plunging her into sorrow. If indeed the family lived in Uvalde when baby P. L. passed, then they had no alternative than to place the body in a small casket and drive to the Vivian Cemetery, some fifty miles south. No doubt other family members made up the sorrowing group, in buggies or on horseback. Certainly, the two Fisher daughters, Florence Fredonia and Eugenia "Minnie," were taken along to the burial services.[28]

The positive changes in King Fisher's lifestyle must have been noticeable to many. One of them might have been the current Uvalde County Sheriff, John Benton Boatright, who needed a good dependable deputy. Boatright was a veteran of the Civil War with a wound that caused him to walk with a limp the rest of his life. He was elected County Sheriff on November 7, 1882.[29] Another Uvalde individual who seems to have recognized value in King Fisher was former Texas Ranger George K. Chinn.[30] O. C. Fisher wrote that when Boatright asked Fisher to be his deputy he "demurred, but the job had an appeal for him." Instead, Fisher informed Boatright that when the position came up for election he would be a candidate running for the office.[31] The election was not until November 1884.

Regardless of whether King Fisher was considering becoming a lawman, he must have become acquainted early on with the family of Thomas and Mary Sheedy Hannahan. Thomas was born in Ireland between 1818 and 1823 and may have served during the Mexican War. His military description shows that he was thirty years of age when he enlisted on June 15, 1853 in San Antonio. He was described as having gray eyes with dark hair and complexion and was but five feet six inches tall. His trade had been listed as "laborer." He was mustered out at Fort Davis on June 10, 1857.[32] We next find Hannahan selected to join the Uvalde County Commissioners, where he swore to the oath of office on May 15, 1868. During Reconstruction, Union-appointed "Federals" replaced many Confederacy officials, such as judges, sheriffs, and so forth, as duly-elected Southerners were considered a hindrance to Reconstruction. Governor E. M. Pease nominated men to replace these vacancies, who were then approved by Brevet Major General J. J. Reynolds. In Uvalde County, Jonathan W. Cummings was named as the new County Judge, and Hugh Cox, William Cox, and Thomas Hannahan were to be the County Commissioners.[33] Prior to the Civil War he had married Mary Sheedy and, by the time of the 1870 Uvalde County census, the family was composed of 52-year-old Thomas, who was raising stock, and wife Mary, keeping house, both proud of their Irish heritage. At that point the family consisted of two sons: eleven-year-old John and ten-year-old James. The daughters were Margaret, eight, Mary, six and Bridget four.[34]

Obviously the lifestyle of the Hannahan family was different than that of the King Fisher family. The Hannahan men and women quickly developed a disreputable reputation. Thomas was indicted for theft of a cow, filed April 27, 1876 in Uvalde District Court. Apparently the charge was dropped due to the death of the defendant, for there is evidence that Thomas Hannahan was killed in July of 1876 by a man named Cook, who disappeared and never was heard of again.[35] Son John also had problems. Accusations were numerous: cause number 502 was filed April 25, 1881 against John for theft of sixteen horses. He was found guilty but appealed the verdict. A similar indictment was filed October 23, 1878. On appeal the verdict was reversed and remanded, and in the second trial he was found not guilty. On October 24, 1878 he was indicted for theft of a steer and found guilty. The punishment demanded he would spend two years in the penitentiary. On appeal the verdict was reversed and remanded and then dismissed by the District Attorney. More serious charges were brought against his brother James Hannahan and his mother Mary along with N. B. Pulliam.[36] Mary, aged fifty, and James, aged twenty-four, were both confined to the Uvalde County jail when the 1880 census was conducted. They were charged with assault with intent to murder. They allegedly intended to murder Edward L. and Susan C. Downes. No details have surfaced as to why and how. In 1880 the Downes were a stock-raising family in Uvalde County, living with brother-in-law Lemuel Sykes and mother-in-law Catherine H. Sykes.[37]

All of this relates to Fisher, because supposedly the El Paso-San Antonio stagecoach was robbed by the Hannahans while Fisher was acting as deputy for Uvalde County. Fisher determined who the thieves were and followed them to the Hannahan residence on the Leona River. When they resisted arrest, one of the robbers was killed and James was captured. The stolen loot was recovered, providing solid evidence of the Hannahans' guilt. A twofold problem arises for the historian: Thomas was supposedly killed in 1876, suggesting that one of the sons, rather than the father, had been killed by Deputy Fisher. The records in the District Court for April 5, 1882, case number 420, show John Hannahan charged with "[t]heft of neat cattle." The case was dismissed from the docket because the District Attorney claimed the defendant was dead. Therefore, it may have been John Hannahan who was killed by Fisher—not Thomas, who apparently was killed in 1876. If this is the case, the other one captured was his brother James.

The details of the robbery of the El Paso-San Antonio stagecoach remain obscure. However, Uvalde sheep raiser Vinton Lee James knew both the Fishers and the Hannahans. He recalled meeting John Hannahan, "who lived on the Leona ... with his mother, a widow, and a one-eyed brother named Jim. John was good looking, pleasant and intelligent, and I liked him. Through some unfortunate reason he did not get along well with his neighbors, who accused him of some rascality." His neighbors went before a grand jury, and John Hannahan was indicted. V. L. James recalled that Hannahan was involved in attempting to steal some horses and then "was soon afterwards killed while resisting arrest, near Laredo, by King Fisher, who was deputy sheriff of Uvalde county."[38] We will learn more about Thomas Hannahan's widow, Mary, later.

In addition to the observable change in King Fisher the man, radical changes were taking place across the state of Texas. For decades the thousands of cattle had roamed at will until rounded up by men eager to drive them to market. The change came in 1876 when John W. Gates demonstrated to doubting cattlemen in San Antonio that his new invention would control the herds and change the industry. This new invention was barbed wire, and no man who called himself a rancher or cattleman could avoid its lasting effect.

In San Antonio in early March 1882, another invention made its appearance which to some may have seemed revolutionary. It was the electric light, and it was exhibited in front of the notorious Vaudeville Theatre, which included a saloon and gambling hall, on the evenings of Saturday, March 4 and Sunday, March 5. The light was clearly visible upon Main Plaza and Commerce Street. The reporter, exhibiting his cosmopolitanism, wrote: "It was not the best of its kind—such as we have seen in London and our northern cities, but it is very satisfactory, and has attracted large numbers to see it." What was special about the Vaudeville was that the proprietor, Jack Harris, had made it a showplace among gambling halls in the Southwest. For the theatrical performances, Harris frequently went to New York to hire new performers and "girls." There was a problem, however, in that occasionally Harris consumed too much of the ardent spirits and settled differences violently. On the morning of March 6, he had to appear in court, where he was fined $5.00 "for an unprovoked assault upon Mr. H. Ryder Taylor," a reporter, no less, for the influential San Antonio *Light* newspaper. Harris "took exception to some criticism in the Light, and struck Mr. Ryder Taylor. He was somewhat under the influence of liquor at the time, and has since apologized for his conduct."[39]

King Fisher may well have been amazed at this electric light exhibition if he was in the Alamo City then. When the phenomenon of electric lights appeared in Uvalde is unknown, but it was certainly much later than in San Antonio. How frequently Fisher visited San Antonio is also unknown, but often when he did, his presence was noted. The *Light* regularly recorded who was staying at the major hotels and noted that on April 28 King Fisher "of Uvalde, is at the Vance Hotel." In the issue of August 2, King Fisher of Uvalde was at Hord's Hotel, and on the following day it was noted that both Fisher and H. R. Patterson,[40] a former sheriff of Uvalde County, were at Hord's.

Fisher may also have occasionally visited the city with his wife and daughters. While King Fisher may not have seemed totally at ease in the halls of the better hotels, that he was becoming a true gentleman was recognized by all. Since, as mentioned previously, he at least made the claim that he had not been taking any toddies, he may not have visited the saloons or gambling halls, such as the Vaudeville or the White Elephant. He probably missed meeting Jack Harris because, during August and September, Harris was in New York City gathering new performers and dancers for the theatre and gambling hall.[41] But he might well have visited such places, given that

Joe Foster was working there at the gambling tables. He and Foster had developed a friendship not long before, when Fisher was incarcerated in the Bat Cave, and Fisher was not a man to forget favors.

Even after King Fisher had reformed, the eastern press managed to keep his name before the readers. In Detroit, Michigan, the editor of the *Free Press* printed a full three and one-half-column article entitled "Riding with the Rangers," by Col. George W. Symonds. Although the focus was on the Texas Rangers and their most noted exploits, considerable ink was given to the outlaws they chased. One was a "Mysterious Dave" who had escaped from the Concho jail and was then still at large. John Wesley Hardin could not be overlooked, and nor could the "Peg Leg" gang of stage robbers of Kimble County or the Jesse Evans gang of Lincoln County, New Mexico Territory. Lesser-known were the "Dick Tutts" gang in Travis County, the "Bill Redding" gang of Llano County, the "Taylor gang" in Lampasas County, and the "King Fisher" gang in Maverick County, not to mention "hundreds of individual operators. The rangers rarely fail in capturing the men they go after."[42] To some readers in Michigan a few of the names may have been familiar, but to most they were names of strangers. None of those mentioned had achieved notoriety due to the "dime-novel" craze.

Whether King Fisher and Jack Harris ever met in or around the Vaudeville Theatre may always remain a mystery, but if they did, it could have been a potentially dangerous situation. Harris's Vaudeville Theatre was located on the Main Plaza and Soledad Street. It had developed a bad reputation and in fact became known as the "Fatal Corner" due to the several killings which had over the years occurred there. In addition to the gambling hall and saloon, there was a theater "that featured scantily clad girls and stock-company entertainment of varied quality." It was the most advertised resort in western Texas, and many a visitor to San Antonio visited the Vaudeville because of its reputation. It was indeed a tourist draw—according to some, it was a trap.[43] Harris and Austin City Marshal Ben Thompson had been feuding over a gambling incident for some time, but apparently in July 1882 Thompson decided to end their differences. Or, perhaps it was Harris who made the decision to quit shouting threats. On the night of July 11, Harris raised his shotgun to kill Thompson. However, he proved to be too slow. Thompson reacted quickly, firing twice with his pistol and mortally wounding Harris. Thompson surrendered and ultimately was tried and found not guilty due to his plea of self-defense. Although he then returned home a hero, the killing and subsequent time in the Bat Cave cost him his position as Austin's City Marshal.[44]

How the killing of Harris by Austin's City Marshal, Ben Thompson, affected the young deputy sheriff of Uvalde is unknown. Thompson, due to his position, had a right to be armed, and Harris had made threats against him. It became clear at the trial that Thompson defended his life and had an obligation to shoot when he did. However, the entire incident was not so simple for Joe Foster, devoted friend of King Fisher, who worked for Harris and presumably was just as good a friend to him as to Fisher. There is also evidence that Harris and Fisher had become friends, although just when this occurred is impossible to say. Also, Fisher's attorney T. T. Teel was hired to prosecute Thompson, which may have created friction between the two noted gunmen.

The writer of the book of Ecclesiastes tells us that "there is no new thing under the sun."[45] In Texas, that idea may have been questioned when Jack Harris lit up his Vaudeville Theatre street corner with the newfangled electric lights and when John W. Gates brought his new barbed wire to Texas, demonstrating in an exhibition how it could hold tough longhorn cattle in check, to the amazement of all. No one who witnessed this dramatic demonstration could envision what the manifold results would be within the year.

Across the state of Texas, barbed wire took hold and ranchers soon fenced their property with it, ostensibly to reduce the amount of rustling. The gamble was that the cost of fencing would be less than the cost of losing their cattle to thieves. But a problem arose which few may have anticipated: some resented the denial of open range and cut the fence wires and burned the fence posts. Miles of fencing could be cut in a single night by a few men. It became a problem, not only for southwest Texas but ultimately in various places all over the American West. In June 1883, some twenty miles of fence in the Devine area of Medina County were reported cut: "Never before has such bitter feeling existed as that now against the pasture company. ... Wire-cutting is not done secretly or underhanded. Those engaged in it can be heard for miles, and it would not be safe for any one not members of the wire-cutting organization to approach them while they are at the work of destruction of fences."[46]

A report from the Waco area, one hundred miles north of Austin, in particular received publicity. In late July, fences were cut, posts dug up and placed on the ground, and pastures burned. A note left on one of the posts threatened the owner if he continued to fence in property. The brazen group who had done this identified themselves as "the owls," just one of the names fence-cutters called themselves.[47]

Threats from fence-cutters were easily ignored by some, but to others the potential for mob law becoming supreme posed a definite possibility. DeWitt County's *Cuero Star* informed its readers that enforcement of the laws was a much nobler action than relying on vigilance committees, or military rule (i.e. martial law). The *Star* editorialized, reminding its readers that the Sutton-Taylor Feud was a reality of not too many years before:

A little wisdom might be gained from the experience of the past, if the writers of such articles were not too wise to their own conceit to think of learning from past experiences. In DeWitt and the counties immediately surrounding there are many graves of men, some of them good and useful ones, who fell as victims to the fury of vigilance committees, under the caption of regulators or moderators.[48]

As mentioned previously, King Fisher had already narrowly escape from a mob intending to lynch him. If he read various newspapers, he certainly became very much aware of the violence taking place in many sections of the state. A man could lose his life during a fiery exchange between two men or suffer the ignominy of losing his life to a lynch mob. A report came from Laredo describing that his acquaintance Ben Thompson had been killed in that town by a man identified only as McLaughlin. No details were given, but supposedly it came from a telegram sent to the express office. A suspicious reporter of the *Galveston Daily News* decided to verify the story and determine if it was a hoax. He finally discovered that the story began with a couple of young fellows who were on a lark and had started the story as a joke. The two young men were both sorry for the joke, and if Thompson should happen to visit Galveston, "two furloughs would be very promptly requested."[49]

In Brazoria County on the Gulf Coast, prairie cattle king Abel Head "Shanghai" Pierce found his fence wires cut: "The pasture contained about three leagues of land, and the wire was cut between each post all around. Pierce at once commenced putting up more wire, and there is every prospect of that being served the same way."[50] Pierce could be as violent as the fence-cutters. A decade before he allegedly had dealt with cattle thieves in a personal way in Matagorda County, stringing them up and leaving them hanging, his own version of mob law.

But cutting fences was not the only cause of additional conflict. In an interview, pioneer real estate man E. S. Graham of west Texas, who owned fenced land in Jack and Stephens Counties west of Fort Worth, said: "There is hardly any doubt but that the pasture men brought this on themselves by fencing up large bodies of land that did not belong to them, and by trampling somewhat on the rights of the public generally." When wire cutting was "inaugurated," he added, "it was no doubt the object of the perpetrators to correct these wrongs, but mobs are uncertain agents to deal out justice and the cutters here degenerated into outlaws ... and where it will stop God only knows." Graham stated that some thought the fence-cutters were farmers, others thought that they were cattlemen who believed in "free range," and still others believed the "outlaws" were unemployed cowboys.[51] Mob law in this form certainly was a concern for ranchers and farmers, as demonstrated by a notice from Wilson County in central Texas pointing out that complaints were reaching the Floresville newspaper of "the burning of grass, cutting pasture fences, etc., and we fear serious trouble will grow out of the matter."[52]

Yet elsewhere an example of good brotherhood in the fence-cutting business was reported. In Gonzales County, one of the best-known cattlemen was Crawford "Doc" Burnett. He was apparently a man who could be at ease with the county sheriff as well as the hunted desperado, as John Wesley Hardin recalled driving cattle for Burnett during the early 1870s. But now in 1883, during a period of no rain, Burnett "found a number of his neighbors [cattle] standing at the gates of his pasture looking longingly at the water within. Mr. Burnet [*sic*] opened the gate and drove them in, and told his neighbors to bring their cattle to his water. He also offered to be one to roll up his wire fence until the drouth was ended."[53]

The Uvalde County sheriff, John Benton Boatright, had requested King Fisher to act as his deputy, not an unusual request as the sheriff realized that Fisher was a respected citizen of Uvalde County and could handle himself in a "fix" whether he was alone or with a group. But Boatright was having problems himself, with an indictment returned against the sheriff on October 1, 1883. King Fisher now became the *de facto* sheriff of the county.[54] Boatright had been elected November 7, 1882.[55] Prior to his election he was a clerk in a store, and although one wonders what qualities the voters had to place him in that important office, they did.[56]

One lawman can only do so much to enforce the law. Mob law can be created at virtually any time and place, no matter how effective a sheriff, constable, or deputy may be. Mob violence arrived in late 1883. Some "nesters" (farmers or squatters who settled on the open range) were accused of destroying the pasture fence of one Robbles in Atascosa County and of one Joseph Carelin in Medina County. Fence cutters destroyed four miles of fencing within three miles of Castroville. Someone estimated that "twenty nesters were engaged in this depredation, as the entire four miles of fencing was cut during one night."[57] But in Wilson County, various "pasturemen" (those who occupied the land legally) armed their ranch employees and gave them instructions to protect their fence from the lawless fence cutters. It was understood that this meant to protect the fences no matter what. The situation quickly changed, and on the twenty-first, "the fence-cutting element held a conference with the pasturemen and asked for quarter." The agreement reached was clear: no more fences would be cut; the pasturemen bound themselves to molest no one, and anyone seen cutting a fence would be "held strictly to account." The reporter concluded that "the lawless element cannot withstand the determination of law-abiding citizens to protect their property, and will always give down before them. It seems that tax-payers must protect themselves, and force must be met with force. The state government has failed to protect property-holders, and a resort to Winchesters and sixshooters is their only refuge."[58]

An agreement for peace was made in Gonzales, and it might have been hoped that, with Christmas coming, peace would settle over the frontier-like areas of Texas for at least a day or two. An *Express* reporter signing his specials "Christmas" happened to be traveling in Del Rio in Val Verde County, as well as in Uvalde, and he sent information on how Christmas was celebrated in those two communities. In Del Rio, citizens consumed "plenty of egg-nog, good whisky and ice-cold lemonade," and the thermometer stood at seventy degrees. He began his report on Uvalde by expressing his apparent surprise: "Nobody has been killed and there has been nary [a] fight, not even a drunk and disorderly." Christmas wondered whether such acts were detrimental to the hoped-for peace and safety of the town:

> However, this quiet status, especially on this occasion—Christmas—
> I am informed, stands to the credit of Sheriff Boatright and his
> very efficient deputy King Fisher and Kelso. I made the acquaint-
> ance of Mr. Fisher (King as he is commonly called), who showed
> me through the city. The entire town was well lit up, as it were by
> sparkling fireworks, and the public halls of Churches adorned with
> beautiful cedar "trees," decorated with Santa Claus' headquarters,
> gave it a holiday appearance. A more hospitable people than at Del
> Rio and here in Uvalde, are not to be found in Texas.[59]

Deputy Alson Algene Kelso remains somewhat a mysterious figure. He was the son of James and Mary Ann Kelso, born November 19, 1844. During the Civil War, he served three years in Waul's Texas Legion before surrendering in May of 1865. When Governor Davis created the Texas State Police, Kelso was commissioned as a private on February 3, 1871. He resigned his position on November 30, 1871.[60] He married Mary Catherine McCarthy on February 24, 1876 in Uvalde, and they had at least two children who survived. In 1880, the census taker identified his profession as a deputy sheriff. Certainly these experiences as a soldier and a member of the State Police gave him the necessary tools to become a trusted deputy alongside King Fisher.[61]

Fence-cutting problems were common in the area where John King Fisher formerly held sway as a master rustler but was now the county sheriff. In the early months of 1884, fence cutters were still at work in Medina and

Uvalde Counties. By early March, there were "thirty-five fence cutters in quod at Castroville," and "under the governor's proclamation," their capture by "the dragnet in this case" would cost the state $7,000 in rewards at $200 each. A dispatch from Castroville dated February 27 reported how Medina County Sheriff William B. Foster, Deputy Marshal Ferdinand Niggli, and other deputies had arrived at Hondo City at 2:00 in the afternoon with thirteen more fence-cutters, "all riding horses tailed together." Ranger Captain Joseph Shely was also instrumental in this roundup of suspected fence cutters. The jail in Castroville was now filled to capacity.[62]

With the threats of fence cutters acting violently, many men felt compelled to arm themselves against those who would cut their wires or burn their posts. Pressure was placed on Governor John Ireland to do something. As demonstrated in this chapter, many believed that making it legal to shoot anyone caught cutting a fence would solve the problem, despite that most of the fences were cut during the night. This dilemma was a central concern to the lawmen of Texas, whether they were deputies, county sheriffs, or United States Marshals.

# Chapter 8

# King Fisher, Peace Maker

**B**eing a sheriff in the 1870s and 1880s held many dangers, a fact of life of which King Fisher was certainly aware. Meanwhile he would make good use of his time as deputy and patiently wait until November 1884 to see if the citizens truly wanted and needed him as their county sheriff. The election for sheriff scheduled to be held in November was a long way off into the future, and many unexpected things could happen before then. Some believed he would run unopposed. O. C. Fisher, having absorbed King Fisher lore, researched John King Fisher and wrote of his findings eighty years later, published in 1966. He did not reveal any doubt when he wrote that the successful election of Fisher was a "foregone conclusion." As Fisher patrolled the streets of Uvalde, children "stared in awe and admiration" and "his worshipers gathered around him wherever he stopped."[1] This may be only slight exaggeration but it is known that Fisher was admired and respected by men who were comfortable on either side of the law. It is likely that parents expressed their positive feelings towards the deputy in their homes and that their children reflected the same emotions when they met Fisher walking his beat or riding on the county roads.

As an acting sheriff, Fisher had more than the quiet streets of Uvalde to patrol, for the entire county was his responsibility, the border lines of which enclosed nearly one hundred thousand acres. In addition, if Sheriff Niggli of neighboring Medina County ever asked for assistance, Deputy King Fisher would go to his aid. In addition to the regular concerns of rustling, fires raging in an age of wooden buildings, burglary, and livestock theft, there was now a new crime to deal with. As mentioned in chapter 7, all over Texas there was a growing concern over fence cutting and pasture burning as a means of intimidation to threaten those opposed to keeping the range open. In general, destruction of private property was among the foremost concerns of every citizen and law officer. To classify that as a misdemeanor or felony—legally, it wasn't yet clear exactly what it would be—had been unheard of when Fisher was a younger man ranching on the Pendencia or shooting up the streets of Eagle Pass.

One must wonder whether King Fisher ever considered how things were different when he was a much younger man, in the early seventies. Fence cutting was becoming a major concern, but he as a husband and father now had another responsibility: another daughter was due in late November 1883. On the twenty-fifth Margurite, who would be called "Mittie," was born in Uvalde.[2]

In 1884, King Fisher made occasional trips to San Antonio. Perhaps due to the proximity to Uvalde the trip was much easier for him, his children, and his wife, who was always ready to ride the railway instead of riding side-saddle on a horse. Travel was much easier than a few years before. One could respond to the "All aboard!" on the Southern Pacific Railroad at Uvalde and, eighty miles later in San Antonio, take the International & Great Northern Railway to arrive in Austin after only a few hours' travel and only the one change of trains.

The Vaudeville Theatre on the Alamo City's Main Plaza was a favorite landmark, or as a San Antonio *Light* reporter described it, the Vaudeville Theatre was a San Antonio "Institution for Amusement, Fun or Recreation." By reputation, it was also a sordid and dangerous place. As mentioned in Chapter 7, it was already infamous due to a number of shootings, stabbings, and suicides in its history and would soon be known as the "Fatal Corner." Fisher was undoubtedly aware of the killing of Vaudeville owner Jack Harris only two years before, by the then-City Marshal of Austin, Ben Thompson. However, according to the *Light* reporter who visited, "The best of order is maintained, a policeman, sworn in as an officer, but paid by the Vaudeville management, is constantly in attendance, and from the first rise of the curtain to the close of the entertainment there was a notable evidence of decorum."[3]

On Monday, March 10, King Fisher visited the Vaudeville Theatre on his way to Austin. His reason for stopping in at the Vaudeville may have been to pay a call on long-time friend Joe Foster and to renew his acquaintance with Foster's partner, fellow gambler William H. Simms. A handful of days later, after the Vaudeville tragedy, Simms explained his relationship with Fisher: "On behalf of myself, Foster and Coy, I intend to ask the grand jury to prefer an indictment against us and to insist on it and have a trial ... a trial by jury and will abide by their decision ... all of us mentioned in the coroner's verdict were acting entirely in defense of our lives. I had no desire to see this trouble come on and would have done, and believe I did, all that any man could have done to avert it, and so did Foster and Coy. The latter risked his life by grabbing Thompson ... [I had nothing] against Fisher either and had a pleasant conversation with the latter a few days before the unfavorable tragedy."

Suspicious minds later questioned what the topic of conversation was that they discussed. What is more, Simms' statement was and remains beyond confirmation: a "few days" before March 11 would have been March 8, and we have no evidence that Fisher or Thompson were in San Antonio then. Publicly proclaiming total innocence, Simms continued with his explanation:

> I had met Fisher a long time ago when our relations were only formal but friendly, and had not seen him for some time until this occasion, when I met him on his way to Austin, when we both remarked that the appearance of each had almost passed out of the recollection of the other, such a long time having passed since our former meeting. King Fisher, I had no idea was ever to be confronted by me in a difficulty of any kind, and if I had been told so I should have scoffed at

the idea, and while I was satisfied that Thompson might attack me on account of the Harris matter, I would not have had a quarrel with him, and had firmly resolved to avoid him as far as I could do so without deserting with cowardice my premises, and I even hoped firmly when we started to the stairs to go to the bar and drink, that all of his resentment had been buried. He and King Fisher had healed their differences, and I hoped that by going with him and drinking he would bury his animosity for me.[4]

Another individual Fisher met in San Antonio on his way to Austin was Vinton Lee James. In 1880 James was a single man raising sheep in Uvalde County. James was born in 1858, so he was only a few years younger than Fisher. Years later he recalled King Fisher as a friend with whom he often shared meals together. At one point, Fisher proposed that the two go into business together, the proposition being that Fisher would raise horses and James would continue raising sheep. Fisher "was such good company and possessed an engaging personality," James recalled, adding, "I was tempted by his offer; but the former reputation was bad, so I declined. He never referred to his past life, and we became fast friends. I admired him when he spoke of the bright future in store for him, as the best element of Uvalde citizens had favored to elect him sheriff of Uvalde County." That was the last time the two ever met. James recalled it was on the corner of Commerce Street and Main Plaza, a few steps away from the doors of the Vaudeville Theatre. James knew that Fisher was traveling to Austin to meet with Governor John Ireland "in regard to the new fence-cutting law" and stopping the unlawfulness, as he was to be the next sheriff of Uvalde County."[5]

When King Fisher was in the Alamo City, both the *Express* and *Light* newspapers frequently reported his presence as if he was a celebrity—and perhaps indeed he was. Although we cannot determine his daily activities, he was in San Antonio on March 10, where a reporter met him and reported briefly on what he was doing. The interview was conducted in the U.S. District Court room. King Fisher explained that he was one of several individuals on their way to Austin on business connected with the fence-cutting issue. Some men identified as fence cutters "had assumed a threatening attitude toward county officials, especially in Medina County."[6]

Unfortunately, what constituted a "threatening attitude" in 1884 Texas was not clarified. Fisher was not only concerned with his own county but neighboring Medina County as well. We can speculate that Ferdinand Niggli, now a Deputy United States Marshal, had requested Fisher's help and Fisher went along, not only because of their friendship but also as a professional courtesy to a fellow officer. Traveling with Fisher was businessman Ed Vance of Castroville. Niggli and Captain Joe Shely of the Texas State Troops may have been part of the group, or the two lawmen may have joined Fisher and Vance in Austin. Upon his arrival in the state capital, Fisher did meet with either Governor Ireland, the adjutant general, or one of the assistants. After possibly finding the answers he was looking for regarding the fence-cutting issues, he then set out to find the former city marshal of Austin, the notoriously dangerous Ben Thompson.

At one point in their lives, Fisher and Thompson had not been the best of friends. Something in their past had caused hard feelings. Thompson resented the fact that Attorney T. T. Teel, Fisher's attorney for years, volunteered to be a special prosecutor during his trial for the Jack Harris killing.[7] Fisher may have resented Harris' killing, since the two had been on cordial terms. Billy Thompson, Ben's younger brother, was a longtime friend of King Fisher, and it seems likely that he intervened before any disagreement between Ben and King became a confrontation. King Fisher, Ben and Billy Thompson, Joe Foster, and William Simms—the latter two now proprietors of the Vaudeville Theatre, taking the place of the deceased Jack Harris—all were strong-willed men, and a disagreement could turn into a volatile situation.

Not long before King Fisher arrived in Austin, Ben Thompson had visited the photography studio of Harvey R. Marks. Thompson posed for an impressive image. It shows him as the quintessential gambler-gunfighter, although not a single weapon is shown. Thompson appears as a tall, slim figure, immaculately dressed, leaning on a studio prop (Marks' draped chair), wearing a beautiful but modest watch and chain.[8] Thompson inscribed on the verso: "To my friend King Fisher/Ben Thompson/Austin, Texas March 11, 1884."[9] The image itself is a mere seven and three-quarter by three and three-quarter inches, mounted on a card eight and a half by four inches. It would seem that this gift to King Fisher was a token of their renewed friendship, a tangible statement that the hard feelings—whatever had caused them—were now a thing of the past. King accepted the gift and placed it in his coat pocket.

Once in Austin, on the tenth the group paid a visit to the *Austin Statesman* office, now accompanied by Ben Thompson. Supposedly Captain Shely wanted to find an issue which contained a letter or article about him, but he was unable to find what he was looking for. The *Statesman* editor published the names of his guests, saying that they "paid the Statesman a pleasant call yesterday, with Capt. Ben Thompson." Editor Isaac H. Julian, editor of the *San Marcos Free Press* in neighboring Hays County, reprinted the notice and added his satirical comment: "Apropos, what are people to think of State and U.S. officers and others claiming respectability, who were found parading around with drunken desperadoes? But then King Fisher was himself a deputy sheriff!"[10] Only Thompson had a reputation as one who abused alcohol—not the others. King Fisher at this stage of his life rarely touched liquor.

After the visit to the *Statesman* office, Fisher and Thompson went to the W. C. Denny and W. R. Brown Cosmopolitan Saloon. where Thompson at least had a drink or two. Perhaps they then visited the Iron Front Saloon, where Ben unofficially had his headquarters, and Ben had another drink or two. After apparently visiting at least two saloons, King Fisher was ready to head home to Uvalde, and he persuaded Ben Thompson to go with him as far as San Antonio. Historians have debated over why Thompson went to San Antonio after he had paid such a high price for visiting the city and the Vaudeville two years before. Perhaps peace maker King Fisher wanted to persuade his friend Ben to end his differences with the present owners of the Vaudeville. At first Ben was reluctant to leave Austin, but after some urging by King Fisher, he consented to accompany his friend. There are various plausible reasons. Brother Billy was in San Antonio, and perhaps a visit with him was in order. There was reportedly a woman in San Antonio who Ben was fond of, and perhaps that was factored into the decision. Ben also wanted to see the play "East Lynne" at the Turner Opera House, featuring the celebrated actress Ada Gray. The same show was to be presented in Austin on March 12 and 13, and Ben wanted to enjoy an advance showing.

Maybe Ben was willing to try and establish a friendly relationship with the new owners of the Vaudeville Theatre. If so, King Fisher could arrange it.

The pair should have been more aware of the time, but they lost track as they enjoyed various establishments in Austin. The International train to San Antonio left at 4:00 p.m., and they were not near the depot. They had to grab a carriage and rush to a place near the Colorado River where the train had to slow down. There they jumped off the carriage and raced to catch the slow-moving train. Fortunately, they were able to jump aboard without incident. Years later Joseph E. Farnsworth told of witnessing King Fisher and Ben Thompson making "a wild dash by hack to catch the train to San Antonio." Farnsworth was a native of New Hampshire and he had seen few incidents as memorable as what he saw in Texas, and in the early 1880s he was a bookkeeper for the *Statesman*, which is why seeing these two noted characters made quite an impression on him.[11]

The pair had been peaceful in Austin, but once on the moving train, which would take four hours to get to San Antonio, Ben allowed his drunken behavior to take over. The question of whether both were intoxicated was arguable in 1884 and remains so today. Thompson certainly was, but Fisher was probably not, though he may have had a drink or two. Thomas L. Houghton of Austin was on the train and talked with Ben. He "remonstrated with him about drinking, and Thompson replied he knew he had been taking too much liquor and would not drink any more" which obviously was a promise not kept.[12] Special telegrams from San Antonio reached both the *Galveston Daily News* and the *Daily Fort Worth Gazette*. The *Gazette* printed a special dated March 12, stating that Thompson and Fisher were "both much intoxicated."[13] The *News* printed a special dated March 11 stating that only Ben "had been drinking freely."[14] At any rate, at least Ben had been drinking—drinking enough for the both of them. Once on the train, Ben brazenly confiscated a bottle of whisky from a fellow passenger identified only as of German descent and then struck the poor man with the bottle. One report stated that Ben then ordered a porter to bring them something. The nervous black man apparently did not move quick enough, and Ben struck him with the bottle of whisky, "or something which caused blood to flow freely from his head." Blood from the porter's head had stained Ben's "fine plug hat," so Ben simply took a knife and "cut the crown out and wore it into town in that manner."[15]

Finally, at about 8:00 p.m., the train arrived in San Antonio. Many of the passengers must have felt a surge of relief, as some ladies had expressed concern for their safety witnessing Thompson's antics. Fisher and Ben stepped off the train and walked across the street to Gallagher's Saloon and Restaurant. Ben kept drinking, and Fisher was seen enjoying cigars. As a lark, Ben continued to wear the remains of his cut-up hat and entertained friends and acquaintances by relating how and why he came to remove the crown. For an unknown reason, it was here that Fisher and Thompson separated and agreed to meet at the Turner Opera House to see the play, "East Lynne." Thomas T. Vanderhaven, a friend of Fisher's and a San Antonio attorney, warned Fisher he should stay away from the troublesome Thompson and even offered the use of his driver and carriage to remove him from any possible danger. Fisher was unconcerned and declined the offer, probably feeling he could avoid or handle any trouble.

Ben Thompson left Gallagher's and headed to San Antonio's Main Plaza. By chance, his brother Billy, while standing with friends in the White Elephant Saloon located on the north side of Main Plaza, learned Ben was in town. Going outside he spotted Ben in a hack and together they were driven to a store where Ben purchased for himself a new hat. For a man to be well-dressed—and Thompson was always conscious of his appearance—a hat was *de rigueur*. The brothers took a drink in a saloon on Commerce Street and then walked west towards Soledad Street. They stopped and stood talking within the shadow of the Vaudeville Saloon. Ben, now with a new hat, wanted a six-shooter, having left Austin unarmed. He may have finally realized that, this close to the Vaudeville, there might be danger due to his past actions. Billy tried to persuade Ben that he didn't need a firearm, but then agreed to get it for him "if he was bound to have one." Ben then went to a barber shop on Soledad Street while Billy walked past the Vaudeville towards the White Elephant several doors down to retrieve his pistol, a past gift from Ben. On returning to the barber shop, Billy learned that Ben had left and had gone to Turner's Opera House. At this point Billy met King Fisher and entrusted him with delivering the pistol Ben wanted so badly. Billy begged King "to keep a watch on Ben and guard him against any trouble."[16] This proved to be somewhat of an ironic twist, as so often Ben had worked to get his younger brother out of trouble. Now the situation was reversed, with Billy expressing concern for Ben to avoid trouble through the aid of his friend King Fisher. Billy then went back to the White Elephant and asked Edward Fowler, the proprietor, to keep a watch on Ben to avoid trouble.[17] By chance Billy met up with Captain Joe Shely and San Antonio Police Captain Phillip Shardein.[18] He requested them to keep a watch on Ben, and they promised to do so. Billy, learning that his brother and King Fisher were both at Turner's watching "East Lynne," now returned to the White Elephant, feeling confident that enough of his friends were looking out for his brother.

This was San Antonio's second opportunity to see Miss Gray as "Lady Isabelle." The play had been performed there the previous evening and, according to one reviewer, she "acquitted herself creditably, but could have thrown a great deal more feeling into her part." The Turner Opera House was managed by Ernest Rische, who years later on the occasion of the death of Ada Gray in 1902 reminisced about the events of March 11, 1884. He recalled that the presence of Fisher and Thompson "caused much anxiety among the ladies present." Ben Thompson "came into the theatre first that night," according to Rische. "He got a seat down near the stage. He had been in the theatre a short time when King Fisher came in and asked for a seat next to Thompson. I gave it to him. He had been seated but a short time when Chris Stafford, who was then head usher, came to me and said the ladies were very much frightened over Thompson's presence." Rische does not explain just how he did it, but he got Thompson to leave the performance before it ended, apparently pacifying the nervous ladies:

> I got him out but King Fisher wanted to see the play finished. Thompson, however, insisted on his coming out with him which he did. As they came out, Charley Watkins, husband of Miss Gray, and I joined them. We walked across the street to get a drink. Watkins wore a high silk hat, and Thompson wanted the worst in the world to shoot some holes through it. We persuaded him out of the notion of doing it, however, and later we went down to the Van Alstine café and it was here that King Fisher told Thompson that Texas was not

big enough to hold them and one of them had better cross the Rio Grande. That was said in jest by King Fisher, but it seems that they had made up that day, having been enemies before.[19]

*King Fisher told Ben Thompson that Texas was not big enough for both of them. ...* This statement appears as a threat. Unfortunately, we cannot now determine if what King Fisher said "in jest" to Thompson was indeed said jokingly or expressed his true feelings, disguised as a jest. He had spent a good portion of the day with Thompson and had observed several examples of his disreputable behavior, his action with the German and then with the porter, two acts which could have resulted in an arrest by a railroad authority.

At the conclusion of "East Lynne," the audience left Turner's "well pleased with the performance."[20] The two who had been earlier escorted from the theatre did not know the audience's response to her performance or how long the applause lasted. The editor of the *New York World* wrote that, having left Ada Gray and her loving patrons soaking their tear-filled handkerchiefs due to the heroine's misfortunes, King Fisher and Ben Thompson now called for a convenient hack to take them the few short blocks to the Vaudeville Theatre.[21]

# Chapter 9

# Into the "Den of Infamy"

T he hack delivered King Fisher and Ben Thompson to the Vaudeville within a few minutes, as it was not far from Turner's Opera House. It would probably have been quicker to walk, but they had chosen to ride. They could not have realized it would be their last visit to the Vaudeville Theatre, where tragedy awaited them. Soon Texas would learn of the basic details of their assassination, and within days the entire nation would also hear of what had happened in that "den of infamy."[1] Yet witness testimony would contain disagreements, raising questions about how the tragedy occurred. Significantly, a telegram to the *Galveston Daily News* stressed the mystery aspects of the tragedy: "No two accounts of the tragedy agree, and when analyzed were self-contradictory."[2] It would remain an unsolved mystery of the Wild West.

What neither King Fisher nor Thompson knew was that word of their arrival in San Antonio had been telegraphed to the proprietors of the Vaudeville, alerting the owners of their approaching visit. This telegram forewarned Joseph C. Foster and William B. Simms of their arrival. What is more, United States Marshal Hal Gosling rode the same train as Fisher and Thompson—in fact, promptly after exiting the train, Marshal Gosling went to the Vaudeville, where he personally informed a theatre employee that Thompson had come down on the train and that they could expect trouble, as "there seemed to be h-ll in his neck."[3] Simms, now fully aware of the impending danger, chose to alert City Marshal Phillip Shardein, who stated that he would send over six police officers to prevent any difficulties.[4]

Having descended from their hack, Thompson and Fisher entered the Vaudeville. Ben, and possibly King as well, stopped at the bar for a drink. It is easy to imagine that Ben may have used this "opportunity" to let every-one know that he was back in town, he was not afraid to enter into the "den of infamy," and he was ready for whatever fate could befall him. Before long, rather than staying at the bar, the pair then went upstairs where a variety show was in progress. San Antonio historian Elton R. Cude wrote that Simms invited waitresses, or "girls in short skirts and red stockings," to wait on them.[5] Thompson consumed yet another drink while Fisher called for a cigar.

As soon as the pair entered, Thompson made a threatening remark about Joe Foster, against whom he held an old grudge.[6] Vaudeville house policeman Jacobo Santos Coy warned Ben to keep quiet. Then Joe Foster and William Simms came into the gallery, and Ben asked them to have a drink with him and Fisher. Drinks were ordered and in the ensuing conversation Ben made more threatening remarks against Foster, including calling him a thief. Foster told him to keep quiet, that he didn't want a fuss. Thompson stated to his old enemy: "Foster, come down stairs." Foster answered: "There is no need; I don't want to have any difficulty with you."

By now all had arisen from their seats. Foster, Simms, and Coy were standing near the door, with Thompson and Fisher to their right, about four feet apart. Coy interfered and told them to quiet down. Ben again called Foster a thief, adding, as the *Austin Statesman* wrote, an "opprobrious epithet" as he struck at him and tried to draw his pistol. Coy interfered, knocking the pistol down, which was a dangerous move as he could have easily been killed as a consequence. Then the shooting began.[7]

"It is impossible to say who fired the fatal bullets," read the *Statesman*.[8] With the first shot, patrons rushed the doors, and several jumped out of the windows. A subsequent examination of King Fisher's pistol found that, unlike the other guns, all of its chambers were still loaded, which means that he must have been shot first. "Thompson died shooting. Both he and Fisher died side by side, and the floor was flooded with their gore." Foster was shot through the right leg, just below the knee, "and bled profusely."

When the shooting stopped, people wanted to see the victims and tried to gain entrance to the building they had just vacated so hurriedly, but the doors were closed to all except officers and reporters. Justice Anton Adams was notified and quickly summoned a jury of inquest. J. M. Emerson was chosen as foreman of the jury and, after searching the bodies for wounds, presented the following conclusions: Ben Thompson had been shot once over the left eye, once in the left temple with the ball coming out under the chin, and also through the abdomen, with another spent ball inflicted a second wound over the left eye. King Fisher had been shot in the heart, the head just over his left eye, and the right leg a few inches above the knee. According to the inquest, two of the deadliest gunfighters in Texas had been gunned down without taking a single adversary with them. Officer Coy had received "only a slight wound in the calf of his right leg."[9] Joe Foster had received a dangerous wound in his leg and was taken to his home, where he received medical attention.

On the morning of March 12, the only conversation on the streets of San Antonio was the double killing at the Vaudeville. Many people believed that the killing of Ben Thompson and King Fisher was an act of premeditated murder, arguing that their deaths could only be accomplished by a carefully planned ambush. No one was arrested, although everyone knew who had been involved in the shooting. The idea was clearly expressed that some person, or persons, had laid a trap for Thompson and that a number of men had fired from ambush—that not only Simms, Coy, and Foster were the shootists but there had been others as well. Rumors of all sorts were floated about the city. Joe Foster was suffering greatly from his wound, and the odds of surviving it were "as much against as in favor of his recovery."[10]

The coroner's findings were reported in the *Statesman* and later in other major newspapers: "That Ben Thompson and J. K. Fisher both came to their deaths on the 11th day of March, A.D. 1884, while at the Vaudeville theatre, in San Antonio, Texas, from the effects of pistol shot wounds from pistols held in and fired from the hands of J. C. Foster and Jacob S. Coy, and we further find that the said killing was justifiable and done in self defense in the immediate danger of life."[11] This verdict, as reported in San Antonio's *Daily Express*, was generally accepted in San Antonio, but in Austin, where people were shocked at the death of Thompson, many reacted differently, including the *Statesman* reporter himself. He clearly did not accept the findings of the coroner's report and explained why: Thompson had ruled Austin, and the San Antonio police were determined that he would not rule their city as well; Thompson was of reckless courage and careless of human life when under the influence of alcohol, as he was that night; Thompson had killed Jack Harris, suggesting the possibility of revenge-seeking Vaudeville workers; the people in the Vaudeville did not like Thompson, and from the moment he entered the Vaudeville he was a doomed man. King Fisher, who perished with Thompson, was merely in the wrong place at the wrong time.

The shooting happened because Thompson had become involved in an altercation with the three men named: Foster, Simms and Coy. In the struggle Thompson and Coy went down together, with Coy holding Thompson's pistol. For this reason, no one could possibly say who fired the shots. "It is believed that Thompson was killed by his own pistol in the hands of Coy," concluded the reporter, going on to state that "Coy's pistol was fully loaded and Fisher's was found in the scabbard." Thus the remaining pistols were those of Simms and Foster, not Coy.

Due to the seriousness of Foster's leg wound, he submitted to amputation, and it was reported that "he will in all probability die." A bit of sympathy was also expressed for Thompson's compatriot: "When the smoke cleared away Fisher was lying across his companion." However, at least one reporter ignored the fact that Fisher was at the time of his death the acting sheriff of Uvalde County and identified him as "the incarnation of desperadoism."[12] Many, on the other hand, regretted Fisher's death, as it was known that he had led a reformed life for the last two years "and hopes were entertained for his future." The reporter from the *Austin Weekly Statesman* must have been among the latter, as he finished his lengthy report philosophically: "It is the irony of fate that men with the reputation for personal prowess possessed by the departed should be shot like dogs and butchered like sheep in the shambles, without one life in exchange for their own."[13]

Police Captain Phil Shardein, as the highest ranking officer, took control of the scene. As mentioned previously, those who had escaped the gunfire when the shooting erupted now wanted to reenter the Vaudeville to see what they had fled from. Shardein must have had his hands full, but the historical record suggests that he was equal to the task. As Shardein was viewing the bodies upstairs, someone yelled from the foot of the stairs that Billy Thompson was coming with a shotgun. Shardein ran down stairs slippery with blood to prevent Billy from coming in and possibly continuing the shooting. He passed Simms helping Foster, who was bleeding badly, descend to the first floor. Shardein took notice that Simms and Foster both had pistols in their hands.

Simms cried out to the passing Shardein, "Give us protection!"[14] Shardein got to the front door, where he met Billy Thompson. As Shardein pushed him outside, someone behind him yelled, "Get out of the way!" as Simms and Foster continued down the stairs. Shardein was probably considering what to do if Billy Thompson was armed, and he may have breathed a sigh of relief when he found that Billy had no weapons. One might well wonder whether the yelling to get out of the way was coming from Simms and Foster or from others, intending to shoot Billy. Shardein commanded Billy to stay out and immediately ordered the Vaudeville closed, allowing only officials and reporters inside. Then he went to Jacobo S. Coy and collected Ben Thompson's pistol, "a large 45-caliber, ivory-mounted, engraved and silver-mounted." Shardein looked at it without revolving the cylinder and found there were five chambers empty.

Such was Captain Shardein's role in the immediate aftermath, coming on the scene after the house had emptied but while gunsmoke was still hanging in the air upstairs. He now was dealing with people wanting to get back in, while Simms and Foster were trying to get out to where Foster could get medical help, and he couldn't be sure of where Billy Thompson might go or what he might do. All this amid the continued crying and screaming of the "drink girls." It was a scene of wild confusion, but Chief Shardein managed to prevent any additional trouble.

In contrast to Shardein's perspective, Jacobo Coy was on the gallery, having participated in the struggle that led to gunfire.[15] Coy, when testifying later, said that, when the touchy subject of Jack Harris came up, Fisher demanded of Thompson, "I thought we were going to have some fun, but don't talk about past times." Thompson had replied, "Don't be uneasy; we will have it soon." At this point the party arose and, according to Coy, Fisher and the others started to go downstairs. Coy and Fisher were in front with Simms and Ben Thompson behind. If all had proceeded down the steps to the main floor, the evening might have ended peacefully. But then, Thompson noticed his old enemy and said to Simms, "Billy, ain't that Joe Foster?" Simms answered that it was and went to Foster, at which point Simms and Foster then rejoined the others. Ben asked Foster to take a drink, but Foster refused, saying, "You know, Ben, I don't drink." Then Ben held out his hand to shake, but Foster replied that he would not shake his hand, which Thompson perceived as a personal insult. Facing Joe Foster, he said, "G-d d-n you, I'm glad you won't drink nor shake hands with me."

Coy testified that he realized then that the situation was approaching the danger point, and he told Ben to behave himself. Ben rudely responded to Coy to get out of his way, saying: "Let me settle this matter with Foster." Coy claimed that he had still hoped to prevent trouble, telling Ben that if he wanted to fight with Foster he should go somewhere else because he intended to prevent trouble in the Vaudeville. Ben Thompson was beyond being reasonable now and again told Coy to get out of the way. He called Foster a thief and then slapped him with his left hand while drawing his pistol with his right hand. Coy realized that it was now too late to prevent trouble, but jumped in and grabbed Ben's pistol by the barrel "when it exploded." Coy held on, fearing that if he let go of the pistol it could be turned against him. Ben said: "G-d d-n you, turn my pistol loose." King Fisher, who had done nothing during this period of yelling and insulting, also said, "Turn that pistol loose."

Then, according to Coy's account, Coy, Foster, and Thompson scuffled from the door to the corner, where they all fell together, with King Fisher pulled, collapsing and falling, in the middle. Coy had not let go of Thompson's pistol, and, in falling, Ben did let it loose. Later Coy turned the gun over to

Captain Shardein. Coy stated that he did not see who else had pistols and that he had not seen King Fisher with a pistol.[16] Such was the testimony of Jacobo Santos Coy, the officer of the Vaudeville whose duty it was to prevent trouble. The pistol Captain Shardein now held with five chambers empty was still warm, having been fired five times only moments before.

When Simms and Thompson first faced each other, Ben seemed to have been in a peaceful mood.[17] "Simms," he had said, "I want to talk to you and tell you I haven't anything against you, but you haven't treated me right." Ben, according to Simms, rambled on. Simms added that Thompson "seemed by his pantomime ... to be half crazy." Thompson continued, according to Simms's statement, "I am rich now. I can get out of any trouble. I was taking chances to come in here, but I am surrounded by my friends. I have a six-shooter, but I won't need to pull it, and if you move you will be killed." To Simms, Ben Thompson's ramblings must have seemed strange. Thompson had boasted about being wealthy enough to be invincible. He had admitted that entering the Vaudeville was risky, but he insisted that he was safe because he was among friends. He had revealed that he carried a six-shooter, but also argued that he wouldn't need it and yet also threatened that, if Simms moved, he would kill him. These odd threatening words suggest that Thompson's thinking was very unclear. After all, he was not surrounded by friends, aside from King Fisher. Simms then responded that he did not want any trouble with Ben.

Ben's temper was getting out of control, and he also felt that Foster had cheated him the last time he had been in the Vaudeville gambling room.[18] Foster, who seemed calm and in control of his emotions, informed Ben that the world was big enough for both of them. As they kept talking, Thompson and Fisher kept backing up. It was a narrow place, with a little elevation. When Thompson got on this elevation, he suddenly jerked out his six-shooter and stuck it in Foster's mouth, cocking it and then pulling it back away from Foster's face. Coy claimed that, upon hearing the click, he grabbed the pistol and said, "Ben, I am an officer, don't do that." Then the pistol Thompson held "exploded," according to Coy, which can be explained by the fact that, in the small enclosure, a shot must have sounded like an explosion. After the first fire, another pistol was drawn, and Fisher said, "Don't you draw that gun, you son of a b–." Firing then commenced on both sides.

When the firing stopped—and no one could have accurately counted the number of shots fired—Joe Foster grabbed Simms by the shoulder and said, "I am shot; help me down stairs."[19] Thompson and King Fisher were both on the floor, dead. Foster said again, "Billy, I am shot all to pieces; help me down stairs." Simms could not have paid any attention to the dead men, because he was now concentrating on getting Foster down the stairs.

According to Simms, it was Thompson who fired the first shot.[20] While Coy was holding the pistol, Thompson fired twice more before anyone else drew a weapon. Simms said that after the first shot he thought his ear had burst because it was so loud. From the testimony given, it would appear Thompson had done all the shooting.

However, Simms' concluding testimony suggests otherwise. He pointed out that Thompson "had taken a drink and asked the boy whether there was poison in it, and Simms took a cigar. Ben would not pay for it, and the boy waited. He asked the boy if he was waiting for that money. The boy said, 'No, I have got plenty of time, Mr. Thompson, and will wait as long as you want me to.' Ben said: 'Well, I'll not pay you for any drinks.'" This strange verbal exchange between a young boy and a drunken Ben Thompson reveals only his confused state of mind. This talk of not paying the boy irritated King Fisher, who interjected, "Ben, pay the boy," and put his hand in his pocket as if to pull out payment for the drink (though Simms couldn't recall who actually did pay for the drink). Once Fisher was in the picture again, Simms related, "I don't think Fisher was drunk. He was very quiet, and when I spoke he wouldn't answer, but got up and faced me. He took a cigar, I think, which I did when Thompson ordered the drinks." Simms saw Foster with a pistol out after the third or fourth shot was fired, but didn't know if Foster had fired, and nor could Simms say whether Coy had fired his pistol. Simms concluded his testimony by saying, "I don't think Thompson slapped Foster, but he was gesticulating rapidly with his hands. I saw Foster cocking a pistol. Don't know that he shot, but he ought to have done so." Officer J. B. Chadwell could offer little with his testimony. He didn't see the shooting, but afterwards took King Fisher's pistol from its scabbard and handed it to Officer Hughes. The revolver had not been fired or even drawn.

Simms was the last to testify as to how the tragedy had occurred. The jury returned its verdict within ten minutes, which was that Ben Thompson and King Fisher came to their deaths at the Vaudeville theater from the effects of shot wounds from pistols held and fired by the hands of J. C. Foster, W. H. Simms, and Jacob Coy. The final statement held that the killing was justifiable and done in self-defense in the immediate danger of life.[21]

In addition to the conflicting statements given at the inquest, wild rumors reported as facts by major newspapers. Due to the similarity of reporting, such as the use of identical terminology, one might think that multiple reporters used the exact same source. The Dallas *Daily Herald* headlined its long article "As Sheep In Shambles," repeating the term used in the *Statesman*, but also in the headline raised the question as to the killing being "A Vendetta or a Vindication—Should San Antonio Shame?" The *Daily Herald* became more thoughtful, but at the same time printed ludicrous tales of King Fisher's supposed exploits, noting that the man "was regarded as a reformed robber. He was chief for years, of a band of Rio Grande banditti and his name inspired terror throughout all the states of Mexico. ... The stories that are told of his adventures would fill a book. He is said to have strung nine pairs of Mexican ears on his bridle reins and with his horse neck gory with the blood of his victims—according to the story—he galloped through the streets of a border town yelling and firing at every swarthy face he could get his eyes on."[22] Although it is doubtful that anyone believed this reporting, the Dallas *Weekly Herald* outdid the *Daily Herald* in what it printed on the same date: "Ben Thompson ... was shot and instantly killed in the Vaudeville at 11:15 to-night by King Fisher, deputy sheriff of Uvalde county, and a desperado of the first water himself."[23] In response to the suggestion that King Fisher killed Ben Thompson, one can only wonder if the reporter wanted his contribution to be more sensational than the next.

# Chapter 10

# A Dozen Carbines

The bodies of King Fisher and Ben Thompson remained on the floor of the upper stairs of the Vaudeville, bloodied from multiple bullet wounds, not only from pistols which Foster, Coy, and Simms claimed were the cause of their deaths, but yet-to-be revealed bullets from Winchester rifles as well as additional pistols. The inquest performed in San Antonio, determined by many to have been perfunctory, would soon be challenged by the results of an inquest on the body of Thompson, which was performed in his own residence.

No inquest was performed on the body of King Fisher. His body was placed on the 6:40 "Sunset" train by Deputy U.S. Marshal Fred Niggli, who, with several other friends, accompanied the body to Uvalde, where it arrived the night of March 12.[1] Details regarding the transportation of the remains from the depot to the Fisher home remain unclear. Perhaps it is true that Marvin Powe, a young boy, was sent on horseback to the Fisher home to inform Sarah that she was now a widow. Among the letters in the Hobart Papers is one written by Powell Roberts of Santa Rita, New Mexico to J. Marvin Hunter. "Mr. Marvin Powe," Roberts wrote, "the present City Marshal of Silver City, New Mexico, was an eleven-year-old boy living in

Uvalde when Ben Thompson and King Fisher were killed in San Antonio, and Powe carried the telegram several miles out to Fisher's wife informing her of his death."[2] The body lay in state at his home where it was viewed by a great many of his friends and general citizens. The funeral took place at 4:00 p.m. on March 13, the largest ever held in Uvalde. Rev. J. W. Stovall of the Methodist Episcopal Church conducted the services.[3]

Anton Adams and the jury of inquest in San Antonio may have satisfied the curious there, but in Austin a much more thorough examination of Ben Thompson's remains took place. Billy Thompson accompanied his brother's body to Ben's residence in Austin. There, Dr. Charles N. Worthington and Dr. Thomas D. Wooten, the latter described as "one of the most scientific gentlemen in Texas," examined the corpse on the thirteenth of March.[4] Their findings were much different than those in San Antonio: the doctors found eight bullet wounds, five of which had entered Thompson's head, whereas the initial autopsy found only three.

The two distinguished doctors found in their autopsy wounds quite different than what the San Antonio newspapers reported after the coroner's hearing. They discovered that all eight bullets had entered the body on the left side, which meant that neither the back, the front, nor the right side were struck at all. The *Statesman*'s conclusion was that the shooting was all done from the left and "that whoever they were shot from the same point." The first wound probed revealed that the ball had "entered the left side of the head near the point where the side head begins to round off to form the crown, and its course was downward, a little backward and slightly inwarded so that if the ball came out its point of exit would have been just back of the right jaw in the neck." An inch and a half below that, another ball had entered and followed a parallel course, and if it had exited, the point of exit would have been an inch and a half below that of the first. A third bullet entered above the left eye, going downward. A fourth ball entered just below the point of entrance of the previous one described. The fifth ball entered the ear and lodged in the brain. The first four balls were fired from above and came down from the same general area and along a similar downward course. The sixth ball struck the jawbone in a downward course. The seventh ball entered the outer center of the heart. The eighth ball had a point of entrance on the left side above the hip and ranged upwards coming out on the other side just below the ribs. Another ball did not enter the body but only grazed across the shoulders from left to right, leaving its mark plainly on the skin.

Some of the bullets were removed and taken to Austin gun shop owner Joseph Carl Petmecky as well as to other gun experts.[5] They were identified as balls from both Winchester rifles and .44-caliber pistol cartridges, proving that two types of weapons were used in the ambush. Six of the eight wounds would have been fatal, proving that the claims of Simms, Coy, and Foster were untrue—that the killing had been done by their pistols alone. The doctors determined that Ben Thompson "would have been powerless in an instant after any of these struck him." The conclusion after the postmortem was that Thompson was shot when standing erect by persons armed with Winchester rifles and revolvers who were above him and also a little to the left, and it was also determined that the balls were fired by as many as five different persons and simultaneously. He would have fallen instantly from the effect of any one of them. The *Statesman* reporter ended his detailed report: "It would be interesting to have a scientific investigation of Fisher's wounds to see what sort of evidence they would give."[6]

Unfortunately, no autopsy was performed on the remains of John King Fisher. Those killing wounds inflicted upon King Fisher by Winchester balls and revolver cartridges would not have differed greatly from Ben Thompson's. A reporter in Uvalde notified the San Antonio *Express* of the funeral and that the remains of "deputy sheriff of Uvalde county, murdered in San Antonio on the night of the 11th, arrived here by last night's express." The reporter also expressed what was probably the opinion of everyone in town: Fisher was assassinated, no question about it. The body lay in state at his home and was viewed by many friends and citizens "at large" in "an elegant casket draped with magnificent wreaths of flowers." The funeral took place at 4:00 the afternoon of the 13th. The procession included two "busses" (vehicles), probably draped in black, as well as most of the other vehicles in town. Rev. J. W. Stovall conducted the services "in an impressive manner." As for the "character and prospects" of King Fisher, it was noted that he had been regarded as a "reformed man, and enjoyed the confidence and respect of our people. Expressions of regret at his untimely end are heard on every hand.

He is believed to have accompanied Ben Thompson in the capacity of a peace-maker. Mr. Fisher was a prominent candidate for sheriff of Uvalde county at the ensuing election, with fair prospects of success."[7] The *Statesman*'s reporter ended the detailed and very informative report with the following thought: "It would be interesting to have a scientific investigation of Fisher's wounds to see what evidence they would give."

Since it was boldly stated that Fisher and Thompson had been murdered, it would make sense to wonder whether any vigilantes attempted to deliver frontier justice to avenge their deaths. Lynch law was not a thing of the past, as every citizen and law officer knew. A brief item in the Austin *Daily Statesman* suggested that these concerns were a reality: It is said by parties from San Antonio, that letters have been received from King Fisher's friends to the effect that unless the law is permitted to deal out justice to King Fisher's murderers, they will be taken care of. Parties in Austin who knew Fisher's followers are certain the murder of him and Thompson is but the beginning of serious tragedies sure to follow.[8]

But there were no such "serious tragedies" following the Vaudeville killings. It is doubtful that any friend of Fisher seriously intended to deter-mine who these murderers were and then deliver mob law justice to them. Enough good citizens of Uvalde did meet and sign a testimonial to King Fisher, suggesting what most people believed that King Fisher had "accom-plished as much for law and order within the last two and a half years as any man in Western Texas, and this assertion will be verified by all officers who may have been thrown in contact with him."[9] This testimonial, which was printed in full in the San Antonio *Daily Express*, was in reaction to how the *Express* had earlier sullied the good name of Fisher. The *Express* had described both Fisher and Thompson as "desperate men, a terror in the neigh-borhood in which each resided, and if they are regretted at all it will not be by the law-abiding element of the state." These were the *Express* editor's true feelings, and of course he had a perfect right to say so. Fortunately for him and the newspaper, the good citizens of Uvalde did not storm the *Express* offices to wreck or burn but thoughtfully prepared their reaction to what they felt was unfair and gathered citizens to sign it. The memorial was signed by two hundred and seventy-one citizens of Uvalde and vicinity.[10]

In San Antonio as well, many citizens found not only the double killing in the Vaudeville but also the findings of Anton Adams's inquest to be an irresistible topic of conversation. On the fifteenth, a representative of the *Statesman* met two gentlemen who were present at the Vaudeville theatre when Fisher and Thompson were killed, took down their story, and shared it with the public. "It is monstrous," said Alexander T. Raymond, "the evidence those fellows gave at San Antonio, and the whole town seems to be in mortal fear of the tough crowd who have their headquarters at that den of infamy, the Vaudeville. Thompson, no doubt, was a bad man, but that crowd who murdered him ought to be hanged, for it was the coldest blooded murder ever committed." This is what the two gentlemen claimed to have witnessed. Raymond and John R. Sublett presumably continued on their business travels, never identifying their friend whose wish to show them the sights of the Alamo City had placed them within inches of the assassination of King Fisher and Ben Thompson. The friend insisted on remaining unidentified for fear of retaliation from the owners of the Vaudeville. The reporter concluded that the account "corresponds with the facts shown by the autopsy, and is no doubt as near the truth as the public will ever get. It is given exactly as related to the STATESMAN representative."[11]

Both were gentlemen from the north and were traveling men, one representing a wholesale liquor house in Kentucky and the other a wholesale tobacco house in Chicago. They were Alexander T. Raymond and John R. Sublett. The pair happened to be in San Antonio that night and were staying with an acquaintance who wanted to show them the sights of the city. Coincidentally, they began their tour at the Turner Opera House, where they saw Ada Gray onstage, perhaps while Thompson and Fisher were there. Then they visited the Vaudeville and happened to be in the barroom when Fisher and Thompson came in. Their host then explained who Thompson was, that he was notorious, that he had killed Jack Harris, and that the current owner was the partner of the deceased Harris. To Raymond and Sublett, neither Fisher nor Thompson appeared drunk: both appeared to be "in the most pleasant humor." Then Simms and officer Coy came in and greeted Fisher and Thompson, shaking hands. Simms then said to Thompson, "Ben, I am awful glad to see you here. Let us forget the past, and be friends in the future."

Thompson responded, "I desire to be friends, and I have come here with my friend Fisher to talk the matter over, and have a perfect understanding. I have a perfect right to do that, have I not?" To this Simms answered, "Yes, Ben, that is right, and I know we can all be friends." Ben responded, "I have nothing against you or Foster, I am not afraid of you. I am here surrounded by my friends, but I want to be friends with you, and I have come here to talk this over." Then Simms answered, "That is all right; come up stairs and see Foster."

According to Raymond and Sublett, at this point in this conversation Thompson and Simms decided a drink was in order. Fisher and Thompson then ascended the stairs, with Raymond and Sublett following with their host, but neither Simms nor Coy went upstairs. Raymond, Sublett, and the unidentified host then took seats to enjoy the show. Shortly after, Simms and Coy did join them, and again some pleasant conversation took place. During this time a "drinks girl" came along and Thompson ordered drinks. Thompson teased the girl about not paying for the drinks, but finally pulled out a large roll of bills saying, "I have lots of money. I have $20,000 in that roll." He then paid the girl for the drinks.

Thompson then turned to Simms, saying, "I thought you brought me up here to see Foster, Billy, don't play any games on me. I did not come here for any fuss and I don't want any, but you must treat me fair."[12] To this Simms answered, "I am, Ben; it's just as I told you, and I will go and tell Foster you want to have a friendly talk with him." Then Fisher, apparently speaking for the first time, said, "Yes, go and get him. I want to make you fellows good friends before I leave. I have invited Thompson here; he did not want to come, but you are all friends of mine, and I want you to be friends. I told him to come and talk the matter over like gentleman together, and bury the past; Thompson is willing to do it, and I want Foster to meet him half way." Simms agreed to this and went to get Foster. As Simms and Foster approached, Thompson, without rising, extended his hand to Foster. As he did so, Fisher said, "I want you and Thompson to be friends. You are both friends to me and I want you to shake hands like gentlemen." Foster refused, saying, "I cannot shake hands with Ben Thompson, nor can he and I be friends, and I want him to keep out of my way."

As Foster spoke these words of rejection, both Simms and Coy stepped to one side, at least two feet from where Fisher and Thompson were seated.[13] Foster was at least that far on the other side. The trap was set, but before it could be set in motion Thompson and Fisher both suspected the foul play and reacted. Before they got to their feet, a volley of shots sounded from a box a little to the left and considerably above the pair, "as though there were a dozen carbines."[14] Both went down instantly. Then either Simms or Coy rushed up and drew Thompson's revolver. Then, bending down close, he put the muzzle close to Thompson's ear and fired. He then fired two other shots into Thompson's head and body while the other man shot Fisher in a similar manner. Joe Foster tried to draw his revolver but it got caught somehow, and he gave it an angry jerk which caused it to discharge, the ball striking him in the leg. Foster then fell.

Will we ever discover who the assassins were that fired the fatal volley? There are potential clues, but the passage of time prevents deeper investigation. George Durham, one of the Texas Rangers who served under both McNelly and Hall, may have learned important information but kept it secret. Durham claimed to "get the record straight" on King Fisher's death, arguing that he "was assassinated by paid killers. I know the three assassins; I know exactly how much money they got, where it come from, and how much each of them got. Them assassins was paid to get Ben Thompson. They didn't want King. But King stuck by Ben as he always stuck by a friend; and King was killed."[15] It may never be known for certain if Durham in fact knew who paid the assassins, or whether this claim just meaningless braggadocio. Unfortunately, then, we may never know for sure the identity of the three assassins. Three years prior to Durham's *West* article, former San Antonio *Daily Express* editor Frank H. Bushick published *Glamorous Days in Old San Antonio*.[16]

The moniker "Canada Bill" could be a fictitious name for any gambler, whether he was from Canada or not. The name McLaughlin remains mysterious. As mentioned in a previous chapter, in August of 1883, a rumor started that Ben Thompson had been killed in Laredo by a man named McLaughlin. Naturally such a statement spread with "cyclonic rapidity," as described by the *Galveston Daily News*. A reporter began to determine the source of the rumor and discovered that two "young fellows who were on a lark" had started the story as a joke.[17] It may be only a coincidence that Thompson's supposed slayer had been named McLaughlin and now one of the proposed assassins was of the same name.

Of interest in the case was a man in San Antonio whose name was John McLaughlin, and he had been employed by the Vaudeville Theater earlier, during the time of the Jack Harris-Thompson feud.[18] At Thompson's trial for the Harris killing, McLaughlin provided evidence for the defense. Whereas Tremaine and Canada Bill immediately left the city after the March 11 killing, John McLaughlin remained. A John McLaughlin also worked as a hack driver during the years before the killings and at least until 1886, according to the San Antonio City Directories. It may be that Frank Bushick was correct in naming McLaughlin as one of the assassins. Or, George Durham may have been right about who the assassins were and how much they had been paid. One reasonable conclusion would be that someone in the Vaudeville proprietor group arranged for three or four men to be ready to kill when Thompson returned to the Vaudeville. The theater's management had been forewarned of his visiting the city, so, in our view, there would have been plenty of time that day to make the necessary arrangements. Determining the placement of the assassins, the money exchanging hands, and just what the right moment to kill would be—all could have been discussed and determined.

By the 1920s, it was generally accepted that Fisher and Thompson had both been killed in an ambush set up by proprietors of the Vaudeville. Henry B. Yelvington, noted newspaperman and author of "innumerable features and short stories," contributed a lengthy article to the *Statesman* in early 1927 stating as much: "There have been different stories of the shooting, but the one most generally accepted is that while Simms, Foster, Thompson and Fisher were talking, Simms and Foster drew to one side, and armed men in the balcony above shot down both Thompson and his friend. A stray bullet struck Foster in the leg, and later on from its effect he too, died."[19]

On the other hand, rather than targeting both Thompson and Fisher, perhaps the plan was solely to eradicate Ben Thompson for entering the

Vaudeville after he had been told to stay away so many times. Once the moment was right for the shooting to begin, it was unfortunate that John King Fisher happened to be so close. This, perhaps, is the main tragedy of King Fisher: that he was where he was when assassins killed Thompson, resulting in Fisher also being killed. Was King Fisher also the target? Or was he simply in the wrong place at the wrong time? Joseph C. Foster provided a sort of "death bed statement" (at the time he believed he would survive the leg wound). After the leg was amputated, he provided a report on the killings for the San Antonio *Express*, reprinted by the *Galveston Daily News*:

> I told him (Thompson) again I would never place a straw in his way and for God's sake to go away and let me alone. He then, at that instant, made a snatch to draw his pistol and said: "You d—d [expletives deleted by the *News*], and thrust his pistol the next moment into my face. The end off [*sic*] the pistol struck me in the mouth, and as I threw up my left arm to ward it off it knocked the skin off my arm from the elbow nearly to the wrist. At that moment Coy spoke to him and reached to catch his pistol. As Coy did so Ben jumped back and struck the chair mentioned above, and as he did so he threw up his hands to regain his balance. That gave me a chance to get my pistol out, which was on my right side in the waistband. I had some little difficulty in getting my pistol out, but as I drew it I fired, striking Thompson in the breast. That was my first shot. From the shock of this shot, I suppose, and from the struggle as well, Thompson, King Fisher and Coy fell together into the corner to the right of the door. I ran up to Thompson, put my pistol to his left eye and turned it loose again. That was my second shot. I was shot next in the leg and fell. I do not know who shot me. As soon as I was shot I caught hold of one of the benches and pulled myself up and fired the remaining shots in my pistol into the crowd. I do not know who killed Fisher.[20]

When Joe Foster made this statement, on or about the eighteenth of March, while recovering from the amputation of his leg, he was lucid enough to state how he fired his first shot in self-defense into Thompson's breast and the second shot into his left eye. As he explained, he then had, at the most, four remaining shots, which he said he fired "into the crowd." He then claimed

that he knew nothing of King Fisher's death. Upon learning Fisher had been
killed, Foster continued: "I am sorry for that, for we had been warm friends.
When he was in jail here in Bexar county I fed him and furnished him
with everything he wanted for his personal comfort at my own expense."[21]
That much we know is true.

However, the Austin *Daily Statesman* called Joe Foster a "boss liar" and
argued that he could not have fired a bullet into Ben Thompson's chest because
the autopsy revealed no such wound. The editor of the *Statesman* further
contended that the dying Foster should have made a full and clear confession
instead of protecting the murderers of King Fisher and Ben Thompson with
a fake statement. Even if J. C. Foster death-bed statement were proven true,
it would not change our opinion of any of the characters involved in the
Vaudeville tragedy. We would feel the same about those involved, because
they killed the two men without given them even a moment's chance.
The Austin public generally had felt, and we after examining this history
today feel, that in spite of the faults of Ben Thompson and King Fisher, they
didn't deserve the death they were given.[22]

But such a confession was never made, and soon there was another
body—that of Joseph C. Foster, who had been severely wounded in the leg
during the gunfire at the Vaudeville. Reportedly Foster had tried to draw
his revolver during the struggle with Thompson and Coy, but it got caught
somehow. Instead of carefully pulling it, "he gave it an angry jerk bringing it out, but the jerk discharged it and the ball struck him in the leg and
he fell."[23] After the amputation of his leg, there was some hope that he
might survive, but he began to fade. At 11:00 on the morning of Saturday,
March 22, eleven days after the Vaudeville killings, Foster "quietly
breathed his last at his house on Soledad street." The doctors initially
had hopes for his recovery, but his leg began hemorrhaging several days
before death came, and on the tenth hemorrhaging again and for the last
time on the twenty-second. He was forty-seven years old and had lived in
San Antonio nearly a quarter of a century. He was survived by his wife and
countless friends. Although of the sporting class, he had earned the respect
and esteem of the "best and most influential citizens." San Antonio showed
its condolences to the widow by attending the funeral in large numbers,

not only members of the sporting fraternity but also ordinary citizens. Over sixty vehicles made up the procession to the grave where he was laid to rest close to the grave of Jack Harris in San Antonio's City Cemetery number 1. Rev. John W. Neil, pastor of the First Presbyterian Church officiated at the obsequies.[24] An item published in a New York newspaper headlined his death with "A Gambler Dies of his Wounds," describing Foster as "the wealthiest gambler in San Antonio, the man who killed Ben Thompson and King Fisher March 11, while they were trying to kill him, and who was himself wounded mortally … He leaves a large estate, valued between $100,000 and $200,000, and a wife to mourn his loss."[25]

Almost ignored by some of the press was that two Mexicans had been arrested and charged with conspiring to assassinate special policeman Jacobo S. Coy, who may have felt he was not safe from would-be avengers. Late on the night of March 13, San Antonio police arrested two Mexicans identified as Cecilio Charo and Santiago Tijerino. They were charged with conspiracy on the basis of statements from two Mexican women who had heard them offer a third party a $50 horse if he would show them where Coy lived. The third party was never identified. Later, policemen Andrew Brown and Thomas C. Rife saw the pair near Coy's house. Charo was a deputy United States Marshal and carried papers as Deputy Sheriff of La Salle County. Neither were armed when arrested in the Washington Saloon.[26] The arrested pair were first escorted to the city jail but then placed in the county jail while the grand jury investigated the alleged conspiracy.[27] A report current among the Mexican portion of San Antonio indicated that Charo and Tijerino were at the Vaudeville the night of the eleventh, but their companions had dissuaded them from "putting their dastardly scheme into force during the fatal struggle" between Shardein and Billy Thompson.[28] The two were eventually cleared of all charges.

While Charo and Tijerino were arrested and being jailed, Billy Thompson had visited the city jail, which is where the bodies of the two murdered men were first placed. During one of the visits, Thompson was quoted as saying to an unidentified bystander, "But for Captain Shardein I would now be lying beside him." It was Shardein who had prevented Billy from entering and getting involved in the shooting fracas.[29] Playing the dangerous game of "What if?" a historian might be tempted to surmise what might have happened if Billy Thompson had continued into the Vaudeville, met the wounded Joe Foster descending the stairs with the assistance of Billy Simms, and there avenged the murder of his brother. Billy Thompson could have killed the three, and he in turn could have been killed in the wild gunfire. Then the stair steps would have become slippery with the blood of another than Joe Foster.

# Chapter 11

# The Times in
# Which He Lived

T he evil reputation of the Vaudeville Theater was solidified as a den of iniquity with the assassination of John King Fisher and Ben Thompson on March 11, 1884. In the following month, violence again erupted, although no one was killed in the later exchange of gunfire. The press intensified the idea that evil was afoot in San Antonio: "The Devil's Den!" exclaimed the lead headline, followed by "Once More the Crack of the Revolver is Heard in the Vaudeville! / And Sims, of Unsavory Memory, Gets the Best of His Antagonist!"[1] The revolver's crack sounded six weeks after the double killing, on the night of Friday, April 25, 1884, and William H. Simms indeed was involved.

For weeks an ominous quiet had been felt in and around the Vaudeville. The calm ended on Thursday, April 24, when Richard Howard Lombard, described as a "warm personal friend" of Fisher, visited San Antonio intending to seek revenge. Lombard, an attorney, was founding editor of the *Eagle Pass Maverick*, the newspaper of Maverick County. That morning Lombard began the day by getting intoxicated. Lombard possibly anticipated trouble from the owners of the Vaudeville, as he did not go alone. With him as he entered the bar was Uvalde County Sheriff John B. Boatright, whose presence perhaps gave Lombard additional bravery as at the bar "he threw down a $50 bill and called for the drinks." This would have passed unnoticed, but the drunken Lombard then stated, probably in a very loud voice for all to hear, that the killing of King Fisher was "a cowardly and cold-blooded murder." Downing their drinks, Boatright demanded of the bartender, "Where are the damn —— [bastards] who murdered the best deputy I ever had?" Without hesitating, the bartender informed him that, if he meant William Simms, then he was not on the premises but could be sent for. Lombard and Boatright replied that it was not necessary to send for him, but that they would see him later. Lombard repeated his statement that Simms had killed the best friend he ever had, and he and Sheriff Boatright then left. It appears Sheriff Boatright was also intoxicated.

If he had been wise, he would have returned to Eagle Pass, but Lombard remained in San Antonio, and on the next day he returned to the Vaudeville and met Simms. The manager, Simms, was aware of Lombard's previous conduct, and although he outwardly considered his behavior nothing more than "drunken hurrah," Simms informed Lombard he had a notion to slap him in the face. Simms probably always carried a pistol with him at that point, and Lombard had obtained a double-action revolver with which he was not yet familiar (he was used to a single-action revolver). As Lombard and an unidentified friend were downing their drinks, Simms approached and asked Lombard if he was not ashamed for threatening the house earlier in the day. "No, I am not," Lombard indignantly responded. With his friend standing between them, Lombard attempted to slap at Simms with one hand and draw his double-action pistol with the other, intending at the time to shoot over the shoulder of the friend. Realizing what was happening, the friend, now terrified, shouted, "For God's sake don't shoot or you will kill me." Lombard now backed up and headed for the exit, snapping off one shot through the same lattice screen Ben Thompson had famously sent the bullet which killed Jack Harris. Lombard's bullet caused no harm, hitting only the wall on the far end of the room. Lombard ran toward the bookstore adjoining the Vaudeville one door to the west. Simms, who may not have intended to kill Lombard but wanted to teach him a lesson, fired off three shots. Two of them struck a waterspout made of tin, and the third chipped the stone casing supporting the bookstore's display window.[2]

Hearing shots fired, Officer Kroeger quickly arrived on the scene. He immediately grabbed Simms, telling him, "Billy, don't be so foolish as to fire again." Lombard continued to fumble with his double-action revolver but managed to fire one more shot, which flew across the Main Plaza but did no damage. Kroeger now released his grip on Simms to chase down Lombard. Simms then discharged his fourth and final shot, striking the door casing of the bookstore entrance and lightly grazing Lombard's forearm, creating only a minor wound. By now two other policemen had arrived and the "gunfight at the Vaudeville" was over.

Both shootists were arrested and hauled before Justice Anton Adams but were quickly released on $2,000 bond. Eventually both Lombard and Simms were fined $100 for their reckless behavior. "And thus by accident or good luck," the reporter concluded, "San Antonio is spared the disgrace of another bloody Vaudeville tragedy."[3]

Whatever the reason Lombard attempted to avenge his friend King Fisher's death, it brought him no respect from anyone. In fact, he was ridiculed for his action. One newspaper described "Dick Lombard" as "the genial and jolly lawyer of Eagle Pass, who had the shooting match with Simms, at the Vaudeville. It certainly was mean whisky—anyway, whisky was the cause of it. Dick is not a desperado. When he gets back to Eagle Pass he ought to hire some one to kick him all around town and clear across the river into Mexico."[4]

Richard Howard Lombard was a native of Mississippi, born in Rankin County, October 29, 1853. He was the son of Ephraim H. Lombard, a native of Maine and likewise a successful attorney. Apparently R. H. studied law in his father's office. When he arrived in Maverick County is unknown, and how long he edited the local newspaper also is unknown. No issue of that newspaper is known to have survived. Reportedly Lombard considered himself a good friend of King Fisher and resented how his friend's life was taken. Unfortunately, we have no knowledge of how a Fisher-Lombard friendship may have actually developed, if it did. The liquor no doubt intensified the anger he felt, to the degree that he felt obligated to avenge Fisher's untimely death. Lombard survived his gunfight with Simms in San Antonio, but not for long, for he died in Del Rio, Val Verde County, May 11, 1890. His grave is lost.[5]

The day after the fine was imposed on Simms and Lombard, the *Light* voiced the fact that a good "many people of late complain about the Vaudeville theatre as a nuisance and want to see the same shut up." Simms was also eager to rid himself of the Vaudeville. He was nervous about how John King Fisher's friends kept coming around to cause trouble and complained to an *Express* reporter that for two nights in a row they had been trying to "hurrah" his place. Simms accused Texas Ranger Captain Joseph Shely and Deputy United States Marshal Ferdinand Niggli, two prominent lawmen, and the Uvalde District Attorney W.R. Wallace, as the culprits attempting to provoke a fight in order to draw him out and murder him. He let it be known in the local newspapers that, if anyone wanting the property would pay anything like a fair price for his lease and the improvements he made in the building, he would sell it off.[6] On July 24 an investor named John Stappenbeck paid $1,753.25 for the effects of the Vaudeville bar and theatre and on August 22 the *Express* informed its readership that the site had been leased to R. Bianchini. His intentions were to open a dining hall and a first-class restaurant. The bloody days of the Vaudeville as a theatre, saloon, and gambling den had ended.[7]

The "bloody days of the Vaudeville" may have ended, but the potential violence remained in that portion of the Alamo City for a few more years. Two years later William Simms was the proprietor of another saloon, the Pickwick. Simms may have moved on, but certain friends of Fisher and Thompson appear to have kept track of his movements. In July of 1886, more than two years after the Vaudeville tragedy, one J. H. Franklin, described as "a bad man from Bitter creek," went into the Pickwick and called out for Simms. He addressed Simms: "You are the man who killed King Fisher, who was my friend, and I am going to kill you." Simms advised Franklin he wanted no trouble and called for an officer to arrest Franklin. The officer and Franklin fought "desperately," but the officer and Simms managed to control Franklin and delivered him to the Bat Cave to reconsider his conduct. Franklin was fined $25 for his action and received advice from the judge to "remain peaceful henceforth." Franklin then apologized and further explained that he was "filled with a peculiar fluid which rendered him oblivious to what had passed," claiming he had no recollection of the struggle with Simms and the officer. Presumably he avoided the "peculiar fluid" henceforth.[8]

***

"An adept with a pistol, possessed of great physical courage and an iron nerve, he was a fitting representative of one of the worst products of the times in which he lived." This statement referring to one-time Austin City Marshal Ben Thompson was authored by A. H. Gregory, who wrote for the *Texas News* of San Antonio. Although the article, later published in the *Uvalde Leader-News*, focused on Ben, the words could have applied as well to the Uvalde County acting sheriff King Fisher, who was also a product "of the times in which he lived."[9]

After the death of her husband, Sarah "Sally" Vivian Fisher could have become an embittered recluse, resentful of the cards life had dealt her. But she was not that type of woman. For a short time, she and the three girls stayed with her father, but she quickly determined that hers was a special task: that of raising her and King's daughters. As she later told an interviewer, "I made up my mind not to let them merely grow up, but to see them educated. I didn't care what self-denial and work fell my lot." She stuck to her guns, returning to the Fisher home in Uvalde, where she stayed until the daughters were grown and educated. In later years, she went to Carrizo Springs to live with her married daughter, Florence Fisher Kellogg.[10]

The subject of King Fisher never seems to tire. In 1993, the *Crystal City Sentinel* reprinted a story from the *Zavala County Sentinel* of fifty years before. It was a society page item recounting that Mrs. Sarah Vivian Fisher "was complimented with a coffee by her daughter," Florence Fisher Kellogg, at their home in Carrizo Springs on Mrs. Fisher's eighty-fifth birthday. Mrs. Fisher, King's widow, we are informed, had come to this section in the early 1860s. Sarah's parents, Mr. and Mrs. John T. Vivian, had moved from Goliad in ox-drawn wagons when Sarah was five years old. They settled on Pendencia Creek, fifteen miles west of Carrizo Springs. At the age of eighteen, we are told, Sarah married King Fisher and they then ranched on the 7-D Ranch near La Pryor before moving to Uvalde. The guests at this coffee also included descendants of other pioneer families: in addition to the Vivians, the Williamses, Vandervoorts, Bells, Englishes, and Doneys.[11]

The body of Ben Thompson was returned to Austin, where a huge crowd waited for its former marshal and troublemaker. The body of King Fisher was returned to Uvalde, where an equally impressive crowd waited for its beloved son and acting county sheriff. Thompson's remains were placed in the family plot in Oakwood Cemetery, and Fisher's were placed in the west side of what is known today as Pioneer Rest Cemetery. Florence Fenley, a Uvalde County native and resident for some forty years and a descendant of the Joel Fenley who had helped Fisher recover some cattle years before, recalled how the location of the apparently lost grave was later found. Sometime in the early 1940s, historian and publisher J. Marvin Hunter and Dean Thomas Ulvan Taylor of the University of Texas went to Uvalde to search for King Fisher's grave. They wanted to visit his final resting place. Unable to find it by following a paper trail, they thought they might locate it somehow by visiting Uvalde. They had no luck at first, but before giving up hope they went to Florence Fenley. She was unable to help and, apparently, Hunter and Taylor returned to their homes disappointed. But a few years later, John Leakey, who had been ranching in Montana, returned to Texas to settle down among his earlier Uvalde County roots. He learned of the search and put Fenley in touch with the Walter Smith family. "Mitt" Smith knew where the grave was, as he had stood in his parents' yard and watched King Fisher's funeral and over the years had been to the unmarked grave "dozens of times." He and his friends had played under the big oak limbs which shaded the grave. Leakey brought King's eldest daughter, Mrs. Florence Fisher Kellogg from Carrizo Springs and they went directly to the grave. Leakey cleared the weeds and brush inside the iron fence and fastened a sign inside stating that it was King Fisher's grave and giving the date of birth and death. "The grave was hitherto unmarked," Florence Fisher Kellogg wrote, "and I was deeply grateful for the work Leakey did in establishing the location of the grave."[12]

About a decade later in October 1959, the city of Uvalde decided to move twenty known graves out of their original sites and into a newly established area of the cemetery for pioneers. The editors of the *Uvalde Leader-News* gave nearly an entire page to the "New Grave for Fisher" article and, not surprisingly, it recreated interest in the life of the former deputy sheriff. It is from this lengthy article by Florence Fenley that we learn details of the first burial and then the interment to where the grave location is today:

> Not only was an iron fence put around the grave, but King Fisher's body had been laid to rest in a cast iron coffin in the popular shape of that day. It was in a state of good preservation after its seventy-five years interment, with only a very small hole in the top where water had rusted through. Brass handles on the sides were still intact and workable. Fisher's body, considering the years it had been laid away, was also well preserved. The body in its iron casket was re-buried in a grave on the east side of the cemetery which is designated as Pioneer Rest Cemetery now.[13]

Photographs and descriptions of the casket and reburial remain, but if any photographs were made of King Fisher in the casket, they have been lost.

A slightly different version of the grave and reburial story appeared in response to the article by Amanda Gardner published in *Texas Highways*.[14] For John R. Seals, the article, titled "King of the Road," brought back memories of his days as principal of the West Main High School in Uvalde. Sheriff Bill Newcomer once called Seals at school, inviting him to come to the Pioneer Cemetery to observe what was happening. Seals related how on the west side of the old cemetery he saw "a cast iron coffin being lifted from a grave which had been enclosed within an iron fence about four feet high and about six by ten feet in perimeter." Newcomer explained to Seals that they were removing this coffin as part of an effort to vacate a small portion of the old cemetery which had been cut off from the main part by what began as foot and horseback traffic back at the turn of the century, developed into usage as wagon and cart traffic to reach North Uvalde, and eventually became a small segment of what is now North Park Street. This small portion of the cemetery was unkempt and interfering with the realty development in the area. All of the identifiable graves were exhumed and moved across the street to the main part of the cemetery, including John King Fisher's. The graves that were crossed over by the street are assumed to be still there.The main purpose of this action was "to attempt to verify that the grave was King Fisher's."[15]

The coffin was loaded onto a truck and taken to the Frazier Funeral Home, unloaded into the freight receiving room and placed on two sawhorses. Seals described that the coffin was "ornate cast iron, had an oval glass window over the head of the deceased, was narrow at the top and tapered rather sharply toward the feet. The glass was deteriorated, much like an old glass bottle, such that we could not see through it." The coffin itself was still in good condition except for a small hole about the size of a dime that had rusted midway through on top. It was necessary for workmen to saw and chisel off the bolts holding the coffin door shut. When they pried the coffin open, "a most strange odor emanating" caused everything to stop for just a moment until the odor dissipated. Inside was "a man with a moustache dressed in a jacket with leather lapels and bow tie, whose chin had dropped and whose features, although somewhat deteriorated, were in such condi-tion to be identifiable." Water had seeped into the coffin through the hole in the top and about an inch had collected in the bottom. This had "caused some deterioration of the body from the lower chest downward." There were about a half dozen individuals at the funeral home, whom Sheriff Newcomer asked to compare the remains in the coffin with a photo he had of Fisher, probably the famous head and shoulders portrait. Everyone agreed the man in the coffin matched the image of the man in the portrait. Then "the coffin was resealed, placed in a concrete vault, and buried under a large oak tree in the Pioneer Rest Cemetery on the east side of North Park Street, where it is today."[16] The only question remaining was whether the iron fence around the grave under the large oak tree was the same as the iron fence around the original grave.

Mementos and relics of King Fisher are virtually nonexistent. The inscribed photograph of Ben Thompson, which Thompson had given to King Fisher on the date of their deaths with King's blood stains, is now in a private collection. At the time of his death, King Fisher had two pistols on his body, legally carried of course as he was a deputy sheriff. Mrs. Fenley was aware of the pistols and indicated one was taken from his body but today its location is unknown: "This was a very fine gun, supposed to be about the last word in guns at that time, and had been a gift from General Porfirio Diaz of Mexico about the time he became president."[17] The other was turned over to Terrell Kellogg, grandson of King Fisher. This is a Colt .45-caliber revolver, which is now in the possession of John Michael Kellogg, King's great-grandson. The serial number is 84630, which was manufactured in 1883.[18] In addition to Florence Fenley explaining the rationale for the existence of a "Diaz pistol" in a lengthy article from the *Uvalde Leader-News*, Eva Sanderlin has also reinforced the idea. In describing Fisher's appearance, she wrote: "Two silver-mounted, ivory-handled pistols nestled in holsters. One pistol was a gift from President Porfirio Diaz of Mexico."[19]

No "Diaz pistol" was ever recovered, but "the other pistol he was wearing was sent to his wife" and then owned by Judge Terrell B. Kellogg, County Clerk of Dimmit County.[20] Few historians today accept that the second revolver found on Fisher's body had been a gift from Mexican President Porfirio Diaz. John Leakey told Florence Fenley the following: "Fisher was wearing two pistols at the time of his death; one was an ivory handled, silver-barreled pistol presented to him in 1870 by his friend, Porfirio Diaz, afterward president of Mexico."[21] There is no evidence that King Fisher, who would have been all of sixteen or seventeen years of age in 1870, ever met Diaz as Leakey claimed—nor of why or where it took place. Possibly King Fisher obtained an ornate pistol and jokingly claimed it came from President Diaz, and his claim was accepted.

Florence Fenley wrote an occasional column published in the *Uvalde Leader-News* called "Old Trails." An undated clipping preserved in the Hobart Papers entitled "The Gun" is of unusual interest as it continues the "Diaz pistol" legend. Fenley began this column by noting that she had read of a Waxahachie gun collector (Robert L. Fowley) "finding an old lever action carbine in Nuevo Laredo and after cleaning it up, beheld the name of King Fisher engraved on the top tang behind the hammer, likewise his initials on the front barrel band. I am hoping now that maybe some day King Fisher's beautiful pistol he was wearing when he was killed and which pistol was given to him by President C. P. Diaz of Mexico, may be found."[22] The present location of the gun that Fowley found is unknown.[23]

It must be noted that King Fisher, although not identified clearly as such, became a character in at least two of the short stories of the celebrated nineteenth-century writer, William Sidney Porter, better known by his pen name "O. Henry." The then-unknown young writer entered central Texas and took on various jobs to support himself. In 1882 he found himself in Austin, where he heard about City Marshal Ben Thompson as well as other interesting frontier characters whom he later placed in his stories without using their real names. Ben Thompson appeared in *The Reformation of Calliope*. Lesser-known perhaps are King Fisher's appearances in two of the O. Henry short stories: "King James" in *The Last of the Troubadours* and "Bud King" in *The Passing of Black Eagle*. Certainly, the best-known example of O. Henry placing historic gunfighters in his stories is in *The Caballero's Way*, in which John Wesley Hardin appears as an evil Cisco Kid.[24]

Nineteenth-century newspapers always found Ben Thompson to be good copy, and at the time of his death he and King Fisher received attention not only from other states but from other countries as well. Their deaths became headline news in such publications as the *Illustrated Police News*, the *Yorkshire Herald*, the *Huddersfield Chronicle*, and *Manchester Weekly Times* of England. Similar articles appeared in the Melbourne *Age* and the *Sydney Morning Herald* of Australia. News of the deaths of these noted desperadoes appeared in newspapers both major and minor in virtually every state in the union, including the *Atlanta Constitution* of Georgia, the *Bismarck Tribune* of North Dakota, the *Cairo Bulletin* of Illinois, the *Evening Herald* of Fort Scott, Kansas, the *Canton Advocate* of South Dakota, and many more.

John King Fisher has not become a celebrity in the film industry, a major oversight on the part of Hollywood, but neither has Ben Thompson. Apparently, Wyatt Earp, "Wild Bill" Hickok, and Bat Masterson have proven to be better draws. However, the character of King Fisher played a small part in one episode of the late 1950s television series *Bat Masterson*, the fictional adventures of the famous Wild West lawman who allegedly used his cane to deal with bad men instead of his pistols. The episode, "Incident in Leadville," aired on March 18, 1959 with Jack Lambert playing the role of King Fisher.

The more popular and longer-lasting television series "Death Valley Days," as mentioned previously, featured Robert Yuro portraying King Fisher in an episode aired on January 1, 1970 entitled "The King of Uvalde Road." The plot involves Fisher placing a sign indicating that a certain road is his only and not to be used by anyone else: "This is King Fisher's Road—Take the Other." A conflict arises because the denial of that particular road prevents the US mail from getting delivered in a timely manner. During the show, Fisher resists the US mail traveling through "his territory" on the grounds that it will allow and encourage other government entities entering as well. The episode may have had some entertainment value: the "love interest" (a virtual necessity in a television show) involves a young lady known as "Chiquita" and there is also a faithful sidekick named "Paco" (another stock character). The conflict is resolved by making King Fisher the county sheriff and Paco his deputy, thus allowing King Fisher to retain control of his region.

King Fisher also appeared in at least one film feature, which proved to be a failure at the box office. *Texas Rangers*, directed by Steve Miner and released in April 2001, was (according to the credits) based on the memoirs of Texas Ranger George Durham, *Taming the Nueces Strip*. It is not an easy task to determine which scenes are from Durham's book and which are from the imagination of the producers. King Fisher, played by Alfred Moline, is the primary desperado working against Ranger Captain McNelly. According to the film's synopsis, Texas in 1875 was "a land without justice, where chaos reigns, [but] one legendary man, Leander McNelly, is chosen to lead a group of unlikely heroes. These young men, out-manned and out-gunned, must battle an army of renegade outlaws led by the ruthless John King Fisher. Sworn to protect the innocent and the women they love, the Rangers risk their lives to put the wrong things right in their beloved homeland."[25]

The prolific novelist William W. Johnstone (with J. A. Johnstone) authored a series of western action novels, one of which included King Fisher: *Flintlock: A Time for Vultures*. In this 2017 work, the historical King Fisher appears bearing the name of "Cage Kingfisher." A synopsis of the novel reads like science fiction more than a typical western: "The stench of death hangs over Happyville. … The citizens … are dead in their beds, taken down by a deadly scourge." Flintlock feels that he has to quarantine himself, but this is broken by the appearance of Cage Kingfisher, "a mad clergyman who preaches the gospel of death." Flintlock orders his followers to round up the survivors of Happyville and bring them home to him. To save the surviving citizens, Flintlock must send Kingfisher to Hell. The deadly deacon however has a mechanical arm which is faster than the eye can follow, leaving the reader wondering how Flintlock can possibly survive the final conflict.[26]

Since 1884, Ben Thompson has overshadowed King Fisher in virtually all ways. Perhaps this is due to the fact that, in 1884, Ben Thompson had already reached the pinnacle of notoriety and was on the descent: he had survived the Civil War and the fruitless escapades of serving under Maximilian in Mexico, and he had gained additional attention during the early 1870s in Kansas cow towns, meeting up with Abilene City Marshal J. B. Hickok as well as the more notorious teenage killer John Wesley Hardin. Adventures in Colorado during the so-called railroad war added to his fame, and, reaching a most unusual summit, he was twice elected Marshal of Austin, Texas, where he proved to be an exceptional peace officer. Only the killing of Jack Harris ended Thompson's rise to popularity. After release from the Bat Cave, he began the downhill spiral which ended in his death at the Vaudeville.

Attorney William M. Walton had interviewed Thompson in an effort to present his biography to the Texas public. When Thompson and Fisher were assassinated, Walton hurriedly completed the manuscript, but it never became the best-selling book which Walton had hoped for and today the few original copies are virtually unobtainable. A serious biography of Thompson did not appear until the 1950s. This was the work of Floyd Benjamin Streeter, Head Librarian at Kansas State College from 1926 until his retirement in 1953. The characters of the Wild West fascinated him, and he became particularly "interested in the doings of the Thompson Boys of Texas. Their names appeared so often in the records of places and happenings—and invariably, wherever they had been, there had also been plenty of excitement, usually caused by one or another of the brothers." The result of his research and writing was *Ben Thompson: Man with a Gun*, published by Frederick Fell, Inc. of New York in 1957.[27] The most recent serious effort to provide a biography of Thompson remains *Ben Thompson: Portrait of a Gunfighter*, by Tom Bicknell and Chuck Parsons, the authors of the present work, published in 2018 by the University of North Texas Press.

The first attempt at a serious biography of King Fisher did not appear until 1966, co-authored by a collateral descendant, Ovie Clark Fisher with J. C. Dykes: *King Fisher: His Life and Times*, published by the University of Oklahoma Press. Congressman Fisher had the advantage of being a relative with access to much of the family lore. Although important and helpful in our research, it leaves much to be desired for modern writers and historians. Ramon F. Adams, in his 1954 *Six-Guns and Saddle Leather: A Bibliography of Books and Pamphlets on Western Outlaws and Gunmen*, had only a few words to say: "One of the few original publications in the Western Frontier Library Series. Has material on King Fisher, Ben Thompson, Bat Masterson, the Taylor-Sutton Feud, and the Texas Rangers."[28]

Of Streeter's work, by contrast, Adams offers much praise, describing it as "reliable"—whose author died before publication and underscored the false claims of Stuart N. Lake. Also, in Streeter's biography, King Fisher enters the narrative only at the Vaudeville, to be assassinated with Thompson, without any biographical information about the man prior to March 11, 1884. But, to Streeter's credit, he does write: "Fisher's part in the tragedy still remains a mystery. Some believed that he pretended to be Thompson's friend and lured him into a trap knowing that he would be ambushed. If he did, he, too, was a victim of treachery. ... It is very unlikely that Foster or Simms used Fisher as a decoy, intending to have him murdered. But the facts hint that some of the gunmen decided to get rid of Fisher along with Thompson."[29]

It was nearly fifty years before another work focusing on King Fisher appeared, this one a dual biography: *The Texas Pistoleers: The True Story of Ben Thompson & King Fisher—Two of the Most Feared Pistol Fighters of the American West*. This significant undertaking was by G. R. Williamson and published in 2009, fifty-three years after O. C. Fisher's.[30]

The conclusion to the above comments is this: King Fisher, although a deadly gunfighter often ranked with Hardin, Longley, and Thompson, was seemingly always kept in the shadow of the more infamous characters. Perhaps the explanation for this is that King Fisher did not begin a violent career while still in his teens, such as Hardin, Longley, and Thompson did. Also, he "roamed" in an area of our country which was not near a metropolitan center. However, even though he may have spent most of his adult years in the brush country far from the larger cities such as Austin, San Antonio, Dallas, Galveston, or Corpus Christi—and their newspapers—he developed friendships with notable individuals such as John Baylor, Ferdinand Niggli, Grey White, and the Vivian clan and, even more significantly, he earned the respect of two of the most prominent Texas Rangers, Captain L. H. McNelly and Lee Hall.

It has been said that America is a country enamored with "Gun Culture." This is possibly true, although trying to categorize the country so offhandedly seems ludicrous. True, the number of victims of the gun since before the days of the Founding Fathers, whether it be revolver or rifle or shotgun, is a number so high it cannot be tallied. In the era of "Manifest Destiny," the westward pioneers considered the weapon as essential as their horses or the availability of water. In the days of the "Wild West," which stretched from before the Civil War to the turn of the twentieth century, certain weapons became well-known: the "equalizer," otherwise known as Colt's .45-caliber "Peacemaker" revolver; Remington's 1875 .44-.40 Single Action Army; and the Winchester Model '73 rifle, "the Gun that Won the West." Many today would argue that the dire necessity for weapons held by citizens as well as law enforcement officers cannot be exaggerated. There are also many who disagree and condemn the proliferation of guns, viewing their easy access as instruments of death and destruction. All of this was as true in the 1880s as it is today.

It is interesting to see how differently newspapers following the tragedies in the Vaudeville treated the question. Newspaper editors could, in the nineteenth century, wage war on other editors and demonstrate freedom of speech with greater intensity than in the press of the twenty-first century, as we are a much more litigious society (in the nineteenth century, an offended editor might challenge an opponent to a duel). A Fort Worth *Gazette* editor, possibly George B. Loving, had choice words to say against the "maudlin and periodical attacks on 'the pistol.'" Certain journals "shriek in chorus" that "the pistol must go" and, "according to the nervous organization of the scribe, write passionately or temperately of the necessity for the departure of the 'little pop.'" The editor asks why, answering that newspapers did not want the "little pop" to go because too many portions of society depend on it for fame, notoriety, or riches. Sales of newspapers also increase greatly with the news of a shooting such as the Vaudeville killings. He reinforces his point with several examples, including that of Jesse James, who, as the entire country knew, with his pistol "stopped railroad trains, rifled mail pouches, murdered conductors and helpless passengers, robbed men, women and children; and yet, when he died as he had lived, was it not the newspapers that howled about the 'deep damnation' and the cowardly treachery of his taking off?"

Ben Thompson's name was also brought in. He, allegedly, with a pistol sent from fifteen to twenty men "to the other world; while he lived and walked the streets of the capital of Texas, a red-handed murderer, which newspaper dared to allude to him otherwise than as 'Capt., Major, or Col. Thompson, the genial companion.'" Then the editor raises the question: "Is not Ben Thompson's life and exploits with the little pistol now in the hands of thousands of boys, and was it not written by a distinguished lawyer who is said to be an aspirant for a high civic honor, in which he would be expected to inspire a respect for *law*?" Obviously, he is here referring to William M. Walton's biography of Thompson, which had just been published.

The editor points out that an unnamed San Antonio newspaper says "the pistol must go" yet does the same paper "denounce the Vaudeville theater when the crack of the little gun has oft reverberated and where human life has so often been endangered and lost?" Other examples follow where the pistol did injustice yet brought notoriety to the shootist. He concludes, "The law as administered takes care of the slayer, and it is the widow and the orphan the little pistol makes who must take care of themselves." Continuing, he declares that the pistol will not go: "Public opinion has devoted the pistol and made it a means to attain fame. It will not go. Newspapers are insincere in denouncing it; lawyers uphold it as productive of rich fees, judges do not discountenance its work, public opinion applauds its performance by acquittal or nominal punishment and even fair women vie with each other in slobbering over red-handed murderers."

The pistol, the *Gazette* says, will not go, as it is "the mark of our civilization, and Texas should inscribe it upon the state arms. *Vox populi, vox Dei.*" Every "decent, law-abiding man [should] buy him one" and then he will be on equal terms with the ruffian or desperado "who would take advantage of his helplessness and shoot him down like a dog [if he did not have one]." Finally, the editor sums up his position: "The law, judges, juries, the people, all glorify the pistol. Why do the heathen journalists rage in the abstract and imagine a vain thing? The pistol will not go."[31]

***

Returning to the life and death of King Fisher, we cannot know the true feelings of Sarah "Sallie" Vivian Fisher on the gun question. Women on the frontier were not prone to sit back and let the men folk defend them. On the contrary, many were proficient with rifles and pistols and viewed it as a natural thing. We are tempted to speculate, however, that she had strong feelings against such places as the Vaudeville, the Revolving Light, or White Elephant, all residing on San Antonio's Main Plaza. It is unfortunate for history that Sarah Vivian Fisher did not keep a journal or in her twilight years compose her autobiography. Her life as faithful wife of such a noted individual as King Fisher would be a most valuable record, not only possibly detailing incidents of his career, but also what it was really like to be a young woman on the edge of the frontier. She may have worried incessantly, never knowing what enemy might attack day or night, having only her husband's reputation to defend her and her little ones. Alternatively, Sarah Vivian Fisher may have had easy access to pistols, and King Fisher (or someone else) may have taught her to be proficient in their use.

Scraps of letters exist and just a few words reveal her intense love for King Fisher's memory as well as revealing the strength of her character: "[Some have named King Fisher] a murderer and a villain. But it is well that they talk publically their hatred for him now and give full swing to their despicable accusations; for they dared not do it while he lived." Writing in the third person, the widow Fisher had this to say:

As there have come to all men of earth, there came a period in Fisher's life—a period of love. He fell in love with a fair damsel, a Miss Vivian, and experienced no trouble in winning her hand. He was loved as well as he loved and the parents of the fair one were more than willing for the daughter to marry him and her mind reverts to bygone days; she remembers the happy years they spent together before his death. She speaks aloud:

"What a handsome man, so brave and true! O, ye gods, how I loved him! How my my heart bleeds for his presence. The curse of God will ever yet rest on the heads of the cowardly villians that robbed me of him."

Then all is quite save the breathing of her three daughters who have drifted sweetly into the Land of Dreams, the light is extinguished, and the picture of King Fisher silently hangs in darkness on the wall.[32]

These aspects of life surrounding John King Fisher were instrumental in the widow Fisher being able to maintain her courage and strength during the many years she lived after his death. He indeed left her a wonderful legacy with the daughters, but also memories of which she and everyone who knew him could be proud.

# Appendix A

# The Pardon of John King Fisher

*"Executive Record Book. E. J. Davis, Richard Coke. 1/8/1870–2/9/1874," microfilm reel # 9, TSAL.*

The State of Texas

To all to whom these presents shall come.

Whereas at the Fall Term A.D. 1870 of the District Court of Goliad County one King Fisher was tried and convicted on a charge of Theft from a house and sentenced therefor to serve a term of Two years imprisonment in the State Penitentiary where he is now undergoing said sentence and

Whereas the statement of facts filed on appeal to the Supreme Court, leaves great doubt in my mind as to the guilt of this youth and

Whereas he was only sixteen years old when tried and seems to have been suddenly taken up, tried and convicted in the absence of his father, when he might have been able to make a better defense of his natural protector had been present

Now therefore, I, Edmund J. Davis, Governor of the State of Texas by nature of the authority vested in me by the Constitutions and Laws of the State do hereby grant unto the said King Fisher a full and free pardon for all the unexpired portion of his term of sentence, and hereby direct and require the Superintendent of the Penitentiary to release him from all further imprisonment for or on account of said conviction and sentence.

In testimony thereof I have hereunto signed my name, and have caused the Great Seal of the State to be affixed at the City of Austin, this 26th day of January A.D. 1871 and of the Independence of Texas the Thirty fifth.

By the Governor                                           Edmund J. Davis
                                                                    Governor

James P. Newcomb
Secretary of State

# Appendix B

# The King Fisher Letter to the *Express*

*This letter dated June 26, 1879 was written by King Fisher to the editors of the* San Antonio *Express and published in the issue of July 18,1879.*

In driving cattle up to Parker's and Ladd's ranch, I happened to come across one of your papers in which I saw and article about myself, which being totally false, I hereby take the liberty to correct.

In the first place, I do not live on the Cariza, but on the Nueces, seventy miles below Uvalde.

In the second place, my revolver did not go off while I was fooling with it, as the person who wrote that article would have known had he been better acquainted with me. I am not in the habit of playing with such things.

Since you have taken the trouble to mention such a small matter in your columns, and it being so far from the true statement of the case, I think it no more than right in me to restate it in the way it took place.

I laid my revolver down previously to going out cow-hunting, and somebody picked it up and didn't put it back as they found it. Not thinking anything was wrong, I got on my horse and started after a cow, but in chasing her my hat came off and I threw myself back in the saddle to catch it, when my revolver struck the saddle and went off, the ball passing through the fleshy part of the leg.

As for being a desperado, all I can say is that I have never killed a man unless it was in self-defense or in defense of my property, and I have very little respect for anyone who would not do the same, especially in certain parts of the state where there are so many horse thieves, etc.

I hope you will excuse me for having taken up so much of your time.

Yours, respectfully,
KING FISHER

# Appendix C

# Sheriff Boatright's Appointment of J. K. Fisher

The State of Texas)
County of Uvalde)

    Know all men by these presents that I, J. B. Boatright, Sheriff of Uvalde County, do here by appoint J. K. Fisher Deputy Sheriff of Uvalde County, Texas giving and granting unto the said J. K. Fisher full power and authority to execute and perform all and singular all the duties required by law to be done and performed in Said Office.

    In testimony whereof I here unto Sign my name and affix my official seal this 15th day of January A.D. 1883.

J. B. Boatright
Sheriff Uvalde County

# Appendix D

# J. K. Fisher's Oath of Office

[I] J. K. Fisher do solemnly swear (or affirm) that I will faithfully and impartially discharge and perform all the duties incumbent upon me as Deputy Sheriff of Uvalde County, Texas according to the best of my skill and ability agreeable to the constitution and laws of the United States and of this State and I do further Solemnly swear (or affirm) that since the adoption of the Constitution of this State I being a citizen of this State have not fought a duel with deadly weapons within this State nor out of it nor have I sent or accepted a challenge to fight a duel with deadly weapons now have I acted as a second in carrying a challenge or aided advised or assisted any person thus offending and I furthermore solemnly swear (or affirm) that I have not directly nor indirectly paid offered or promised to pay contributed nor promised to contribute any money or valuable things or promised any public office or employment as a reward for the giving or withholding the appointment at which I was appointed So help me God.

J. K. Fisher

Sworn to and subscribed before me this 15th day of January 1883.

[Seal]                              T. J. Spencer County Judge Uvalde County

Filed January 15th 1883 and duly recorded September 13th A.D. 1883.

A. J. Spencer
County Clerk U.[valde] C.[ounty]

# Appendix E

# Uvalde and Vicinity Communication

*Citizens of Uvalde County took issue with some of the statements about King Fisher after the Vaudeville tragedy and communicated to the press their objections. The following appeared in the Austin* Daily Statesman *of March 16, 1884 and again in the* Austin Weekly Statesman *of March 20, 1884.*

King Fisher

The San Antonio Express stated, in substance, that King Fisher was a desperate man, a terror in the neighborhood in which he resided, and if he were regretted at all it would not be by the law-abiding element of the state; that he had a record of having taken the life-blood of many men in his day, and was noted for his handsome appearance and gentlemanly disposition when sober; that he died with his boots on, a death which is considered quite genteel by desperate men, and two hundred and seventy-one citizens of Uvalde and vicinity, including the names of all the more prominent, signed the following communication in replay:

"While we do not propose to discuss or enter into a discussion of the early life of J. K. Fisher (better known as King Fisher) we desire to refute the assertions contained in the above, and we will speak of the deceased as we have known him since he has been a citizen of our county for about two and a half years past. Instead of the "bravado, desperado and terror in the neighborhood where he lived", his character and deportment have been diametrically the opposite. Kind, courteous, affable and generous, always ready and willing to ferret out crime and bring criminals to justice. And as a matter of fact, he has been the means of bringing to justice some of as bad criminals as ever infested western Texas. His ever vigilance and willing-ness to ferret out crime, and to assist the officers of the law, procured for him the esteem of all law-abiding citizens, and also the appointment of deputy sheriff of the county. Since he was thus installed as an officer of the law, his deportment as such commends him to all; even violators of the law that he was compelled to arrest, were treated with that kindness and courtesy coupled with a firmness and decision that at once commanded respect and submission without a murmur.

We feel that we do not exaggerate when we assert that King Fisher has accomplished as much for law and order within the last two and a half years as any man in Western Texas, and this assertion will be verified by all officers who may have been thrown in contact with him.

In justice to the dead, and in justice to his family, we ask that this correction in the above paragraph be made.

# Appendix F

# King Fisher Family Tree

| | | |
|---|---|---|
| **Job/Jobe/Joseph FISHER** | **wed** | (1) **Lucinda Warren** |
| (1827–1869 or 1870) | | (1832–1856) |
| | | (2) Minerva Coffee |
| | | 1834–1868) |

**Issue:**

John King Fisher (1855–1884)
Jasper Fisher (1856–?)
John Fisher (1857–?)
Sarah (1860–?)

| | John King Fisher | |
|---|---|---|
| **John King Fisher** | **wed** | **Sarah Elizabeth Vivian** |
| (Oct. 1855–1884) | Apr. 7, 1876 | (Dec. 18, 1856–Aug. 10, 1946) |

**Issue:**

| | | |
|---|---|---|
| Florence Fredonia | wed | Frank Rea Kellogg |
| (Oct. 18, 1877–June 9, 1952) | July 3, 1898 | (June 17, 1878–Sept. 8, 1954) |
| Eugenia "Minnie" | April 17, 1901 | Benjamin F. McDonald |
| (May 1, 1879–Feb. 22, 1912) | | (1873–?) |
| P. (Paul?) L. Fisher | | |
| (Nov. 25, 1881–Jan. 2, 1882) | | |
| Margurite "Mittie" | wed | Edgar Oliver Campbell |
| (Nov, 25, 1883–Sept. 7, 1958) | May 25, 1904 | (July 4, 1881–Dec. 19, 1924) |

# Appendix G

# Texas State
# Historical Marker

*This Texas State Historical marker (# 2946) gives special recognition to John King Fisher. It was erected in 1973 in the Pioneer Rest Cemetery in Uvalde, Texas, where Fisher's grave is located. This cemetery is located at the intersection of North Park Street and West Leona Street. Its size is 27" × 42".*

King Fisher

(1854–1884)

Celebrated outlaw who became a peace officer, once undisputed ruler of a 5,000-square-mile area of southwest Texas, centered in Eagle Pass and known as King Fisher's territory.

Son of Jobe and Lucinda Fisher, at age 17 Fisher settled on Pendencia Creek in Dimmit County, hired by ranchmen to guard their herds from bandits who frequently raided from Mexico, across Rio Grande.

A complex and forceful individual, he imposed order in lawless border area. His henchmen rustled cattle and terrorized resisting settlers but also protected them from outside intruders. Near his ranch was sign reading: "This is King Fisher's road, take the other." Many prominent men, including Porfirio Diaz, President of Mexico, counted him a friend.

Tall, charming, and quite handsome, Fisher wore fine clothes and tiger skin chaps. An expert shot—with either hand—he was indicted on six murder charges and fifteen lesser counts but was never convicted.

Devoted to wife and daughters, he reformed after being arrested in 1876 by ranger Capt. L. H. McNelly. He was acting Uvalde County sheriff, when, on March 11, 1884, he and the notorious Ben Thompson were killed from ambush at a vaudeville theatre in San Antonio.

(1973).

# Endnotes

## Notes for Preface

1. "Congressman to Speak at Marker Dedication" (press release), typescript, Hobart Papers, box 2, folder 1. The Frank L. Hobart Papers are preserved in the El Progreso Memorial Library, Uvalde, Texas. Hereafter, cited as "Hobart Papers."
2. *Uvalde Leader-News*, March 23, 1980.
3. "Fee Book County Court Uvalde Co., Tex.," Hobart Papers, box 3, folder 13.

## Notes for Chapter 1

1. O. C. Fisher and J. C. Dykes, *King Fisher: His Life and Times* (Norman: University of Oklahoma Press, 1966), x. Ovie Clark Fisher's father Jobe Fisher, born 1859, was a first cousin of King Fisher.
2. Ibid.
3. David Minor, "Collin County," *New Handbook of Texas*.
4. Anonymous, "Sister Grove Creek," *New Handbook of Texas*.
5. Fisher and Dykes, 3.
6. Ibid.
7. The 1850 Collin County census shows the Fisher family residing in household number 24 and the Hiram Warren family "next door" in household number 25. O. C. Fisher wrote that Jobe Fisher married Lucinda Warren of McKinney (7), which agrees with the census. Additional genealogical information is available in "The Dameron-Damron Family Newsletter," Vol. 13, Fall 1987, 409. Courtesy of Larry G. Shaver (hereafter, cited as Shaver collection).
8. Fisher and Dykes, 3.
9. Fisher Family Bible, photocopy of entries in authors' possession.
10. Amanda Gardner, "King of the Road," *Texas Highways*, December 1998, 58.
11. O. C. Fisher, "The Texas Heritage of the Fishers and the Clarks," 3, typescript, Hobart Papers. Published under same title in Salado, Texas by Anson Jones Press in 1963. Hereafter, cited as Fisher, "Texas Heritage."
12. 1850 Collin County census, 19. Alfred Coffee was from North Carolina; Sarah Coffee, from South Carolina. The Coffees covered much ground:

sister Naomi was born in Kentucky, Minerva was born in Illinois, and three younger siblings were born in Missouri.

13. 1860 Karnes County census, 5. The three-year-old John and perhaps the two-months-old Sarah are the children of Minerva before her marriage to Jobe. Their post office was in Helena, today a popular ghost town attraction with a historical museum.

14. Abstracts of Muster Rolls of Civil War Soldiers, Texas State Archives and Library (hereafter, cited as TSAL).

15. Fisher and Dykes, 4. When the Fisher family relocated in Williamson County is unknown. Even O. C. Fisher contributes to the uncertainty of the early years of King Fisher and his family. According to his treatment of the early years, once in Texas, Jobe Fisher lived in Jack County, then Denton County during the Civil War years, then Williamson County, then Goliad County, then Lampasas County, and then, again, in Goliad County. See Fisher, "Texas Heritage," 54.

16. Texas Voter Registration Lists, 1867–1869, 436. TSAL.

17. Fisher and Dykes, 6.

18. Widow's Application for Pension, no. 2394, Elizabeth J. Vivian, prepared October 1911. [National Archives?]

19. *Fort Worth Star-Telegram*, April 10, 1936.

20. Widow's Pension for Indigents, application of Jane O'Neal Vivian, Dimmit County, 41028, National Archives. The bill for expenses for burial of Mrs. Vivian from Leonard Funeral Home of Uvalde gives the date of her death.

21. Widow's Application for Pension, no. 2394, Elizabeth J. Vivian.

22. Fisher and Dykes, 17. French Strother Grey White was the son of Peter and Martha McCulloch White, born November 24, 1840 in Texana, Jackson County, Texas. He died on January 24, 1915 in Carrizo Springs and is buried there in the Mount Hope Cemetery. Throughout the census years, White was identified as a cattle raiser or stock raiser. O. C. Fisher dedicated his biography of King Fisher to White: "To the memory of Grey (Doc) White, who never claimed a calf that was not following a White brand; a stalwart frontiersman and homesteader who established the first permanent settlement on the Pendencia in Dimmit County."

23. Mr. and Mrs. Ben C. White, interview conducted by Frank L. Hobart, Carrizo Springs, January 18, 1966, transcript, Hobart Papers. Hereafter, cited as White, Hobart Papers.

24. Our spelling of the Vivian name deserves clarification here as it appears both "Vivian" and "Vivion" in various sources. Census records

are by no means consistent. We have chosen the Vivian spelling for the following reasons: the family is "Vivian" in the 1860 Goliad County census (60B); her headstone reads "Sarah Vivian Fisher" in Mount Hope Cemetery, Carrizo Springs; the death certificate for daughter Florence Fisher Kellogg spells her parents' name as "John King Fisher and Sarah Vivian"; the 1920 Dimmit County census enumerates the Kellogg family with Florence as head of household, Maurine and Gladys as daughters, Sarah Fisher as mother and Jane Vivian as grandmother (family 147). A deep kinship has endured no matter how the name is spelled. There is no ill will from any family member regarding the spelling of the family's name. Large Vivion/Vivian family reunions are still held today.

25. Younger sister of Grey White, Alpha Idania White married Lafayette Vivian on October 26, 1876 in Goliad County. She was born February 1, 1859 and lived until November 28, 1926, dying in San Antonio. She is buried in Mission Burial Park South in San Antonio.

26. Sarah Elizabeth Vivian was born December 18, 1856 and wedded to King Fisher on April 7, 1876.

27. Paul S. Taylor, "Historical Note on Dimmit County, Texas," *Southwestern Historical Quarterly* 34, no. 2 (October 1930).

28. *Northern Standard*, Clarksville, Texas, July 12, 1851, *Civilian and Galveston Gazette*, Galveston, Texas, June 17, 1851. Levi English was born August 24, 1817 in Arkansas and came to Texas with relatives in 1824. He died May 14, 1894 in Carrizo Springs. The fenced-in grave in the Mount Hope Cemetery has a plaque informing the viewer that he was "The Father of Carrizo Springs" and donated land for the Baptist Church, the Mount Hope Cemetery, and the first school of Carrizo Springs. Within the fenced area is a Texas Ranger memorial cross. Family tradition places him at the Battle of San Jacinto, but there is no documentation showing he was there. Muster Rolls of the Texas Revolution. TSAL; Laura Knowlton Tidwell, *Dimmit County Mesquite Roots* (Austin: Wind River, 1984).

29. White, Hobart Papers, 2.

30. White, Hobart Papers, 3.

31. Fisher and Dykes, 18. Durham's memoirs were first published in *West* (magazine) and then serialized in *The Valley Evening Monitor* of McAllen, Texas, as well as other south Texas newspapers, during October and November 1959. This particular quote is from the *Monitor* issue of November 8, 1959.

32. Fisher and Dykes, 19.
33. Fisher and Dykes, 7. This information was verified in the Bell County census, enumerated July 1860, 333. The census shows A. J. Turnbow as a twenty-nine-year-old farmer from Tennessee with wife Louisa and two sons: Hugh, age four years, and William, age two years. A. J. Turnbow, age thirty-two, enlisted April 16, 1862 in Williamson County, Company G, with Colonel R. T. P. Allen, commanding. Texas Muster Rolls Civil War Index, 1838–1900.
34. Fisher, unnumbered notebook, 5, Hobart Papers.
35. White, Hobart Papers, 5.

# Notes for Chapter 2

1. Goliad County authorities wanted a man identified as Charles Fulcrod, with the only information added: "Theft from house; negro." Fulcrod was also listed in Gillett's personal copy of the 1878 fugitives list. Could Willis and Charles Fulcrod be one and the same man? James B. Gillett, *Fugitives from Justice: The Notebook of Sergeant James B. Gillett*, 1878, facsimile reprint (Austin: State House Press, 1997), 24. Original title: *A List of Fugitives from Justice*, compiled by William Steele, Adjutant General, January 1, 1878. This document was a list of names sent to the adjutant general's office. The State House Press used Gillett's copy for the facsimile edition. Hereafter, cited as Gillett, *Fugitives*. W. H. Brooking and Lark Ferguson are two additional names listed on the same page. They both will enter into the King Fisher story.
2. Box 3, Folder 11, Hobart Papers. These pages are very faded and nearly impossible to read. The first page however does give the accepted name of Willis Fulcrod.
3. James H. Greenly was a single man, born in New York. 1870 Federal census, 385. He is listed as a merchant with $500 in real estate and an $800 personal estate. His headstone shows he was born October 24, 1827 and died December 22, 1875. He is buried in the Woodlawn Cemetery in Goliad, Texas. His grave stone has sunk and the stone is cracked, but the lettering is visible and the wording is legible.
4. Record of Arrests [by Texas State Police], 54–55. Ledger Book # 401-1001. TSAL.
5. Ibid. Writers generally consider these two as acting together in the robbery, but the official record of arrests shows that Fulcrod was

charged with "attempt to kill" and arrested seven days later than Fisher with no mention of the house burglary.

6. E. H. Wheelock, contributor. *Reports of Cases Argued and Decided in the Supreme Court of the State of Texas during the Latter Part of the Galveston Session, 1870* (St. Louis: Gilbert Book Company, 1872), 715–17. Hereafter, cited as Wheelock, *Reports of Cases*.

7. Minutes of District Court Book A, Goliad County. Details on this case are from our notes taken many years ago from the actual court books. Presumably they are still available for public examination. My thanks go to Gail M. Turley, District Clerk, for assistance.

8. Minutes of District Court Book A, Goliad County, October term, 13–14. "Richard" Vivian was in reality Henry Calvin Vivian, but everyone knew him as "Dick" Vivian. Born September 10, 1839 he enlisted at Goliad in Company D, 25th Texas, Wilkes' Regiment of Cavalry. In the spring of 1862 he was captured at Arkansas Post, Arkansas but was paroled or exchanged and then sent to the Army of the Tennessee. He fought in the battles of Chickamauga and Missionary Ridge, receiving two severe wounds during the conflict. He lived until November 25, 1927 and is buried in the Mount Hope Cemetery in Carrizo Springs. His grave is marked. Pension Application of Henry Calvin Vivian, Dimmit County, 34126, National Archives. Charles Bluford Bruton was the son of William Wesley and Cynthia Ann Vivian Bruton, born July 1850 in Goliad County and died September 5, 1922 in Engle, Sierra County, New Mexico. Charles Bruton married Elizabeth Agnes Cornett in 1883. Genealogical research courtesy of M. L. Cornett, Murchison, Texas. Findagrave.com was consulted for the locations of graves throughout our research.

9. Fisher and Dykes, 14.

10. See Thomas C. Bicknell and Chuck Parsons, *Ben Thompson: Portrait of a Gunfighter* (Denton: University of North Texas Press, 2018), 106–07.

11. Convict Record, Texas State Penitentiary, Huntsville, Walker County, Texas, 82.

12. "Fisher v. State, 35 Tex. 792 (Tex. 1870)," in Wheelock, *Reports of Cases*, 717.

13. If the numerous petitions for Fisher's pardon still exist, the Texas State Archives has not been able to locate them. This is unfortunate, as it would be interesting to see the names of those who wished the young man released.

14. For the full text of the pardon, see Appendix A.
15. *San Antonio Daily Express*, March 13, 1884.
16. Willis Fulcrod remains a mysterious figure. Convict Record, Texas State Penitentiary, at Huntsville, Walker County, Texas, microfilm record. TSAL. Fisher's and Fulcrod's records both appear on page 82. The prison record's handwriting is difficult to read. Fulcrod's death may have been November 1 or November 14, 1874. A "Willis Fulckrod" has been found in Bee County, age twenty-three years, a "mulatto" working as a "Stock Hand," who perhaps is the same man. Perhaps the prejudice of the day precluded anyone appealing the court's verdict. 1870 Bee County census, 571. The county seats of Beeville and Goliad are only thirty miles apart.
17. Fisher and Dykes, 15.
18. The 1870 Goliad County census lists the members of the William Bruton family. Head of household William is forty-eight years of age, raising stock, and a Kentucky native, as is his wife Cynthia. Six children are listed: William, twenty; Charles, eighteen; Wiley, seventeen; Mary, fourteen; Medora, eleven; and Eliza, eight years of age. All the children were born in Texas. 1870 Goliad County census, 384.
19. Fisher and Dykes, 15; Gary P. Fitterer, biography of Alfred Y. Allee, unpublished and untitled manuscript. Gary P. Fitterer private collection. Fitterer cites Minute Book D, District Court, Goliad County.
20. French Strother Grey White was the son of Peter and Martha McCulloch White, born November 24, 1840 in Texana, Jackson County, Texas and died on January 24, 1915 in Carrizo Springs. He is buried in the Mount Hope Cemetery in Carrizo Springs. All through the census years White was identified as a cattle raiser or stock raiser.
21. The 1860 Williamson County census lists the Mrs. M. Thompson family; the head of household is a twenty-three-year-old female, occupation farming; her apparent younger siblings are listed as Pennelope, nineteen; brother Edward, eight; and younger sister Lucy M., six years of age. We believe that this is the Edward A. "Bud" Thompson wbo may have found friendship with King while living in Williamson County. Williamson County census, Georgetown (the county seat), 273.
22. Fisher and Dykes, 15.
23. Crystal S. Williams, "History of Dimmit County," photocopy of unpublished typescript, 1960. Hobart Papers, 18.
24. Memoirs of George P. Durham, serialized in *The Valley Evening Monitor* of McAllen, Texas, November 8, 1959.

25. Mary Brock, "Life of Sally Vivian Fisher Reflects Stirring Texas Days," *Austin-American Statesman*, June 18, 1939. The shifting perspective of the quotes may reflect that the article was based on an interview.

26. Paul S. Taylor, "Historical Note on Dimmit County, Texas," *The Southwestern Historical Quarterly* 34, no. 2 (1930): 81, 83–84.

27. Fisher and Dykes, 29.

28. *Austin Weekly Statesman*, October 5, 1871, citing an item from an undated *Corpus Christi Advertiser*.

29. Fisher and Dykes, 29. Arguably O. C. Fisher was inclined to make King Fisher into a Robin Hood figure.

30. Fisher and Dykes, 30.

31. 1870 Kinney County census, Post Office Uvalde, 181A. When conducting the 1870 Uvalde County census enumerator F. A. Kendall listed five Fenley/Finley families, household numbers 116–120: a John D. Finley, the Joel C. Fenley, a James T. Finley, a Dempsey Finley, and another James Finley. The five Fenley/Finley families were all from South Carolina, Georgia, or Alabama, settling in close proximity to each another. Joel Clinton Fenley was born November 2, 1839 in Georgia and died April 30, 1920, according to an official Uvalde County death certificate numbered 15165. His son George W. was born December 2, 1866 and died June 28, 1940 in Nogales, Santa Cruz, Arizona, according to a death certificate numbered 442. In 1880 the Joel C. Fenley family consisted of wife Margarite A. [née Miller]; G. W., age thirteen; and brothers L. A., ten; G. B., eight; and E. J., age three years. 1880 Maverick County census, 73. If the incident in question happened closer to 1880, then son George W. would have been old enough to go along with his father and carry a Winchester.

32. A death notice in the *Arizona Daily Star*, described George W. Fenley as "a resident of Amado for the past eleven years, died at Nogales, Friday afternoon at 6:30. Funeral services for Mr. Fenley will be held in Nogales tomorrow." *Arizona Daily Star*, June 30, 1940.

33. Guy T. Fenley, interview conducted by Frank L. Hobart, March 14, 1966, Crystal City, Texas. Box 2, folder 3, Hobart Papers.

34. 1880 Maverick County census, settlement on La Muela, precinct number four, 73. Enumerated by Charles W. White.

35. An article contributed by the Dallas correspondent of the *New York Sun* found in the *Evening Gazette* of Cedar Rapids, Iowa, April 28, 1884.

36. A. H. Gregory, "Death of Ben Thompson and King Fisher," *Frontier Times* 5, no. 9 (June 1928). From an undated *Texas Argus* of San Antonio then reprinted in *Frontier Times*. Typescript in Hobart Papers.

37. Roy B. Young, Gary L. Roberts, and Casey Tefertiller , *A Wyatt Earp Anthology: Long May His Story Be Told* (Denton: University of North Texas Press, 2019). This nine-hundred-page tome is among the most recent publications dealing with the life and adventures of Earp.

38. Stuart N. Lake, *Wyatt Earp Frontier Marshal* (Boston: Houghton Mifflin Co., 1931), 168–69.

39. Ranald Mackenzie letter to General C. C. Augur, written at Fort Clark, July 18, published in the *Daily Herald* and then in the *Galveston Daily News* of August 5, 1873.

40. Ibid.

41. J. A. Hicklin letter from Nuecesville, Uvalde County, written July 25, 1873 and sent to the *Daily Herald* and then published in the *Galveston Daily News* of August 5, 1873.

42. Letter from A. J. Potter written from Frio city, July 26, 1873 and published in *Galveston Daily News* of August 5, 1873; Letter to Editor of *San Antonio Daily Herald* and published in the *News* of August 5, 1873.

43. A. J. Potter letter from Frio City, written July 26 to the *Herald* and published in the *Galveston Daily News* of August 5, 1873.

44. List of Fugitives from Justice, from Records in the Adjutant General's Office. TSAL. See also Gillett, *Fugitives*. The Coryell County entry appears on page 16. Occasionally James B. Gillett, whose personal copy is preserved in the Texas State Archives and which State House Press used for its facsimile publication, made notations by the names of some of the fugitives, such as "Killed" or "Captured." The facsimile is the only known copy of the list.

45. Fisher and Dykes, 62–63.

# Notes for Chapter 3

1. For a thorough treatment of the border conditions, see Michael L. Collins, *A Crooked River: Rustlers, Rangers, and Regulars on the Lower Rio Grande, 1861–1877* (Norman: University of Oklahoma Press, 2018). A significant companion piece is Collins's *Texas Devils: Rangers and Regulars on the Lower Rio Grande, 1846–1861* (Norman: University of Oklahoma Press, 2008).

2. *Galveston Daily News*, reporting from *Corpus Christi Gazette* and *Indianola Bulletin*.

3. *Galveston Daily News*, January 19, 1873, citing undated reports from the *Corpus Christi Gazette* and the *Indianola Bulletin*.

4. "Rio Grande Matters," *Galveston Daily News*, February 12, 1873.

5. Of interest is the belief that "Doc" White got Fisher appointed as a constable of Pendencia "to take a job chasing rustlers and bandits." This is the only reference to the early foray into law enforcement yet found and may be folklore. Jack Mitchell, "King Fisher," in *A Proud Heritage: A History of Uvalde County, Texas* (Uvalde: El Progreso Club, 1975), 454.

6. Augustus A. Dial later lived in Uvalde during the time King Fisher and his family lived there. Dial was born November 4, 1845 in Louisiana and died May 18, 1897 and is buried in the Uvalde Cemetery. The 1880 Uvalde County census shows him as a lawyer living with his wife and children, on page 524.

7. O. C. Fisher, "King Fisher: Texas Gunman, Lawman," *Corral Dust* 4, no.1 (1959): 1–3. A presentation given at the February 1959 meeting of the Potomac Corral of the Westerners, subsequently published in their journal (from personal notes taken on typescript manuscript by Mandy Gardner).

8. *Daily Democratic Statesman*, February 13, 1874.

9. *Daily Herald*, April 3, 1874.

10. Darren L. Ivey, *The Ranger Ideal: 1874–1930 Texas Rangers in the Hall of Fame*, vol. 2 (Denton: University of North Texas Press, 2018), 79–80.

11. *Galveston Daily News*, August 2, 1873, citing a special report from San Antonio, August 1, 1873.

12. Ibid.

13. *Galveston Daily News*, August 5, 1873, citing a letter from A. J. Potter at Frio City dated July 26, 1873.

14. *Galveston Daily News*, September 11, 1874, citing a special telegram from San Antonio dated September 10, 1874.

15. Record of Criminals by Co[unty] Crime, Description, Ledger 401-1081, 144–45. TSAL.

16. *Galveston Daily News*, October 21, 1875, citing news from Maverick County.

17. *Galveston Daily News*, November 27, 1874, citing a letter from Goliad written by "Edmond," November 27, 1874.

18. Fisher and Dykes, 64.

19. Kathy Weiser, "Fort Duncan, Texas—Protecting the Rio Grande." Accessed online January 14, 2020.

20. Ben Pingenot, "Eagle Pass, TX," *New Handbook of Texas Online*, https://www.tshaonline.org/handbook/entries/eagle-pass-tx.

21. M. L. Crimmins, "Old Fort Duncan: A Frontier Post," *Frontier Times* (1938): 379–85.

22. *Galveston Daily News*, May 4, 1875. This is from a reporter's visit to the Adjutant General's office and "Special Correspondence" to the *News* dated April 30, 1875.

23. Ibid.

24. *Galveston Daily News*, May 5, 1875, citing a special to the *News* from Brownsville dated May 4, 1875.

25. *Galveston Daily News*, May 14, 1875.

26. *Galveston Daily News*, May 15, 1875, citing a report from Brownsville dated May 14, 1875.

27. *Brenham Daily Banner*, April 9, 1875.

28. Ibid.

29. Irish-born Edward Dougherty had a successful career as a legislator after his military career. Having immigrated to the United States with his parents, he traveled from New York City to Texas in 1846, which is where he was raised. During the Mexican War, he served with David Emanuel Twiggs's dragoons and participated in the first battles of the conflict at Palo Alto and Resaca de la Palma. In 1852 he was admitted to the bar at Brownsville; he then served as county judge and justice of the peace in Cameron County. In 1874 he was appointed commissioner for the extradition treaty between the United States and Mexico. He served as judge of the 15th District at Brownsville in 1877. The date and place of death is uncertain. *Handbook of Texas Online* gives the dates of his life as 1819 to 1877, but the year of his death is uncertain. J. L. Bryan and Laurie E. Jasinski, "Edward Dougherty," accessed March 23, 2020, https://www.tshaonline.org/handbook/entries/dougherty-edward.

30. Michael L. Tate, "Black Seminole Scouts," *Handbook of Texas Online*, https://www.tshaonline.org/handbook/entries/black-seminole-scouts. Tate writes: "Confrontations with members of John King Fisher's gang around Brackettville, Texas, resulted in some later killings of scouts." However, no specific scout is identified.

31. *Daily Democratic Statesman*, October 19, 1875.

32. Judge W. A. Bonnet, "King Fisher, a Noted Character," *Frontier Times* July, 1926, 37. William Andrew Bonnet was born April 15, 1867, died May 9, 1930, and is buried in Eagle Pass. He married Maude Vivian Ellis in Durango, Mexico, exact date uncertain. She was born May 12, 1873 in Bandera County, Texas and died April 22, 1960.

33. Fisher and Dykes, 65.

34. Creaton was born near Carlisle, Pennsylvania on January 12, 1856. He lost his father in the Civil War. With his widowed mother and younger sister Ida, the Creaton family moved to Texas about 1870. Curiously, in his manuscript, he identifies neither of his parents by name, mentioning only his younger sister, Ida. Creaton wrote considerably about his experiences around Fort Griffin before locating in Eagle Pass.

35. Autobiography of John Creaton, typescript. TSAL. Quotation 32–33. The manuscript is forty-three pages in length and typed on legal-size paper.

36. Undated and unidentified newspaper clipping King Fisher Collection, box 2, folder 4. Hobart Papers.

37. Military Muster Rolls, Seminole Negro Scouts, Fort Duncan, Texas. National Archives; Larry G. Shaver, "This is King Fisher's Road: A Biography of John King Fisher," unpublished manuscript. Copy in authors' possession.

38. Seminole Indian Negro Census, conducted by Lt. Alfred C. Markley, March 12, 1875, Microfilm Publication Microcopy 234, roll 805, frame 075. National Archives. Cited in Larry G. Shaver's unpublished manuscript.

39. List of Seminole Indian Negroes at Fort Duncan, Texas, May 9, 1875. National Archives Record Group 393, Records of the U.S. Army Continental Commands 1871–1920, Division of the Missouri, E2547, Special Files Box 15, Seminole Negro-Indians, 1872–1876, frame 090.05. Cited in Larry G. Shaver's unpublished manuscript.

40. Fisher and Dykes, 65–66.

41. Maverick County District Court Records, State of Texas v. J. K. Fisher, Case number 122. Cited in Larry G. Shaver's unpublished manuscript.

42. *Austin American*, November 25, 1925 and *Taylor Daily Press*, November 25, 1925, providing obituaries for Judge Kelso.

43. *Daily Herald*, June 8, 1875, San Antonio. Fisher was arrested the previous day. Mr. Perrin is not further identified. Attempts to learn more about Thomas Dashiell arresting King Fisher have proven unsuccessful. By occupation he was a stock raiser. He was born February 11, 1838 in

Issaquena County, Mississippi, the son of Jeremiah Yellot and Mildred Hornsby Dashiell, but spent much of his life in Bexar County, Texas. He married Mary Estes, who preceded him in death. His obituary in San Antonio papers stressed that he had been a Confederate veteran. Dashiell died December 4, 1921 in San Antonio and is buried in the Confederate Cemetery there. 1870 Bexar County census; *Evening News*, December 5, 1921, San Antonio.

44. *Daily Herald*, May 30 and 31 and June 1, 1876, San Antonio. This same item appeared in the *Galveston Daily News*, June 4, 1876. It was incorrectly reported that Alejo Gonzales made the arrest: "He captured, and lodged in our jail, the notorious horse thief King Fisher, with several of his gang [who] afterwards escaped."

45. Fisher and Dykes, 65–66.

46. *Daily Herald*, July 23, 1875, San Antonio.

47. *Galveston Daily News*, July 22, 1875, reporting news from Frio County. In Arizona John Horton Slaughter became sheriff of Cochise County from 1886 to 1890. For a full-length biography of Slaughter see Allen A. Erwin, *The Southwest of John Horton Slaughter, 1841–1922: Pioneer Cattleman and Trail-Driver of Texas, the Pecos, and Arizona, and Sheriff of Tombstone* (Glendale, California: Arthur H. Clark Company, 1965).

48. *Dallas Daily Herald*, March 13, 1884, headlined "AS SHEEP IN SHAMBLES" with numerous sub-headlines. This relates in detail to the double killing at the Vaudeville Theatre.

49. 1870 Cameron County census, post office Brownsville, enumerated by Henry Haupt, 22.

50. *Galveston Daily News*, June 20, citing a special telegram from Austin dated June 19, 1876. This incident is from an 1876 newspaper, but it could be referencing the incident of the killing at the Zimmerman ranch.

51. Box 2, spiral notebook 3, transcript. Hobart Papers. These were the instructions to the jury by Thomas J. Paschal, Judge 24th Judicial District: "The defendant [J. K. Fisher] is indicted and on trial for the murder of an aged Mexican whose name other than Estanislado is unknown to the Grand Jurors. The State has failed to prove that said Mexican ever was killed and unless the death is proven you cannot convict of Murder hence you will return a verdict of not guilty."

52. "Transcript of Minutes of District Court, Uvalde County, Texas," box 4, folder 13. Hobart Papers. Jury foreman Celestin Pingenot's father was

the great-grandfather of the late historian Ben E. Pingenot. Celestin Pingenot was born February 17, 1838 in France, the son of Pierre Francois Pingenot and Alexis Pingenot. The 1850 Medina County census shows Celestin as 2 and 1/2 years of age (394); the 1870 Medina County census shows him with the family (189). On April 18, 1876 Celestin took the oath of office of Tax Assessor of Medina County. "Texas, Bonds and Oaths of Office, 1846-1920," microfilm. TSAL. Pingenot died November 18, 1901 in Cline, Uvalde County and is buried in the Uvalde Catholic Cemetery.

53. C. S. Broadbent, "King Fisher, A Ranchman's Story of Early Days," *McKay's Weekly*, April 9, 1910. Courtesy Larry G. Shaver.

54. Ironically King Fisher had had his picture taken that very day with his fiancée, thus providing a date for the image of the armed Fisher and Sarah Vivian. One cannot help but wonder if Parrott had also taken pictures of others of King Fisher's associates. No one seems to know if the photographs still exist and, if so, where they might be located.

55. Nicholas Reynolds may have been an orphan taken in by the Charles Vivian family. The 1870 Maverick County census shows him living with Charles and Ann Vivian, although the relationship to head of household is not shown. Reynolds was then a fifteen-year-old boy living with them (536). The 1880 Dimmit County census shows him as a family man, twenty-five years old, working as a "Cow Boy" (two words) born in Texas with parents born in Massachusetts and Illinois. His wife, Mollie, is twenty-two and also a Texan. The couple had a two-month-old daughter, Juliann. They lived on Pendencia Creek (216B).

56. This is the only time Canterbury enters into the story of King Fisher. He was the son of Henry and Elizabeth Menefee Canterbury, born June 17, 1853. In 1870 he was a clerk in an unidentified store in San Antonio and single. He died June 2, 1928 and is buried in Brownsville, Cameron County, Texas. 1870 Bexar County census. Why Canterbury was in the immediate area of Charles Vivian's ranch that day is unknown.

57. Some of the details of the Donovan killing are from Larry Shaver's unpublished manuscript, reflecting court records originally in Maverick County and then Uvalde County, cases 172 and 379.

58. This is from the testimony of William T. Cavin in the manuscript authored by Larry G. Shaver.

# Notes for Chapter 4

1. State News from Goliad to the *Galveston Daily News*, January 15, 1876.
2. *Galveston Daily News*, July 20, 1875, citing county news from Goliad County.
3. *Chicago Daily Tribune*, January 25, 1876. This article headlined "Texas Border Outrages / Capt. McNelly's Story" was a special dispatch to the *Chicago Tribune*.
4. *Texas Frontier Troubles*. House of Representatives 44th Congress, 1st Session, testimony of L. H. McNelly delivered January 24, 1876, 10.
5. *Galveston Daily News*, March 8, 1876.
6. Fisher and Dykes, 65–66.
7. *Galveston Daily News*, March 22, 1876.
8. Fisher and Dykes, 110.
9. Gillett, *Fugitives,* 16. Austin: State House Press, 1997. Of interest is that from Goliad County the names of several appear who played a part in the King Fisher story. A Charles Fulcrod is listed for "Theft from house; negro." Could this be Willis Fulcrod who was sent to Huntsville with Fisher for that early house-breaking? Also listed is W. H. Brooking, wanted for "several cases" of theft. A description is given and suggests he is "probably in the Indian nation." One other name is that of Lark Ferguson who will be suspected of the Goliad Bank robbery with Fisher allegedly aiding and abetting. Ferguson will become known as "Pete Spence" and gain notoriety in the conflict between the Earp brothers and the Clanton-McLaury clan in Tombstone, Arizona Territory. Following Ferguson's name is that of John H. Martin, wanted for "Theft of cattle"; one cannot help but wonder if this is the same John Martin who was killed in the battle of Espantosa Lake in September of 1876 by a squad of rangers commanded by John B. Armstrong. Of additional interest is that in the index Gillett wrote by the name: King Fisher, "Killed." His name is repeated on page 193 "Fisher, J. King." And in Gillett's hand "Killed." So in 1884, perhaps in April, James B. Gillett became aware that John King Fisher had been killed. One other mention is made of Fisher in the original *Fugitives* book published in 1878. On page 153 the entry from Webb County appears: "Fisher, J. King … Theft of geldings; committed February '76; indicted April, same year."
10. Historian Larry G. Shaver found some District Court Minutes for the 1870s that had been bound in the county court's minute book:

cause # 880, theft of a mare, and cause # 882, theft of a gelding, in Book 4, 393.

11. Fisher and Dykes, 43. 1880 Maverick County census, 71. Trinidad San Miguel died April 10, 1938 and is buried in the Catholic Cemetery in Eagle Pass. Brown, *Indian Wars and Pioneers of Texas* (189?; facsimile reprint, Austin: State House Press, 1988), 580–81. Hereafter, cited as Brown, *Indian Wars*.

12. Trinidad San Miguel Jr., interview conducted by Frank L. Hobart, Eagle Pass, March 8, 1966, 6–7. Hobart Papers.

13. Gillett, *Fugitives*, 153; Sammy Tise, *Texas County Sheriffs* (Albuquerque: Oakwood Printing, 1988), 526 (hereafter, cited as Tise, *Texas County Sheriffs*).

14. William Stone was the first appointed judge of Maverick County. He had an extensive career as an entrepreneur and pioneer. Born in New Orleans on May 25, 1835, he came to Texas in 1847 and served in the Mexican War. During the Civil War he became wealthy with his activities in the cotton business. The 1870 Maverick County census shows him at age thirty-six, a general merchant with $9,600 in real estate and $18,000 in personal estate (512). In 1875 he was appointed county judge. He had married Josepha Martinez, age twenty-five in 1866 and the couple would have four children. William Jr., Lucretia and James were Texas born; the oldest child, twelve-year-old Ubenslado Stone, was born in Mexico. Judge Stone died January 23, 1880 in Eagle Pass and is buried in Our Lady of Refuge Cemetery in Eagle Pass. At the time of his death he owned 100,000 acres of land and 30,000 head of sheep as well as extensive real and personal property. Brown, *Indian Wars*.

15. This may have been the *Wipff* Saloon, although the spellings vary. The John Michael Wipff family was prominent in the affairs of Maverick County during this time.

16. *Galveston Daily News*, March 8, citing a special from San Antonio to the *News* of March 7, 1876; *San Antonio Daily Express*, March 8, 1876.

17. *Galveston Daily News*, March 23, 1876. The 1860 Maverick County census, enumerated by Lorenzo Castro, identifies the seven-year-old son of Robert and Maria Porter as "Andres" (19). The 1870 Maverick County census enumerated by Lieut. F.A. Kendall identifies him as Andrew, now nineteen, and a "Farm Laborer" (520). Andres/Andrew, as well as his mother, were born in Mexico. Presumably the young Porter answered to both versions of his name.

18. Details from Larry G. Shaver's unpublished manuscript on King Fisher, reflecting court records originally in Maverick County and then transferred to Uvalde County, cases 172 and 379.

19. Charles Sykes Brodbent was born April 3, 1842 and died March 23, 1931. His name is spelled both Brodbent and Broadbent; the headstone in Alamo Masonic Cemetery in San Antonio spells it Broadbent. He was a sheep raiser when he entered the story of King Fisher, but by 1880 he was a clerk in a merchandise store in Brackettville, Kinney County. 1880 Kinney County Census, 296.

20. Fisher and Dykes, 50–51. O. C. Fisher tends to remove any deliberate murders from Fisher, blaming his men who were desperadoes.

21. Transcript of indictment, case 279. Hobart Papers.

22. *San Antonio Daily Express*, January 4, 1877.

23. *New Orleans Republican*, September 3, 1876.

24. *Galveston Daily News*, April 7, 1876, reporting news from Goliad County.

25. *Galveston Daily News*, April 9, 1876, reprinting an article from an undated *Victoria Advocate*.

26. *Galveston Daily News*, July 20, 1876.

27. *Galveston Daily News*, April 9, 1876.

28. *Galveston Daily News*, June 2, 1876, citing a special telegram from Austin directed to the governor dated June 1, 1876. The "organizations" of former times in eastern Texas is a reference to the so-called war of the early 1840s, a bloody conflict which Sam Houston and the Texas Militia finally quelled. See *War in East Texas: Regulators vs. Moderators* by Bill O'Neal (Denton: University of North Texas Press, 2006.)

29. Fisher and Dykes, 76.

30. Fisher Family Bible.

31. Bruce Roberts, *Springs from the Parched Ground* (Uvalde, Texas: Hornby Press, 1950), 68.

32. *Galveston Daily News*, headlined "Frontier Telegraph" citing a special telegram from Denison dated May 17, 1876.

33. *San Antonio Daily Express*, May 30, 1876.

34. John Franklin Claunch at the time of this incident was a fifty-one-year-old rancher from Alabama as was his forty-seven-year-old wife Martha, living in Wilson County. At this time they had six children, born in Arkansas and Texas. George was born about 1857. 1870 Wilson County census, 484. A few years later the family is found in Zavala County with the head of household listed as a carpenter.

1880 Zavala County census, 471. Franklin Claunch, born in 1828 in St. Clair County died March 24, 1898 in Merkel, Taylor County, Texas and is buried in Rose Hill Cemetery there.

35. J. E. and William T. Cavin were brothers who ranged over a good portion of the Texas frontier. Earlier they had been wanted in Burnet County along with companion Clay Stinnet. Ed Cavin was then described as twenty-four years old, five foot and eleven inches tall, slender with brown hair, blue eyes and "regular features" and brown mustache, who "travels from Burnet County to Rio Grande, frequently in Gillespie and Kimble Counties. Captured with K. Fisher." Brother William T. was two years younger, six foot tall weighing two hundred pounds with dark complexion, black hair, brown eyes, no beard, "youthful homely features. Ranges thro San Saba, Mason, Gillespie and to Rio Grande." Record of Criminals by Co[unty] crimes, description, 148–49. TSAL. This ledger, 401-1081, shows that the crime of murder was committed on September 1, 1873 and the three were indicted on August 8, 1874. No other source known indicates Cavin was arrested with King Fisher in 1874.

36. Augustine Montaigue Gildea led an adventurous life, although his autobiographical writings are sometimes contradictory and repetitive. He was born in DeWitt County April 23, 1854, the son of James E. and Mary Adelaide Cashell Gildea. Philip J. Rasch did extensive research on the man and provides corroboration for Gildea being in King Fisher's territory: "In 1876 Gus sold a small bunch of cattle which he owned in Dimmit County and started for Arizona." In Texas he served under Captain Frank Jones in Company D. Later in Arizona Gildea had further adventures. He died August 10, 1935 in Douglas, Arizona and is buried in Bisbee, Arizona. The cabinet card image of Gildea in his early twenties showing only the white handled pistol was made in 1877 by A. Lewison, 203 W. Commerce Street, San Antonio. See Rasch's entire article in "Gus Gildea – An Arizone Pioneer," *Brand Book* (English Westerners Society), 1985. The article was reprinted in *Desperadoes of Arizona Territory*, a collection of published articles by Philip J. Rasch (Stillwater, Oklahoma: Western Publications, 1999).

37. *San Antonio Daily Express*, August 28, 1877.

38. *Galveston Daily News*, May 31, citing a special telegram dated May 30, 1876 from San Antonio.

39. "State News" from Maverick County in the *Galveston Daily News*, June 4, 1876.

40. *San Antonio Daily Express*, March 13, 1884.

41. N. A. Jennings, *A Texas Ranger* (1899; reprint, Chicago: Lakeside Press, 1992), 230–31. Hereafter, cited as Jennings, *Texas Ranger*.

42. Jennings, *Texas Ranger*, 231.

43. George Durham and Clyde Wantland, "On the Trail of 5,100 Outlaws," *West*, 1937. Later published as *Taming the Nueces Strip: The Story of McNelly's Rangers* (Austin: University of Texas Press, 1962). It had first appeared in the *Brownsville Herald* as a Sunday feature in the seven weeks of October 4, October 11, October 18, November 1, November 15, November 22, and November 29, 1959 under the title of "On the Trail of 5100 Outlaws." Hereafter, cited as Durham and Wantland, "On the Trail."

44. Durham and Wantland, "On the Trail," 106.

45. English was born August 25, 1817 in Little Rock, Arkansas and died May 14, 1894 in Carrizo Springs, and is considered the Founder of Carrizo Springs. He married Matilda Jane Burleson and the couple had eleven children. English donated land for the city cemetery, the Baptist Church and the first school of the county. His grave has a Texas Ranger Memorial Cross. Drew Kirksey Taylor, the son of M. J. and A. R. Taylor was born April 16, 1857 and died January 31, 1942. He is buried in Austin's Memorial Park Cemetery, where famed Texas Ranger Frank Hamer is also buried. Taylor's small headstone bears a lone star at the top with the statement "A Texas Ranger" on the top line, followed by his name and date of birth and death. A brief obituary appeared in the *Austin Statesman* February 2, 1942. He married Anne Hardeman on October 26, 1881. Durham calling Taylor "a gangling youngster" seems out of hand, as he was nineteen at the time of leading McNelly to Fisher's camp. Durham was born on March 11, 1856, so he was but a year older than Taylor. George Preston Durham Sr. died on May 28, 1940.

46. Jennings, *Texas Ranger*, 235.

47. Ibid., 236.

48. Allen was elected on April 18, 1874 and served until July 18, 1874 when he resigned. Tise, *Texas County Sheriffs*, 312.

49. Jennings, *Texas Ranger*, 237.

50. Ibid.

51. Ibid., 238.

52. One source wrote that King Fisher "sported two silver-plated ivory-handled six-shooters, especially manufactured for him. He could

use them, too." Curtis Bishop, "King Fisher's Road," *True West* (January–February 1963). Although this may be true we have found no other confirmation of these two pistols.

53. Jennings, *Texas Ranger*, 237–38.

54. The fancy "leggins" worn by King Fisher is a constant theme of writers of fiction and non-fiction. Curtis Bishop continues the notion that Fisher wore "hand-made high-heeled boots of alligator hide— and *chaparijos* of real tiger skin! (The King had boldly robbed a traveling circus to secure this prize.)" (36). To reinforce this idea of raiding a circus, a half-page illustration shows Fisher shooting an escaping Bengal tiger as it leaps out of the circus cage. Unfortunately no contemporary source has yet been found to confirm this act. The illustrations provided were by Ben Carlton Mead, the noted artist and illustrator. Among other accomplishments are his illustrations appearing in J. Frank Dobie's *Coronado's Children* (1931 edition) and various murals in the Panhandle-Plains Historical Museum in Canyon.

55. Durham and Wantland, "On the Trail," 108.

56. *San Antonio Express*, June 6, 1876.

57. *San Antonio Express*, June 9, 1876.

58. George Durham and Clyde Wantland. *Taming the Nueces Strip: The Story of McNelly's Rangers* (Austin: University of Texas Press, 1962), 142. Hereafter, cited as Durham and Wantland, *Taming the Nueces*.

59. Ibid., 138.

60. Jennings, *Texas Ranger*, 239.

61. L. H. McNelly to William Steele, June 4, 1876. McNelly did not list the names of those outlaws captured, only King Fisher. It is unknown how Jennings and later Durham determined the identity of those arrested. Certainly they could not have "remembered" them so many years after the June 1876 arrest. Perhaps Jennings somehow obtained the names from his own experiences and Durham merely repeated them, as we know he was familiar with Jennings's writings.

62. *Galveston Daily News*, June 22, citing a special telegram from Austin, dated June 21, 1876.

63. Tise, *Texas County Sheriffs*, 363; *Daily Democratic Statesman*, July 21, 1877; *Dallas Daily Herald*, July 31, 1877.

64. Report of the Adjutant General of the State of Texas for the Year Ending August 31st, 1876. Shaw & Blaylock, Galveston. Entry compiled by William Steele.

65. *Daily Democratic Statesman*, June 9, 1876.

66. Jennings, *Texas Ranger*, 241.

67. Durham and Wantland, *Taming the Nueces Strip*, 147–48.

68. Archelous L. "Arch" Parrott remains a mysterious figure in Texas Ranger history. He was the son of William and Martha Parrott, born about 1852 in Lee County, Virginia. William Parrott farmed with $6,200 worth of real estate and $2,000 worth of personal estate in 1860. Both parents were from Claiborne County, Tennessee. The 1860 census shows eight children, Archelous L. being eight years old. His service record, always simply "A. L. Parrott," shows he mustered into McNelly's company on July 26, 1876 at Clinton, DeWitt County. By December 1, 1878 he had risen to the rank of 1st Sergeant in Hall's company of Special State Troops. He and Charles B. McKinney signed the oath there before Rudolph Kleburg, District Clerk, together. Sources dealing with McNelly and Hall agree that Parrott was in 1875–1876 an itinerant photographer, traveling among outlaws such as King Fisher and his men. He is listed as "Parrott & Quesenberry" working in Maverick County in 1875 and Starr County in 1876 in David Haynes's work, *Catching Shadows: A Directory of 19th Century Texas Photographers*. As yet no examples of his photography are known to exist, other than the image of Fisher with his fiancée Sarah Vivian. He married Annie S. Morris October 16, 1884 in Jack County, Texas. Although his origins remain obscure, it is known that he died in Jacksboro, Jack County, Texas on March 24, 1899 and is buried in Jacksboro's Oakwood Cemetery. His grave is marked.

69. Durham and Wantland, *Taming the Nueces Strip*, 136.

70. Jennings, *Texas Ranger*, 32–33.

71. Ibid., 276.

72. Ibid., 277.

73. *San Antonio Express*, June 10, 1876.

74. Ibid.

75. L. H. McNelly to William Steele, May 31, 1876. Adjutant General Correspondence, Vol. III. TSAL.

76. *Weekly Democratic Statesman*, June 1, 1876.

77. *Daily Democratic Statesman*, June 27, 1876.

78. Captain L. H. McNelly to Adj. Gen. William Steele, written from Laredo, May 31, 1876. "Adj. Gen. Correspondence," Box 401-394, Folder 7. TSAL.

79. *Galveston Daily News*, June 20, citing a special telegram from Austin dated June 19, 1876.

80. *Daily Democratic Statesman*, June 20, 1876.

81. *San Antonio Daily Herald*, June 23, 1876, citing a report from an undated Austin *Gazette*. This article also reported the arrest but identified the brothers as John Smith and Turk Smith (some sources identify him as "Pink") and that they had been convicted in McLennan County of murder. Having escaped the Waco jail after conviction, they went to the Rio Grande but operated under the name of Burnes "and were connected with the Hardin gang until it was broken up, and then joined the King Fisher band." The breakup of the Hardin gang was in May and June of 1874. If they were really considered part of the Fisher band it was because Fisher did not carefully concern himself about who he associated with.

82. Gillett, *Fugitives from Justice*, 32; Tise, *Texas County Sheriffs*, 312.

83. *Galveston Daily News*, June 28, 1876.

84. *Galveston Daily News*, June 20, 1876.

85. This first appeared in the *St. Louis Republican* of St. Louis, Missouri, June 15, 1876, and later reprinted in the *San Antonio Herald* of June 30, 1876.

86. The rumor had appeared in the *San Antonio Daily Express* of July 13 and was also brought up in the *Galveston Daily News*, July 15, 1876.

87. *San Antonio Daily Express*, July 13, 1876.

88. From testimony of William T. Cavin.

89. *Galveston Daily News*, July 27, 1876.

90. *The Inter Ocean* (Chicago, Illinois), August 23, 1876.

91. *Victoria Advocate*, August 17, 1876.

92. The name of William Brooking appears frequently in the literature of the Wild West yet no one has yet attempted his biography. The 1850 Goliad County census shows the family as living in Goliad town in the household of William and Martha Meller, both from Virginia and aged sixty years old. Beveon, thirty-five, and Joanna, thirty, were from Virginia and Tennessee respectively, with their then four children. Haret [Harriet?], age ten, and Martha J., age seven, were both Arkansas natives. Son Edward U., three years of age and William H., eight months, both born in Tennessee, rounded out the household. This man William, who shot at the bank robbers, later would be accused of aiding and abetting them in the robbery along with Bill Taylor, King Fisher, Doc Cornett, and others. Of particular interest is that later, in September, 1877, rumors were about that the Brooking brothers had both been killed, yet according to the *Goliad Guard* E. U. Brooking came in and "put himself

under the protection of Lieutenant Hall, ... but after remaining two or three days, took fright, and, mounting a horse belonging to Mr. Miller, left for the Rio Grande." In October, a Will Brooking and a group of drovers were on their way to the Black Hills. William Hargrove, one of the group, wrote of a fight between Will Brooking and a Peter Preston in which Brooking was killed. He lived but a short time but managed to ask that his family be notified. Hargrove also explained that Preston had since been killed in Kansas during an attempted train robbery. Hargrove's letter to the *Galveston Daily News*, dated October 15, 1877, was written from camp in Lavaca County and published in the *Galveston Daily News*, October 25, 1877.

93. *Victoria Advocate*, October 13, 1877, citing a report from an undated *Goliad Guard*. This is the only mention of Bob Holt in the King Fisher saga. The *Guard* described him as a man "with many aliases" and as "the same kinky-headed gent who was with Wm. Brooking and Bill Taylor [who] pretended to be firing at the robbers as they left."

94. *Victoria Advocate*, August 24, 1876.

95. Ibid.

96. Ibid., August 31, 1876, reporting news from an undated *Goliad Guard*.

97. Victor M. Rose, *The Texas Vendetta, or, The Sutton-Taylor Feud* (1880; facsimile reprint, Houston: The Frontier Press of Texas, 1956).

98. *The Inter Ocean*, August 29, 1876.

99. *Galveston Daily News*, September 13, 1876.

100. *New Orleans Republican*, September 3, 1876.

101. For a complete biography of Armstrong and further details on the Espantosa Lake fight, see Chuck Parsons, *John B. Armstrong: Texas Ranger and Pioneer Texas Ranchman* (College Station: Texas A&M University Press, 2007).

102. *Dallas Daily Herald*, October 3, 1876, citing a special to the *Herald* from San Antonio. This report appeared in several other newspapers as well, significantly in Austin's *Daily Democratic Statesman* of the same date.

103. *Galveston Daily News*, October 22, 1876.

104. Monthly Return of Lieutenant Hall, Special State Troops. TSAL.

105. *Victoria Advocate*, October 13, 1877, citing an undated article from the *Goliad Guard*.

106. William Riley "Bill" Taylor gained notoriety during the infamous Sutton-Taylor Feud of the 1870s in the DeWitt County and surrounding area. His most serious offense was the killing of Gabriel Webster

Slaughter in 1874. Later, he was involved in the killing of Reuben H. Brown, the City Marshal of Cuero, Texas. He was arrested for this latter offense but charged with the Slaughter killing. During a hurricane in 1875, he escaped from the Galveston jail. His ultimate fate is uncertain, but it is believed he was killed in 1895 in Oklahoma. "Doctor Cornett" is how the 1860 Goliad County census taker identified James Richard Cornett, son of Samuel and Lucretia Pigg Cornett, born July 30, 1851 in Johnson County, Missouri. Why he was charged with aiding and abetting the bank robbers is unknown, other than that the only other charge against him was one of exhibiting a monte bank in Frio County in 1885. He died in San Antonio, Texas of a heart attack on March 9, 1924. A sister, Elizabeth Agnes Cornett, married Charles Bruton of the Bruton family. See David Johnson, *The Cornett-Whitley Gang: Violence Unleashed in Texas* (Denton: University of North Texas Press, 2019).

107. James M. Smallwood, *The Feud That Wasn't: The Taylor Ring, Bill Sutton, John Wesley Hardin, and Violence in Texas* (College Station: Texas A&M University Press, 2008), 170.

# Notes for Chapter 5

1. *Galveston Daily News*, December 30, 1876, reporting state news from Nueces County. San Diego is the county seat of Duval County.
2. *Daily Express* (San Antonio), January 4, 1877.
3. Ibid. The headline reads: "King Fisher on the War Path," all in uppercase bold letters, followed by a smaller sub-headline: "He and his men 'take' Eagle Pass, and give Judge Stone a Piece of their minds."
4. *Galveston Daily News*, February 9, 1877.
5. *Galveston Daily News*, February 15, 1877.
6. Fisher and Dykes, 92–93.
7. Report of Operations of State Troops Since August 1, 1876 to December 31, 1881, Vol. 1, File No. 401-1082. TSAL.
8. *Galveston Daily News*, February 23, 1877, reporting news from Goliad County.
9. There are two biographies of J. L. Hall: Dora Neill Raymond, *Captain Lee Hall of Texas* (1940; facsimile reprint, Norman: University of Oklahoma Press, 1982); Chuck Parsons, *Texas Ranger Lee Hall: From the Red River to the Rio Grande* (Denton: University of North Texas Press, 2020).

10. Webb County Court records. Box 4, Folder 11. Hobart Papers; 1870 Webb County Non-Population (Agricultural) Schedule.

11. Fisher and Dykes, 101–02.

12. *Daily Express*, March 29, 1877, San Antonio.

13. *Galveston Daily News*, March 30, 1877, citing "State News" from Webb County, initially published in the *San Antonio Daily Express*.

14. *Daily Express*, April 15, 1877.

15. *St. Louis Globe-Democrat*, April 21, 1877, reprinting an item from an undated *San Antonio Daily Express*.

16. *Galveston Daily News*, April 28, 1877, reporting news from Brackettville.

17. Williams, also known as Jim Jones, "escaped across the border but was arrested by Mexican authorities. ... On May 14 Lieutenants Lee Hall and John B. Armstrong and Sergeant A.L. Parrott ... brought him back from Piedras Negras." Robert K. DeArment, *Alias Frank Canton* (Norman: University of Oklahoma, 1996), 323 n. 85.

18. *Galveston Daily News*, May 15, 1877, citing a special telegram from Eagle Pass dated May 14, 1877.

19. Monthly Return of Special State Troops, May 1877, in Results of Operations of State Troops, vol. 1. Box 401-1082. TSAL.

20. Details from Larry G. Shaver's unpublished manuscript on King Fisher, reflecting court records originally in Maverick County, cases 172 and 379.

21. Fisher and Dykes, 96.

22. *Galveston Daily News*, May 20, 1877, citing a special telegram from Austin dated May 19, 1877.

23. *Brenham Weekly Banner*, May 25, 1877. McNelly's hometown was Burton, a small community only a few miles west of Brenham, hence the frequent reporting of McNelly's activities.

24. Monthly Return of Special State Troops, May 1877. TSAL.

25. *Galveston Daily News*, May 25, 1877, citing correspondence by "Ourdab" from Eagle Pass dated May 17, 1877. "Ourdab" was a term referring to a small group of men sharing meals while on a scout.

26. Rick Miller, *Texas Ranger John B. Jones and the Frontier Battalion, 1874–1881* (Denton: University of North Texas Press, 2012), 147–50.

27. *Galveston Daily News*, September 26, 1877. "Mervyn" contributed at least four letters published in the *News* between September 26 and December 7, 1877. His real name was Mervyn Bathurst Davis. The complete set of letters with annotations appears in Chuck Parsons,

"'Mervyn' A Poetical Correspondent," in "The Annotated Letters of Texas Ranger Mervyn Bathurst Davis," *Brand Book* (English Westerners Society), Winter 1988–1989, 1–9.

28. *Daily Express* (San Antonio), May 22, 1877. The news was reported by special telegram to the *Express* from Uvalde.

29. *Galveston Daily News*, May 23, 1877, citing news from Medina County.

30. "Grand Jury Work," *Daily Express*, June 12, 1877.

31. Chicon Creek, during King Fisher's lifetime, was one of several creeks feeding into Espantosa Lake in Dimmit County. A map in the Hobart Papers has Chicon Creek south of Palo Blanco Creek and north of Pendencia and Comanche Creeks. The creeks were over one hundred miles southeast of San Antonio. It is possible that in Medina County there was also a Chicon Creek which no longer exists due to the building of dams.

32. *Burnet Bulletin*, December 22, 1877, from the *San Antonio Herald* of December 12, 1877.

33. Ferdinand Niggli was first elected Medina County sheriff on February 15, 1876; was reelected November 5, 1878 and November 2, 1880; and served until he resigned on June 1882. He became a deputy United States Marshal under Hal Gosling. Niggli and Fritz Thumm allowed themselves to get into a feud over unknown causes, which ended with Thumm shooting Niggli the night of August 25, 1885, from which several wounds he died on August 31, 1885. Niggli is buried in Mission Burial Park South in San Antonio. His grave is marked. Tise, *Texas County Sheriffs*, 369; *Galveston Daily News*, August 27, 1885, citing a special telegram from Castroville, August 26, 1885. See also Robert Ernst, *Deadly Affrays: The Violent Deaths of the United States Marshals* (Avon, Indiana: ScarletMask Enterprises, 2006), 262–63.

34. *Galveston Daily News*, May 30, 1877.

35. *Daily Express* (San Antonio), June 2, 1877, written May 31, 1877 from Hondo, Texas. The correspondent has taken the word "malleus" from the book *Malleus Maleficarum*, a well-known treatise on witchcraft written by Heinrich Kramer in 1486, written in Latin and first published in Germany. It broadly endorsed the extermination of witches. The latest translation into English is the 2009 *The Hammer of Witches* published by the Cambridge University Press.

36. *Daily Express*, June 2, 1877.

37. Ibid. Cortina had been arrested on February 24, 1877 in Matamoros and was awaiting execution, but he was saved from the firing squad by

the intervention of Col. John S. "Rip" Ford. Jerry Thompson, *Cortina: Defending the Mexican Name in Texas* (College Station: Texas A&M University Press, 2007), 236–38.

38. *Daily Express*, May 25, 1877.
39. Ibid.
40. Ibid.; Monthly return of Hall's Special State Troops, May 1877. TSAL. The Biblical quote is from Proverbs 13:15: "Good understanding giveth favour: but the way of transgressors is hard" (King James Version).
41. *Galveston Daily News*, May 25, 1877, citing a special report from Eagle Pass dated May 17, 1877.
42. Ibid.
43. Robert Ernst, *Deadly Affrays: The Violent Deaths of the US Marshals* (Avon, Indiana: ScarletMask Enterprises, 2006).
44. *Weekly Democratic Statesman*, May 31, 1877.
45. *Galveston Daily News*, June 8, 1877, printing a letter from Rockport signed "Nym Myrtle," dated June 5, 1877 and headlined "Lieut. Hall's Command / West Texas Demands that it be Retained in Service."
46. *Dallas Weekly Herald*, June 9, 1877.
47. *Galveston Daily News*, July 4, 1877, citing a report from an undated and unidentified San Antonio newspaper.
48. *Daily Fort Worth Gazette*, July 11, 1877.
49. *Daily Express*, July 11, 1877.
50. *New Orleans Daily Democrat*, July 24, 1877, in the "Texas News" column.
51. *Daily Express*, July 15, 1877.
52. *Daily Democratic Statesman*, August 14, 1877.
53. *Daily Express*, July 27, 1877.
54. *Daily Democratic Statesman*, July 29, 1877, in the "Texas—Facts and Fancies" column.
55. *Daily Express*, October 16, 1877; *Daily Democratic Statesman*, October 20, 1877.
56. *Dallas Weekly Herald*, August 25, 1877.
57. *San Antonio Express*, December 31, 1934. San Antonio native August Hornung was involved in law enforcement for many years. He was born on February 15, 1850 and died on December 30, 1934. He died in Hondo but is buried in Mission Burial Park South in San Antonio. His obituary states he was formerly a Texas Ranger and had been a tax collector, tax assessor, and justice of the peace. He served under Governor E. J. Davis in the First District as a private in the Texas State

Police for one month, from July 29 to August 29, 1870. The 1880 census shows him as a deputy sheriff. 1880 Medina County census, 78A; obituary in *San Antonio Express*, December 31, 1934; Adjutant General Service Records. Guarding King Fisher from Castroville to Uvalde may have been his "claim to fame."

58. *Daily Express*, September 2, 1877.
59. *San Antonio Light*, November 22, 1883.
60. *Weekly Democratic Statesman*, July 8, 1875, from the popular "Texas—Facts and Fancies" column.
61. Thomas McCall was first elected sheriff of Medina County on August 2, 1858; was reelected on August 6, 1860; and served until April 1862. Tise, *Texas County Sheriffs*, 369. He then was elected sheriff of Bexar County on November 5, 1878; was reelected on November 2, 1880 and on November 7, 1882; and served until November 4, 1884. Then two others, E. A. Stevens and Nat Lewis, served as sheriff, but McCall was again elected on November 6, 1888 and November 4, 1890 and served until November 8, 1892. Ibid., 43.
62. *Daily Express*, September 4, 1877.
63. *Daily Express*, August 10, 1877.
64. *Victoria Advocate* of October 6, 1877, reprinting an item from an undated *Pleasanton Journal* (Atascosa County).
65. *Daily Express*, March 13, 1884.
66. *Galveston Daily News*, October 27, 1877.
67. *Galveston Daily News*, November 8, 1877.
68. *Daily Democratic Statesman*, August 29, 1877.
69. From Durham's memoir serialized in the *Brownsville Herald*, November 15, 1959. A "swap-out," as used by Durham, meant that the two men met face-to-face and had a gunfight. Fisher won and Donovan lost.

# Notes for Chapter 6

1. *The World* (New York), January 6, 1878.
2. W. A. Bonnet, "King Fisher, a Noted Character," *Frontier Times*, July 10, 1926.
3. Ibid.
4. *Marshall Messenger*, July 17, 1926. Curiously, the *Marshall Messenger* identifies the judge as W. A. Bonnett, but Judge Bonnet died May 9, 1930, having lived fifty years in Eagle Pass.

5. *Galveston Daily News*, February 2, 1878, reporting news from Medina County.

6. *Galveston Daily News*, February 13, 1878, reporting news from Medina County.

7. *Daily Herald*, San Antonio, February 19, 1878.

8. *Galveston Daily News*, February 19, 1878, quoting a special telegram from Castroville dated February 18; *Galveston Weekly News*, February 25, 1878. Efforts to determine if Merritt died or recovered from these dangerous wounds have not been successful.

9. *Galveston Daily News*, February 22, 1878.

10. *Daily Herald*, February 19, 1878.

11. *Galveston Daily News* (Austin), April 25, 1878, citing news in the "Texas—Facts and Fancies" column.

12. Texas, Convict and Conduct Registers, 1875–1945, 663, microfilm. TSAL. The word "strike" could mean refusing to work, or might possibly refer to a hunger strike, but the record gives no indication.

13. Convict Record, Texas State Penitentiary, at Huntsville, Walker County, Texas, 51. TSAL.

14. *Tri-Weekly Herald* (Marshall, Texas), May 18, 1878, citing an item from an undated *Goliad Guard*.

15. Fisher and Dykes, 99–101.

16. Details of the difficulties in Maverick County and change of venue to Uvalde County are found in transcriptions by Frank Hobart preserved in Box 3, Folder 13 of the Hobart Papers.

17. *Weekly Democratic Statesman*, May 30, 1878, in the "Texas—Facts and Fancies" column.

18. *Brenham Weekly Banner*, May 31, 1878.

19. *Texas Siftings*, April 5, 1884. Alexander E. Sweet was Texas's most important early-day humorist. Born in Canada, he came to San Antonio with his parents in 1849, studied law, became a newspaperman, and worked for the *Galveston Daily News*. In 1881 he took on as a partner J. Armory Knox. They were extremely successful with *Texas Siftings*, and the circulation reached fifty thousand. C. L. Sonnichsen, editor, *Texas Humoresque: Lone Star Humorists From Then Till Now* (Fort Worth: TCU Press, 1990), 36.

20. *Galveston Daily News*, May 14, 1878, citing a letter to Congressman Schleicher first printed in the *St. Louis Republican*.

21. The 1880 Bandera County census shows the Joseph and Anna Kalka family, whose daughter Rose was then nineteen years of age.

Both parents were born in Poland, while all the children were born in Texas. Bandera County Census, eight. Rose, born on September 3, 1862, married Phillip Henry Mazurek. They raised fifteen children. She died on April 25, 1918, according to her death certificate, but on April 29 according to the double headstone in the Saint Stanislaus Cemetery in Bandera.

22. Mrs. Albert Maverick Sr., "Ranch Life in Bandera County in 1878," *Frontier Times* (April 1978): 270. Albert Maverick Sr. was born on May 7, 1854 and died on January 24, 1947. Jane Lewis Maury was born on December 14, 1858 and died on February 15, 1954. The Mavericks had eleven children. The one she held fast in fear of Fisher was daughter Jessie, born on December 27, 1877, assuming this event did happen in 1878.

23. Oliphant, prior to the Civil War, advertised his services in the *San Antonio Ledger and Texan*. The September 22, 1860 issue informed potential clients that his office was on the North Side of Commerce Street. The 1850 Nelson County, Kentucky census shows him living with his father, Andrew Oliphant, and an older sister. The mother was apparently deceased. Perhaps his first initial stood for Andrew, his father's name, but this is uncertain. In 1870 he was listed as a resident of Bandera, Bandera County, thirty-four years of age, and born in Kentucky. He may have relocated in the Oklahoma territory by the turn of the nineteenth century. The *Daily Gazette* of Stillwater, Oklahoma of May 22, 1902 reported a train wreck in which several men had been killed and injured, among them A. M. Oliphant, "a prominent attorney of Tishomingo" described as being fatally injured. The construction train was part of the Choctaw, Oklahoma & Gulf railway system. The wreck was caused when the train plunged through a high trestle twelve miles west of Ardmore, May 20, 1902. The news of the wreck was reported throughout the United States.

24. A. M. Oliphant's use of the term "Hoodoos" to describe Hall's rangers is curious, as generally the term was applied to vigilantes, such as those active in Mason County during the early 1870s. Various explanations of the term exist. See David Johnson, *The Mason County "Hoo Doo" War, 1874–1902* (Denton: University of North Texas Press, 2006), 5–6.

25. *Galveston Daily News*, January 23, 1879, letter from A. M. O. dated January 18, 1879 from Eagle Pass.

26. Ibid.

27. Ibid.
28. *Daily Democratic Statesman*, June 18, 1879. This item was reprinted in the *Tri-Weekly Herald* of Marshall, Texas on June 21, 1879.
29. *Daily Express* (San Antonio), June 15, 1879.
30. *Daily Express*, July 18, 1879.
31. *Weekly Democratic Statesman* (Austin), July 17. 1879; *Times-Picayune* (New Orleans), July 24, 1879. The latter article also appeared in the *Weekly Bazoo* of Sedalia, Missouri on July 29, 1879 and perhaps in numerous other newspapers as well.
32. Lieutenant T. L. Oglesby's Semi-monthly Report, dated September 30, 1879. Special Forces Correspondence, RG 401-1157-19, TSAL. *Galveston Daily News*, September 26, 1879, citing an undated report from the *Castroville Quill*.
33. *Gonzales Inquirer*, November 1, 1879.
34. *Galveston Daily News*, October 16, citing a special telegram report of October 15, 1879 from Uvalde County.
35. *Valley Evening Monitor*, November 15, 1959. This incident appears in Durham and Wantland's story, later published as Durham and Wantland's *Taming the Nueces Strip*. In this *Monitor* selection, Durham is quoted as saying that Allen "had been a Ranger before. He was one of them notched-gun badmen that enlisted at the beginning under McNelly. ... He was a Ranger, but he wasn't a McNelly Ranger." This incident does not appear in *Taming the Nueces Strip*. According to our research, George Henry Allen had mustered into McNelly's company as a private on June 22, 1875 and was discharged on February 1, 1877. He then was mustered into Hall's company of "Special Force State Troops" on March 31, 1877 and served until November 30, 1879, having served from August 1 as a 2nd Corporal. His final record shows he had earned $140 for service from August 1 to November 30, 1879. Nothing in his record indicates that Fisher's escape was due to a neglectful act, nor does his last pay statement indicate his discharge was either honorable or dishonorable. Adjutant General Service Records. TSAL. According to a news report, Allen later served as City Marshal of Weimar, Colorado County, Texas. He was in Coleman County when death came on December 15, 1893 due to pneumonia. Born July 8, 1853, he was only forty years of age when he passed. He is buried in the Odd Fellows Cemetery in Weimar, and his grave is marked. *Weimer Mercury*, December 23, 1893.
36. 1880 Zavala County census, 472B.

37. The same headline also adorned a lengthy column in the San Antonio *Daily Express* of January 4, 1877.

38. *Daily Express*, April 8, 1881. Citizens of Zavala County may have seriously considered Fisher for their sheriff, but it never happened that he was elected. At the time of this report, Zavala County was not yet organized, and would not be until February 1881. The first sheriff was J. E. Ragland. Tise, *Texas County Sheriffs*, 561.

# Notes for Chapter 7

1. Bruce Roberts, *Springs from the Parched Ground* (Uvalde: Hornby Press, 1950), 67. In 1950 Baptist pioneer preacher Roberts was eighty-two years of age. Roberts was also Chaplain of the Texas Old Trail Drivers' Association. *Star Telegraph* (Fort Worth), April 30, 1950, citing an article from an undated Uvalde newspaper.

2. Roberts, *Springs from the Parched Ground*, 66.

3. Ibid., 67.

4. Curiously the sign appeared in a television production of the popular television show *Death Valley Days*. The program aired on January 1, 1970, with Robert Yuro playing the role of King Fisher. The production was aptly entitled "King of the Uvalde Road" and highlighted the famous sign in Uvalde County. In the television version, fortunately for all concerned, a way was found to avoid violence over the use of the sign, and the Uvalde community made King Fisher into a much-admired hero.

5. Some writers have questioned whether the road sign ever actually existed, although Roberts and Bonnet both accepted it as a reality, as did Ranger George Durham. His reminiscences, as told to Clyde Wantland, first appeared in *West*, a pulp western magazine, and then were serialized in various south Texas newspapers prior to their 1962 publication in book form as *Taming the Nueces Strip*. It was perhaps inevitable that Hollywood would discover Durham's account of his experiences with McNelly. However, in 2001 the *Texas Rangers* movie appeared on the big screen and was a disappointment to virtually all who attended. King Fisher (played by Alfred Molina) was portrayed as a heartless bully on horseback. Among the screen credits one sees George Durham's book, but the adaptation was so loose as to be beyond recognition. Durham's reminiscences were serialized in the *Brownsville Herald*, and the quote is from the issue dated November 8, 1959.

6. Roberts, *Springs from the Parched Ground*, 67.

7. Dr. O. C. Pope was a giant among nineteenth-century Baptist ministers. During his long career, he established Baptist churches from Fort Worth to El Paso and into Mexico as well. He was born on February 15, 1842 in Washington County, Georgia and graduated from Mercer University in 1860 with a bachelor of divinity degree. Shortly afterward, he married Miss Mollie Sinquefield and soon was called to preach at the Baptist Church in Linnville, Georgia. He was ordained as a minister in 1861. As a Confederate he preached nightly to the troops, but his health was never strong after the war. For years he taught school, preaching continually to rural churches, since few churches could afford a full-time minister. In 1878 he moved to Houston, Texas and later became managing editor of the *Texas Baptist Herald*, a journal which continues today. In 1880 he was awarded an honorary doctor of divinity degree from Baylor University. In 1898 he became the third president of Simmons College, which later became Hardin-Simmons University in Abilene, Texas. Dr. Pope died November 18, 1901. Dr. and Mrs. Pope are buried on the Hardin-Simmons University Campus.

8. Roberts, *Springs from the Parched Ground*, 74–77.

9. *Daily Express*, April 8, 1881, citing a letter from Carothers dated April 7, 1881.

10. This item appeared initially in the *Austin Daily Statesman* on April 15, 1881 in the "Texas—Facts and Fancies" column and was reprinted in the *Austin Weekly Statesman* of April 21, 1881.

11. Box 3, Folder 13. Hobart Papers.

12. April 20, 1881 Dallas *Daily Herald* special to the San Antonio *Daily Herald*, reporting news from Uvalde; April 28, 1881 Dallas *Weekly Herald* reporting telegraphic news from San Antonio. Some reports identify the family as Gilchrist, but the report from Fort Clark describing the fatal fight that cost the lives of the father and son identified the family as Gilcrease. For the version provided by John R. Baylor's brother George W., see George Wythe Baylor, *Into the Far, Wild Country: True Tales of the Old Southwest*, edited by Jerry D. Thompson (El Paso: Texas Western Press, 1996). The young Baylor was Henry W. Baylor, who was elected Sheriff of Uvalde County on November 4, 1884, reelected on November 2, 1886, and reelected ten more times, serving until November 6, 1906. Tise, *Texas County Sheriffs*, 503.

13. Fisher and Dykes, 108. The most detailed report of the final confrontation between the Baylors and the Gilcreases appeared in the *Galveston*

*Daily News* of April 28, 1881, printing a version from an undated *Fort Clark News*. Curiously, it concluded: "We do not know much about General Baylor, but he is represented to us as a man who does not seek for a fight, but one who is always ready to defend himself whenever occasion requires it."

14. *Austin Weekly Statesman,* June 30, 1881, citing a special to the *Statesman* from Eagle Pass dated June 28, 1881.

15. Notes from Larry G. Shaver's unpublished manuscript reflecting court records in Maverick County and Uvalde County; Fisher and Dykes, 108–09.

16. Florence Fisher Kellogg, "Incidents in the Life of John King Fisher," unpublished manuscript, Maverick County Deed Records, 1880 Zavala County census, Hedrich interview. Hobart Papers. Florence was a granddaughter of King Fisher. Frances Wipff Hedrich said in an interview that it was a combined saloon and livery stable, and that the saloon "was about as tough a place as it could possibly be!" Dancing and violin music were features. Fisher and Balis A. Bates were co-owners and -operators. Bates was also a farmer with a family. The 1880 census shows that Bates and his family then resided in Zavala County. Deed records in Maverick County show that Fisher sold his interest in the Sunset Livery Stable/Saloon on June 28, 1883 for $2,000.

17. *Las Vegas Gazette* (New Mexico), July 12, 1881.

18. *Las Vegas Daily Optic,* July 12, 1881.

19. *Daily Gazette* (Fort Wayne, Indiana), December 21, 1881. This is an interview with a "Colonel Davis, U.S.A." identified only as a brother of General Jeff C. Davis, not to be confused with the Confederacy's Jefferson Davis.

20. *Galveston Daily News,* October 27, 1878, citing a special telegram from Uvalde dated October 26, 1878.

21. *Brenham Weekly Banner,* March 16, 1882.

22. *Galveston Daily News,* May 14, 1882, citing news from Uvalde dated May 13, 1882.

23. *San Antonio Light,* April 26, 1882.

24. *Daily Statesman,* June 6, 1882.

25. *San Antonio Light,* September 16, 1882, citing news from Uvalde dated September 15, 1882.

26. Hobart Papers. Hobart's research indicates the baby was a son, although some sources identify the baby as a daughter. Also, T. H. McKinney knew the Fisher family well and, in a letter correcting some statements

in a *Frontier Times* article, wrote: "King Fisher left a family, a wife, two, little girls and a baby boy, I heard. I never saw the baby boy, but I have seen the little girls many times—as nice a family as you [would] meet anywhere, and all devoted to each other." T. H. McKinney, "In Defense of King Fisher," letter to editor, *Frontier Times* 12, no. 4 (January 1935).

27. Fisher and Dykes, 114; TexasEscapes.com, accessed May 23, 2020. The Vivian Cemetery is on private property. Once Cometa was a small but thriving village, but according to the 2000 census it now has a population of only ten. TexasEscapes.com wrote of the community: "The most noticeable proof of a substantial past is the Vivian Cemetery." Cometa was located about ten miles west of Crystal City, county seat of Zavala County. The other identifiable graves include: Albert L. Osgood (April 22, 1866–June 29, 1869), Lloyd Thomas "John" Vivion Jr. (December 10, 1836–May 28, 1896), Alpha Vivion (November 19, 1877–February 16, 1895), Clarence Vivion (July 21, 1896–January 3, 1897), Effre Maud Vivion (November 5, 1882–May 29, 1898), R. Riley Ware (March 7, 1862–September 18, 1907), Pearl L. White (May 17, 1877–September 13, 1877), Romey Gertrude White (January 13, 1888–February 8, 1888). A brief history of Cometa is found in Zavala County Historical Commission, *Now and Then in Zavala County* (Crystal City: Zavala County Historical Commission, 1985),132–34. The articles on Cometa are by Camillo Flanagan and Beatrice W. Franks.

28. O. C. Fisher leaves no doubt that the Fishers were living in Uvalde when P. L. was born, not on a ranch in Zavala County. Fisher and Dykes, 114.

29. Boatright was born on March 10, 1835 in Vigo County, Indiana and died on April 12, 1929 in Austin. He is buried in the Confederate Field, Section 1, Row U, # 12 in the Texas State Cemetery. Other sources indicate he was born in Crawford County, Illinois.

30. George Kerfoot Chinn mustered into Company "F" of the Frontier Battalion on September 1, 1877, serving under Captain Pat Dolan. Although some papers of his service record appear to be missing, he probably served continually from that date until his honorable discharge on April 30, 1879. TSAL. He was born in Hopkinsville, Christian County, Kentucky on June 15, 1852, the son of John W. and Eliza C. Kerfoot Chinn. When he came to Texas is uncertain, but an item in the Dallas *Weekly Herald* of December 5, 1874 perhaps gives the answer: "G. K. Chinn, Esq., of Hopkinsville, Kentucky, is at the San Jacinto

[Hotel]. He has his eye on a sheep ranche and will make a good Texan." Following his service with the Frontier Battalion, he settled down in Uvalde County, where he married Ella Nunn in October 1882. G. K. Chinn, who had a high regard for King Fisher, died July 11, 1928, and is buried in the Uvalde Cemetery.

31. Fisher and Dykes, 114.

32. Description and Historical Register of Enlisted Soldiers of the Army, for during the war with Mexico under the Acts approved January 12th and February 11th, 1847. Microfilm copy online, 118. TSAL.

33. "Military Items," *Daily Picayune* (New Orleans), April 28, 1868.

34. 1870 Uvalde County census, 542B. Mary Hannahan was born on March 24, 1818 and died on April 13, 1905 in Uvalde County.

35. *Daily Express*, July 14, 1876. Thomas Hannahan had been found dead, "having been shot through the body by some unknown party." From Larry G. Shaver's unpublished manuscript.

36. This is Needham B. Pulliam, son of William and Matilda Pulliam, born in Texas about 1857 and residing in Uvalde at the time of the 1870 census. His father and three older brothers are identified as stock raisers. 1870 Uvalde County census, 539.

37. 1880 Uvalde County census, 526.

38. Vinton Lee James, "Recollections of the Sheep Range," transcript, Box 2, Folder 3. Hobart Papers. James, the son of John and Annie Milby James, was born on July 3, 1858 and died on January 5, 1939, according to his Bexar County death certificate. He is buried in San Antonio's City Cemetery number one, and his grave is marked. The 1880 Uvalde County census shows him living as a single man, twenty-one years of age, and his occupation is given as sheep raiser. Among the Hobart Papers is a note, attached to the listing of fees paid by the district court of Uvalde County, which contains the following: "Vinton L. James states that Fisher killed John Hannahan near Laredo for stealing horses—we're not sure who he killed or where but the court records show the Hannahans—including the mother—to be a tough bunch! As an Officer, Fisher was probably justified in his dealings with them." Frank L. Hobart to Harry L. Chrisman, Box 3, Folder 13.

39. *Daily Statesman* (Austin), March 7, 1882, reporting by special telegram news from San Antonio of March 6, 1882. Henry Ryder Taylor was born in England in May 1850 and died on July 13, 1908. The 1900 Bexar County census identified him as "Rep. Notary Publ."

40. H. R. Patterson was how the reporter read the name on the hotel register, but it is more likely his name was James L. H. Patterson, who was a former sheriff of Uvalde County. On page 518 of the 1880 Uvalde County census shows that he claimed sheriff as his occupation and also that he had a wife, Cordelia, and three children. Enumerated June, 1880. He was elected on November 5, 1878, reelected one time, and served until August 31, 1881 when he resigned. Tise, *Texas County Sheriffs*, 503.

41. *Daily Express*, August 17 and September 20, 1881.

42. *Free Press*, July 30, 1882.

43. Fisher and Dykes, 120.

44. Bill O'Neal, *Encyclopedia of Western Gunfighters* (Norman: University of Oklahoma Press, 1979), 319–20. For a much more detailed description of the Harris-Thompson feud, see Bicknell and Parsons, "Gunfire at the Vaudeville," *Ben Thompson: Portrait of a Gunfighter* (Denton: University of North Texas Press, 2018), 347–90.

45. Ecclesiastes 1:9, King James Version.

46. *Galveston Daily News*, June 30, 1883. For additional information about fence cutting, see Wayne Gard, "The Fence-Cutters," *The Southwestern Historical Quarterly* 51 (July 1847); Wayne Gard, "Fence Cutting," in *The New Handbook of Texas* Vol. 2, 976–77.

47. *Galveston Daily News*, August 9, 1883, reporting news from Waco, Texas.

48. *Galveston Daily News*, August 8, 1883, reporting "State News" from various places.

49. *Galveston Daily News*, August 21, 1883.

50. *Galveston Daily News*, September 11, 1883, citing news from an undated Brazoria County source.

51. *Daily Fort Worth Gazette*, September 19, 1883. This was part of a long article contributed by "Slade."

52. *Galveston Daily News*, September 17, 1883, citing a report from an undated *Floresville Chronicle* of Wilson County.

53. *Austin Daily Statesman*, October 5, 1883. Crawford Burnett was born in Harris County, April 19, 1835 and died in Gonzales County, January 12, 1915. According to J. Marvin Hunter: "He was one of the first to drive herds to Kansas in the late '60's and has the credit of driving the last herd out of Gonzales county to the northern markets. No man was better or more favorably known in Texas, on the trail, and on Northern markets than Doc Burnett." *The Trail Drivers of Texas* (Austin: University of Texas Press, 1985), 796.

54. Fisher and Dykes, 114.

55. Tise, *Texas County Sheriffs*, 503.

56. 1880 Uvalde County census, enumerated June, 518B. Boatright was accused of stealing $7,500 of Uvalde County tax revenue. He had left for Austin to pay it to the state's comptroller, "but of whom nothing has since been heard." *Austin Daily Statesman*, October 8, 1884. Boatright was a native of Illinois, born in 1835. In 1880 when the census was taken, he and his wife Mary Elizabeth Holcomb Boatright were the parents of seven children. In all, ten would be born to the couple. Boatright outlived whatever disgrace he experienced when charged with embezzlement of county funds. After eleven months in office, Boatright had to resign as sheriff and King Fisher became the new acting sheriff of the county. Years later Boatright was a resident of the Confederate Home in Austin. When he died on April 12, 1929, he was buried in the Confederate Section in the Texas State Cemetery.

57. *Galveston Daily News*, December 8, 1883.

58. *Galveston Daily News*, December 26, 1883, citing a special report from Gonzales dated December 25, 1883.

59. *Daily Express*, December 28, 1883.

60. Barry A. Crouch and Donaly E. Brice, *The Governor's Hounds: The Texas State Police, 1870–1873* (Austin: University of Texas Press, 2011), 275.

61. 1850 DeWitt County census, 119; 1860 Gonzales County census, 85; 1850 Uvalde County census, 524; Pension application #12179 of Kelso and of widow Mary C. Kelso. At his death on September 29, 1917, he was buried in the Sabinal Cemetery, Uvalde County. On his pension application he had written: "I am Naturally not Strong and was wounded in battle."

62. *Austin Weekly Statesman*, March 6, 1884.

# Notes for Chapter 8

1. Fisher and Dykes, 116.

2. Most sources, such as the 1920 census, give her name as "Margurite." At that time, the Oliver Campbell family consisted of head of household Oliver, thirty-eight years old, a cotton farmer; his wife Margurite, thirty-six, and their two children, Noris, their thirteen-year-old son and their four-year-old daughter Ruth. They lived in Calexico Township in Imperial County, California. Census enumerator Mrs. Nora J. Weis

certainly understood correctly the spelling of Mrs. Campbell's name. She, like her grandmother Jane O'Neal Vivian, would also have a good long life, dying in San Francisco, California on September 7, 1958.

3.  *Light* (San Antonio), November 12, 1883.

4.  *Austin Daily Capital*, March 15, 1884.

5.  Vinton Lee James, *Frontier and Pioneer Recollections of Early Days in San Antonio and West Texas* (San Antonio: Artes Graficas, 1938), 76. By 1900 James was the City Auditor of San Antonio, living there with his wife Mary and their six children. James, the son of John and Annie James, was born on July 3, 1858 and died on January 5, 1939. He is buried in City Cemetery No. 1 in San Antonio. 1880 Uvalde County census, 527B; 1900 Bexar County census.

6.  *Galveston Daily News*, March 12, 1884, citing a special from San Antonio dated March 11, 1884.

7.  Fisher and Dykes, 126.

8.  It is believed that the watch and chain visible in the photograph were a gift from Phil Coe to Ben Thompson, presented in Abilene, Kansas in 1871. Coe, a Gonzales County native, was killed by J. B. "Wild Bill" Hickok in October 1871 in Abilene. *Galveston Daily News*, March 14, 1884.

9.  This description of the actual photograph is from *The Robert G. McCubbin Collection Catalogue* by Brian Lebel (Santa Fe: 2019), 179. Thompson had also presented a print to his daughter: "To my daughter Katie / Ben Thompson / Austin Texas Feb 22nd 1884."

10. *San Marcos Free Press*, March 13, 1884.

11. *Austin American*, January 20, 1927. At the time of relating this incident, Farnsworth was Vice President of Southwestern Bell Telephone Company. He was speaking at a banquet given in his honor by company executives and attended by local newspapermen and others. He told of the wild days of Austin in the early 1880s. Born in Manchester, New Hampshire on January 31, 1862, in Texas he first worked for the *Austin Statesman*, then the *Waco Examiner*, and later the San Antonio *Daily Express*. He died at his home in California on October 16, 1935 and is buried in Forest Lawn Memorial Cemetery in Glendale. Biographical information is from the *Austin Statesman* of October 17, 1935.

12. *Light* (San Antonio), March 12, 1884.

13. *Daily Fort Worth Gazette*, March 13, 1884.

14. *Galveston Daily News*, March 12, 1884.

15. *Austin Weekly Statesman*, March 20, 1884, citing a special from San Antonio dated March 12, 1884.
16. *Light* (San Antonio), March 12, 1884.
17. The White Elephant Saloon, rivaling the Vaudeville in its reputation for quality food, drinks, and entertainment, was operated at this time by Edward Fowler and Sam Berliner. It was located at 315 W. Commerce on the north side of the Main Plaza.
18. Phillip Shardein was born January 11, 1839 in Kentucky. During the war he was mustered in as a 2nd Lieutenant in Company "G," 3rd Regiment of the Texas Infantry. When the war ended, he had risen to the rank of captain. By 1880 he was Captain of the Police in San Antonio. Later he became a Judge. He died of a heart attack on September 13, 1905 and is buried in the Alamo Masonic Cemetery. A visit to his grave in 2019 revealed that his headstone had been toppled off its base, whether by vandals or by nature, and was on the ground face down. In an email, historian Kurt House of San Antonio maintains that he is "90% certain that it was vandals since the stones are too heavy to have been moved under natural forces and those nearby with similar vulnerability have not been toppled." House to Parsons, November 19, 2020.
19. *Fort Worth Telegram*, September 7, 1902. Ada Gray had died only ten days before, and Ernest Rische had reason to remember her. This Fort Worth article first appeared in the *San Antonio Express*.
20. *Light* (San Antonio), March 12, 1884.
21. Ibid., March 12, 1884. Ada Gray was a beautiful actress and extremely popular, especially in small venues: "in a hundred smaller cities and towns she was as well known as [Sarah] Bernhardt." She died on August 28, 1902 in a New York hospital. According to the *New York Evening World*, "In point of tears shed over her 'East Lynne' she was the most bewept member of her profession in America. In the emotional role of the injured wife returned from exile she had saturated more hemstitched handkerchiefs with dewy teardrops of rural eyes than any other actress on record." One notice of her passing stated she began her acting career at the age of sixteen, making her first appearance in Rochester, New York. She was the first woman to appear in "East Lynne" in the United States. She was twice married, and her second husband was Charles F. Tingay, "an English actor who was her leading man the last few years of her career." The *Farmers Vindicator* (Valley Falls, Jefferson County, Kansas), September 12, 1902. She died at the

Home for Incurables and was buried in the Actors Field plot at Evergreen Cemetery, New York. The extremely popular play was based on the novel of the same name written by Ellen Wood, under the name of Mrs. Henry Wood. The play was first staged in New York in 1861. The play has had many different arrangements, and motion pictures have been based upon the novel, which was characterized by infidelity and double identities.

# Notes for Chapter 9

1. The expression "den of infamy" (used in the title of this chapter as well) is from William M. Walton's 1884 biography, *Life and Adventures of Ben Thompson, the Famous Texan*, edited by Lisa Lach (self-published, 2016), 195. By chance, the expression was also used in the San Antonio *Daily Express* of April 25, 1881 in the write-up of the gunfight between Billy Simms and Lombard.
2. *Galveston Daily News*, March 13, 1884.
3. *Daily Fort Worth Gazette*, March 13, 1884, citing a special from San Antonio, March 12, 1884. This is an expression which has lost its nineteenth-century meaning except in certain circles. Today it is more likely heard in references to the trucking industry: gooseneck trailers when mishandled have "hell in the neck." In the 1880s, of course, it referred to a troublesome horse or individual. Cattleman Ab Blocker contributed an article titled "The Man Who Had Hell In His Neck" about his own experiences having "hell in the neck," which appeared in J. Marvin Hunter, *The Trail Drivers of Texas* (Austin: The University of Texas Press, 1985), 504–13.
4. 1880 Bexar County Census, 20. Captain Shardein was about forty-five years old, born in Louisville, Kentucky in 1839 of Prussia-born parents. He had a strong desire to succeed in everything he did, and by 1884 he was Chief of Police in San Antonio. At the time of the census, he had a wife, Mary Ann Colton Shardein, who was a year younger and Texas-born. Captain Shardein lived with his wife and mother-in-law, Elizabeth Colton. Shardein was born on January 11, 1839 and died on September 13, 1905 in San Antonio. He is buried in the Alamo Masonic Cemetery in San Antonio. Elton R. Cude, *The Wild and Free Dukedom of Bexar* (San Antonio: Manguia Printers, 1978), 113.
5. Cude, *The Wild and Free Dukedom of Bexar*.
6. *Galveston Daily News*, March 13, 1884.

7. *Austin Daily Statesman*, March 13, 1884.

8. Ibid.

9. *Austin Weekly Statesman*, March 12, 1884, citing a report from San Antonio.

10. Telegraph published in *New York Herald* on March 29, 1884 in the *Texas Siftings* section.

11. This wording of the coroner's verdict is from the San Antonio *Daily Express*, March 13, 1884. Other newspapers contain slight variations of the report.

12. *Light* (San Antonio), March 15, 1884.

13. *Austin Daily Statesman*, March 12, 1884, citing a report from San Antonio.

14. *Galveston Daily News*, March 13, 1884, citing specials from San Antonio dated March 12, 1884.

15. Ibid.

16. Ibid.

17. Ibid.

18. Ibid.

19. Ibid.

20. Ibid.

21. Ibid.

22. *Daily Herald* (Dallas), March 13, 1884.

23. *Weekly Herald* (Dallas), March 13, 1884.

# Notes for Chapter 10

1. Fisher and Dykes, 144.

2. Hobart Papers. Excerpt from a letter written by Powell Roberts of Santa Rita, New Mexico, dated March 2, 1931, to historian and publisher J. Marvin Hunter. Marvin Powe is listed in the 1930 Grant County census as a fifty-five-year-old deputy sheriff, living in the town of Hurley, Grant County. If he was eleven in 1884, then he was born about 1873, which agrees closely to the census.

3. *Daily Express* (San Antonio), March 14, 1884, citing a special from Uvalde dated March 13, 1884. This also appeared in the *Galveston Daily News*, March 14, 1884.

4. *Austin Weekly Statesman*, March 27, 1884.

5. Joseph Carl Petmecky was born August 12, 1842 in Prussia and, when brought to the United States by his parents when he was seven years of age, he remained. After the Civil War, during which he served with

the Sibley Brigade and its invasion of New Mexico Territory, Petmecky opened a gunshop on Congress Avenue. He married Adolphina Helene Sterzing and together they raised five children. His advertisement in the Austin City Directory showed he was a gunsmith, a dealer in guns, pistols, ammunition, and sportsmen's supplies. Petmecky died on August 16, 1929 in Austin and is buried in Oakwood Cemetery in Austin. His grave is marked.

6.  *Austin Daily Statesman*, March 14, 1884. During fall of 2019, in an effort to solve the mystery of the Vaudeville tragedy, a group of Wild West historians and several esteemed pathologists assembled by the authors of this biography appealed to a descendant of John King Fisher to exhume his body and perform an examination. The intent was to determine the angle of the shots that took his life and perhaps recover the fatal bullets laying in his coffin with his remains, which would have revealed the caliber and type of weapons used. The descendant decided to refuse the request.

7.  *Daily Express*, March 14, 1884, citing a telephone message from Uvalde of March 13, 1884.

8.  *Daily Statesman*, March 15, 1884.

9.  *Daily Statesman*, March 20, 1884. See Appendix E.

10. *Daily Express*, March 15, 1884. The testimonial to King Fisher is printed in full in Appendix E.

11. *Austin Daily Statesman*, March 16, 1884. The *Statesman* placed the interview under the headline: "The Facts. /An Interesting Interview With Two Gentlemen Who Saw the Shooting. /A Far Different Story From the One Told by Those Who Planned the Murderous Work. /A Fearful Den of Iniquity and Vice Where the Bloody Work Was Done."

12. J. S. Coy testimony as reported in *Galveston Daily News*. Special to the *News* dated March 13, 1884.

13. Ibid.

14. *Austin Daily Statesman*, March 16, 1884, 4.

15. Durham and Wantland, "On the Trail," later published as *Taming the Nueces Strip: The Story of McNelly's Rangers* (Austin: University of Texas Press, 1962). This material regarding Durham is largely omitted from the later version. However, the incident appears briefly in the "sanitized version" on page 163: "King even tried to hold Ben back [from going up the stairs], but he broke loose and started up the steps. King had run to his side when the shooting began and they were both dropped. The place was forted." In the later edition, there is no mention

of Durham knowing who the assassins were, much less knowing how much each of them were paid.

16. Frank H. Bushick, *Glamorous Days in Old San Antonio (A Never to be Forgotten City)* (San Antonio: The Naylor Company, 1934). Charles B. Myler, "A History of the English Speaking Theatre in San Antonio Before 1900," PhD dissertation, University of Texas, 1968. Bushick identifies three previously unmentioned men as the assassins. The trio were "hangers-on at the theatre": Harry Tremaine, an English Jew variety performer, a gambler known only as "Canada Bill," and a bartender named McLaughlin. Efforts to flesh out these names with biographical information have produced little. Vaudeville theater manager Frank Sparrow kept a record book of performers, their names, their engagements, and additional comments relative to their effectiveness, but the name of Tremaine does not appear. Sparrow's record book is archived in the rare book room of the Genealogy Department of the San Antonio Public Library.

17. *Galveston Daily News*, August 21, 1883.

18. San Antonio City Directory, in which McLaughlin's name is listed.

19. Henry B. Yelvington, "Single Living Witness Describes How Editor Outdid Ben Thompson," *Sunday American-Statesman*, February 13, 1927. Yelvington worked for the *American-Statesman*, *Houston Chronicle*, *San Antonio Express*, and *The Oklahoman*. The "innumerable features and short stories" quotation is from an obituary for Yelvington who died on February 28, 1944, which appeared in the *Austin American* of February 29, 1944.

20. *Galveston Daily News*, March 20, 1884. Citing a report from San Antonio of March 19.

21. Ibid.

22. *Daily Statesman*, March 20, 1884.

23. *Daily Statesman*, March 16, 1884.

24. *Light* (San Antonio), March 22 and March 24, 1884. The graves of both Joseph C. Foster and D. A. "Jack" Harris are marked. They are located just inside the entrance from Commerce Avenue. An official Texas State Historical Marker has been placed at the grave of Harris.

25. *Tribune*, March 23, 1884, New York. Telegram from San Antonio.

26. *Light* (San Antonio), March 14, 1884.

27. *Light* (San Antonio), March 15, 1884.

28. Ibid.

29. Ibid.

# Notes for Chapter 11

1. *Daily Express*, April 25 and 26, 1884.
2. *Daily Statesman*, April 25, 1884, Austin; *Daily Express*, April 25 and 26, 1884, San Antonio.
3. *Daily Statesman*, April 25, 1884, Austin; *Daily Express*, April 25 and 26, 1884, San Antonio.
4. *Light* (San Antonio), May 3, 1884, San Antonio, citing a report from an undated *Floresville Chronicle*.
5. 1860 Rankin County, Mississippi census, 868.
6. *Light* (San Antonio), May 3, 1884; *Daily Express*, June 1, 1884.
7. *Light* (San Antonio), July 24, 1884; *Daily Express*, July 25, 1884.
8. *Daily Express*, July 14, 1886. Article headlined: "Wanted Gore."
9. *Uvalde Leader-News*, April 20, 1928.
10. Mary Brock, "Life of Sally Vivian Fisher Reflects Stirring Texas Days," *Austin American-Statesman*, June 18, 1939.
11. *Crystal City Sentinel*, January 1, 1943.
12. "Old Trails," *Uvalde Leader-News*, October 11, 1959.
13. "New Grave for King Fisher Recreates Interest in Former Deputy Sheriff," *Uvalde Leader-News*, October 11, 1959.
14. Amanda Gardner, "King of the Road," *Texas Highways*, 38–42.
15. Letter from Jack R. Seals to Amanda Gardner, November 17, 1998. Copy in authors' possession.
16. Ibid.
17. *Crystal City Sentinel*, November 6, 1959
18. Ibid.; Pat Horn, article in *The Junior Historian*, March 1927 in Frank L. Hobart Papers.

    *The Junior Historian* was the publication of the Texas State Historical Association and was the idea of TSHA Director Walter Prescott Webb. The idea of such an organization was announced in the October 1939 issue of the *Southwestern Historical Quarterly*. The secondary high school organization still exists.
19. Eva Sanderlin, "King Fisher dies in San Antonio gambling Hall," *Uvalde Leader-News*, March 11, 1984. Folder 4, Box 2, Hobart Papers. This article appeared on 100th Anniversary of Fisher's death.
20. Leakey, John. *The West that Was: From Texas to Montana.* As told to Nellie Snyder Yost (Dallas: Southern Methodist University Press, 1958), 30.
21. John Leakey, "King Fisher," as told to Florence Fenley, transcript. Folder 3, Box 2. Hobart Papers.

22. Robert L. Fowler owned the King Fisher carbine at the time of the Fenley column. Florence Fenley, "The Gun," clipping. Box 2, Folder 4, "King Fisher—Interviews—News Clippings—Photographs." Hobart Papers.

23. Diaz was president of Mexico from February 17, 1877 to December 1, 1880 and from December 1, 1884 to May 25, 1911. The southern province of Oaxaca, far from the Rio Grande valley, was Diaz's birthplace and where he rose to power.

24. J. S. Gallegly, "Background and Patterns of O. Henry's Texas Badman Stories," *Rice University Studies* 42, no. 3 (1955): 1–31.

25. Review and cast listing on IMDb.com.

26. "A Movie in Your Mind," synopsis from GraphicAudio webpage. In the audio version, Chris Genebach plays Kingfisher. The CD was directed by Terence Aselford.

27. Quotation is from the dust jacket of the book.

28. Ramon F. Adams, compiler, *Six-Guns and Saddle Leather. A Bibliography of Books and Pamphlets on Western Outlaws and Gunmen.* (1954. Revised edition, Norman: University of Oklahoma Press, 1969).

29. Floyd B. Streeter, *Ben Thompson: Man With A Gun* (New York: Frederick Fell, 1957), 201.

30. G. R. Williamson, *The Texas Pistoleers: The True Story of Ben Thompson and King Fisher – Two of the Most Feared Pistol Fighters of the American West* (self-published, 2009).

31. *Fort Worth Daily Gazette*, May 11, 1884.

32. These reminiscences appear in a brief typescript titled "King Fisher" provided by Amanda (Mandy) Gardner to Thomas C. Bicknell.

# Selected Bibliography

## Primary Sources – Texas State Archives and Library, Austin

Abstract of Muster Rolls of Civil War Soldiers.

Adjutant General Correspondence, Vol. III.

Adjutant General Records, Muster Rolls and Monthly Returns, Letters To and Received.

Autobiography of John Creaton. Typescript.

Description and Historical Register of Enlisted Soldiers of the Army, for during the War with Mexico under the Acts Approved January 12th and February 11th, 1847.

Executive Record Book. E. J. Davis, Richard Coke. 1/8/1870-2/9/1874. Microfilm reel 9.

List of Fugitives from Justice, from Records in the Adjutant General's Office.

Muster Rolls Civil War Index.

Muster Rolls of the Texas Revolution.

Record of Arrests [by Texas State Police]. Ledger 401-1001.

Record of Criminals by Co[unty] Crime, Description. Ledger 401-1081.

Report of the Adjutant General of the State of Texas for the Year Ending August 31st, 1876. Shaw & Blaylock, Galveston.

Report of Operations of State Troops since August 1, 1875 to Dec. 31, 1881. File 401-1082.

Semi-monthly Report. Sept. 30, 1879. Original. Special Forces Correspondence.

Texas, Bonds and Oaths of Office, 1846–1920.

Texas, Convict and Conduct Registers, 1875–1945.

Texas Voter Registration Lists, 1867–69.

## Primary Sources – Other Archives

"The Damerson-Damron Family Newsletter." Fall, 1987. Shaver collection.

Fenley, Guy T. Interview conducted by Frank L. Hobart. Transcript in Frank L. Hobart Papers.

Fisher, Florence. Diary excerpts. Frank L. Hobart Papers.

Fisher, O. C. "The Texas Heritage of the Fishers and the Clarks." Typescript in Frank L. Hobart Papers.

Fitterer, Gary P. Biography of Alfred Y. Allee. Untitled manuscript. Gary P. Fitterer, private collection.

Horn, Pat. Article in *The Junior Historian*, March 1927 in Frank L. Hobart
    Papers.
James, Vinton Lee. "Recollections of the Sheep Range" Transcript in Frank
    L. Hobart Papers.
Larry G. Shaver, private collection.
Leakey, John. "King Fisher." As told to Florence Fenley. Transcript of her
    article written for *Uvalde Leader-News*. Frank L. Hobart Papers.
Minutes of District Court Book A. Goliad County.
Pension application of Henry Calvin Vivian, Dimmit County. 34126. National
    Archives.
San Miguel, Trinidad Jr. Interview conducted by Frank L. Hobart. Transcript
    in Frank L. Hobart Papers.
Seals, Jack R. Letter to Amanda Gardner in Frank L. Hobart Papers.
Texas Frontier Troubles. House of Representatives Report, 44th Congress,
    1st Session, Washington, DC, 1876. Original. National Archives.
White, Mr. and Mrs. Ben C. Interview conducted by Frank L. Hobart, Carrizo
    Springs, January 18, 1966. Transcript in Frank L. Hobart Papers.
Widow's Application for Pension, no. 2394, Elizabeth J. Vivian, prepared
    October 1911. [National Archives?]
Widow's pension for indigents, application of Jane O'Neal Vivian, Dimmit
    County. 41028. National Archives.

# Census Records – Texas

Bandera County, 1880
Bee County, 1870
Bell County, 1860
Bexar County, 1870, 1900
Cameron County, 1879
Collin County, 1850
Dimmit County, 1880, 1920
Goliad County, 1850, 1860, 1870
Karnes County, 1860
Kinney County, 1870, 1880
Maverick County, 1860, 1870, 1880
Medina County, 1880
Uvalde County, 1870, 1880
Webb County, 1870 (Non-population schedule)
Williamson County, 1860

Wilson County, 1870
Zavala County, 1880

# Census Records – Other States

Claiborne County, Tennessee, 1860
Imperial County, California 1920
Rankin County, Mississippi, 1860

# Newspapers – Texas

*Austin American*, Austin
*Austin-American Statesman*, Austin
*Austin Daily Capital*, Austin
*Austin Weekly Statesman*, Austin
*Brenham Daily Banner*, Brenham
*Brenham Weekly Banner*, Brenham
*Brownsville Herald*, Brownsville
*Burnet Bulletin*, Burnet
*Castroville Era*, Castroville
*Castroville Quill*, Castroville
*Civilian and Galveston Gazette*, Galveston
*Corpus Christi Advertiser*, Corpus Christi
*Corpus Christi Gazette*, Corpus Christi
*Crystal City Sentinel*, Crystal City
*Cuero Star*, Cuero
*Daily Democratic Statesman*, Austin
*Daily Statesman*, Austin
*Express*, San Antonio (weekly and daily)
*Daily Fort Worth Gazette*, Fort Worth
*Daily Herald*, San Antonio
*Daily Statesman*, Austin
*El Paso Times*, El Paso
*Evening News*, San Antonio
*Fort Worth Star-Telegram*, Fort Worth
*Free Press*, San Marcos
*Galveston Daily News*, Galveston
*Goliad Guard*, Goliad
*Gonzales Inquirer*, Gonzales
*Herald*, Dallas (weekly and daily)

*Indianola Bulletin*, Indianola
*Light*, San Antonio
*Marshall Messenger*, Marshall
*McKay's Weekly*, San Antonio
*Northern Standard*, Clarksville
*Pleasanton Journal*, Pleasanton
*San Antonio Ledger and Texan*, San Antonio
*San Antonio Light*, San Antonio
*San Marcos Free Press*, San Marcos
*Star Telegraph*, Fort Worth
*Taylor Daily Press*, Taylor
*Texas Argus*, San Antonio
*Texas Siftings*, Austin
*Tri-Weekly Herald*, Marshall
*Uvalde Leader-News*, Uvalde
*Valley Evening Monitor*, McAllen
*Victoria Advocate*, Victoria
*Weekly Democratic Statesman*, Austin
*Weekly Herald*, Dallas
*Weimer Mercury*, Weimer

# Newspapers – Other States

*Arizona Daily Star*, Tucson, Arizona
*Daily Democrat*, New Orleans, Louisiana
*Daily Gazette*, Fort Wayne, Indiana
*Daily Gazette*, Stillwater, Oklahoma
*Daily Kansas Tribune*, Lawrence, Kansas
*Daily Picayune*, New Orleans, Louisiana
*Daily Tribune*, Chicago, Illinois
*Evening Gazette*, Cedar Rapids, Iowa
*Farmers Vindicator*, Valley Falls, Kansas
*Free Press*, Detroit, Michigan
*Las Vegas Gazette*, Las Vegas, New Mexico
*Las Vegas Daily Optic*, Las Vegas, New Mexico
*New Orleans Republican*, New Orleans, Louisiana
*New York Evening World*, New York, New York
*New York Sun*, New York, New York
*Inter Ocean*, Chicago, Illinois

*Salt Lake Tribune*, Salt Lake City, Utah
*St. Louis Globe-Democrat*, St. Louis, Missouri
*St. Louis Republican*, St. Louis, Missouri
*Sedalia Weekly Banner*, Sedalia, Missouri
*Times-Picayune*, New Orleans, Louisiana
*Tribune*, New York, New York
*Weekly Bazoo*, Sedalia, Missouri
*The World*, New York, New York

# Books, Pamphlets, and Articles

Adams, Ramon F., compiler. *Six-Guns and Saddle Leather. A Bibliography of Books and Pamphlets on Western Outlaws and Gunmen.* Revised edition. Norman: University of Oklahoma Press, 1969.

Baylor, George W. *Into the Far, Wild Country: True Tales of the Old Southwest.* Edited by Jerry Thompson. El Paso: Texas Western Press, 1996.

Bicknell, Thomas C., & Chuck Parsons. *Ben Thompson: Portrait of a Gunfighter.* Denton: University of North Texas Press, 2018.

Bishop, Curtis. "King Fisher's Road." *True West*, January–February 1963.

Bonnet, Judge W. A. "King Fisher, a Noted Character." *Frontier Times*, July 1926.

Brock, Mary. "Life of Sally Vivian Fisher Reflects Stirring Texas Days." *Austin-American Statesman*, June 18, 1939.

Brodbent, C. S. "King Fisher, A Ranchman's Story of Early Days." *McKay's Weekly*, April 9, 1910.

Brown, John H. *Indian Wars and Pioneers of Texas.* 189?. Facsimile reprint, Austin: State House Press, 1988.

Bushick, Frank H. *Glamorous Days in Old San Antonio (A Never to be Forgotten City).* San Antonio: The Naylor Company, 1934.

Collins, Michael L. *Texas Devils: Rangers and Regulars on the Lower Rio Grande, 1846–1861.* Norman: University of Oklahoma Press, 2008.

Collins, Michael L. *A Crooked River: Rustlers, Rangers, and Regulars in the Lower Rio Grande, 1861–1877.* Norman: University of Oklahoma Press, 2018.

"Cometa, Texas" in *TexasEscapes.com*, accessed May 23, 2020. http://www.texasescapes.com/SouthTexasTowns/Cometa-Texas.htm.

Crimmins, M. L. "Old Fort Duncan: A Frontier Post."*Frontier Times*, June 1938.

Crouch, Barry A., & Donaly E. Brice. *The Governor's Hounds: The Texas State Police, 1870–1873*. Austin: University of Texas Press, 2011.

Cude, Elton R. *The Wild and Free Dukedom of Bexar*. San Antonio: Manguia Printers, 1978.

DeArment, Robert K. *Alias Frank Canton*. Norman: University of Oklahoma Press, 1996.

DeMattos, Jack. "King Fisher." *Real West*, September 1972.

Durham, George, & Clyde Wantland. "On the Trail of 5,100 Outlaws." *West*, 1937.

Durham, George, & Clyde Wantland. *Taming the Nueces Strip: The Story of McNelly's Rangers*. Austin: University of Texas Press, 1962.

Ernst, Robert R. *Deadly Affrays: The Violent Deaths of the United States Marshals*. Avon, Indiana: ScarletMask Enterprises, 2006.

Erwin, Allen A. *The Southwest of John Horton Slaughter, 1841–1922: Pioneer Cattleman and Trail-Driver of Texas, the Pecos, and Arizona, and Sheriff of Tombstone*. Glendale, California: Arthur H. Clark Company, 1965.

Fisher, O. C. "King Fisher: Texas Gunman, Lawman." *Corral Dust* 4, no. 1 (1959).

Fisher, O. C. "The Life and Times of King Fisher." *Southwestern Historical Quarterly* 64, no. 2 (October 1960).

Fisher, O. C., & J. C. Dykes. *King Fisher: His Life and Times*. Norman: University of Oklahoma Press, 1966.

Gallegly, J. S. "Background and Patterns of O. Henry's Texas Badman Stories." *Rice University Studies* 42, no. 3 (1955): 1-31.

Gardner, Amanda. "King of the Road." *Texas Highways*, December 1998.

Gillett, James B. *Fugitives from Justice: The Notebook of Sergeant James B. Gillett*. 1878. Facsimile reprint, Austin: State House Press, 1997.

Gregory, A.H. "Death of Ben Thompson and King Fisher." *Frontier Times* 5, no. 9 (June 1928).

Haynes, David. *Catching Shadows: A Directory of 19th Century Texas Photographers*. Austin: Texas State Historical Association, 1993.

House, Kurt. "San Antonio's Most Famous Gunfight." *The Texas Gun Collector*, Spring 2003.

Hunter, J. Marvin. *The Trail Drivers of Texas*. Austin: University of Texas Press, 1985.

James, Vinton Lee. *Frontier and Pioneer Recollections of Early Days in San Antonio and West Texas*. San Antonio: Artes Graficas, 1938.

Jennings, N. A. *A Texas Ranger*. 1899. Reprint, Chicago: Lakeside Press, 1992.

Johnson, David. *The Mason County "Hoo Doo" War, 1874–1902*. Denton: University of North Texas Press, 2006.

Johnson, David. *The Cornett-Whitley Gang: Violence Unleashed in Texas*. Denton: University of North Texas Press, 2019.

Kellogg, Florence. "Incidents in the Life of John King Fisher." Unpublished manuscript.

Lake, Stuart N. *Wyatt Earp, Frontier Marshal*. Boston: Houghton Mifflin, 1931.

Leakey, John. *The West that Was: From Texas to Montana*. As told to Nellie Snyder Yost. Dallas: Southern Methodist University Press, 1958.

Lebel, Brian. *The Robert G. McCubbin Collection Catalogue*. 2019.

Maverick, Mrs. Albert, Sr. "Ranch Life in Bandera County in 1878." *Frontier Times* Magazine, April, 1928.

McKinney, T. H. "In Defense of King Fisher." Letter to editor. *Frontier Times* 12, no. 4 (January 1935).

Miller, Rick. *Texas Ranger John B. Jones and the Frontier Battalion, 1874–1881*. Denton: University of North Texas Press, 2012.

Mitchell, Jack, contributor. *A Proud Heritage: A History of Uvalde County, Texas*. El Progreso Club, 1975.

Myler, Charles B. "A History of the English-Speaking Theater in San Antonio before 1900." PhD diss., University of Texas, 1968.

O'Neal, Bill. *Encyclopedia of Western Gunfighters*. Norman: University of Oklahoma Press, 1979.

O'Neal. Bill. *War in East Texas: Regulators vs. Moderators*. 2006. Reprint, Denton: University of North Texas Press, 2018.

Parsons, Chuck. "'Mervyn' A Poetical Correspondent." In "The Annotated Letters of Texas Ranger Mervyn Bathurst Davis," *Brand Book* (English Westerners Society), Winter 1988–1989.

Parsons, Chuck. *John B. Armstrong: Texas Rangers and Pioneer Ranchman*. College Station: Texas A & M University Press, 2007.

Parsons, Chuck. *Texas Ranger Lee Hall: From the Red River to the Rio Grande*. Denton: University of North Texas Press, 2020.

Rasch, Philip J. "Gus Gildea – An Arizone Pioneer." *Brand Book* (English Westerners Society), 1985.

Rasch, Philip J. *Desperadoes of Arizona Territory*. Stillwater, OK: Barbed Wire Press, 1999.

Raymond, Dora N. *Captain Lee Hall of Texas*. 1940. Facsimile reprint, Norman: University of Oklahoma, 1982.

Roberts, Bruce. *Springs from the Parched Ground*. Uvalde, Texas: Hornby Press, 1950.

Rose, Victor M. *The Texas Vendetta, or, The Sutton-Taylor Feud*. 1880. Facsimile reprint, Houston: The Frontier Press of Texas, 1956.

Sanderlin, Eva. "King Fisher Dies in San Antonio Gambling Hall." *Uvalde Leader-News*, ND. Frank L. Hobart Papers, El Progreso Memorial Library, Uvalde, Texas.

Smallwood, James M. *The Feud that Wasn't: The Taylor Ring, Bill Sutton, John Wesley Hardin, and Violence in Texas*. College Station: Texas A & M University Press, 2008.

Sonnichsen, Charles L. *Texas Humoresque: Lone Star Humorists from Then till Now*. Fort Worth: Texas Christian University Press, 1990.

Streeter, Floyd B. *Ben Thompson: Man with A Gun*. New York: Frederick Fell, 1957.

Taylor, Paul S. "Historical Notes on Dimmit County." *Southwestern Historical Quarterly* 34, No. 2 (October 1930).

Thompson, Jerry. *Cortina: Defending the Mexican Name in Texas*. College Station: Texas A & M University Press, 2007.

Tidwell, Laura K. *Dimmit County Mesquite Roots*. Austin: Wind River Press, 1984.

Tise, Sammy. *Texas County Sheriffs*. Albuquerque: Oakwood Printing, 1988.

Walton, W. M. *Life and Adventures of Ben Thompson, the Famous Texan*. 1884. Edited by Lisa Lach. Self-published, 2016.

Wheelock, E. H., contributor. *Reports of Cases Argued and Decided in the Supreme Court of the State of Texas during the Latter Part of the Galveston Session, 1870*. Vol. 23. 715–17. St. Louis: Gilbert Book Co., 1872.

Williamson, G. R. *The Texas Pistoleers: The True Story of Ben Thompson and King Fisher—Two of the Most Feared Pistol Fighters of the American West*. Self-published, 2009.

Yelvington, Henry B. "Single Living Witness Describes How Editor Outdid Ben Thompson." *Sunday American-Statesman*, February 13, 1927.

Young, Roy B., Gary L. Roberts, & Casey Tefertiller. *A Wyatt Earp Anthology: Long May His Story Be Told*. Denton: University of North Texas Press, 2019.

Zavala County Historical Commission. *Now and Then in Zavala County*. Marcus A. "Buddy" Johnson, chair. Crystal City, Texas: Zavala County Historical Commission. 1996.

# New Handbook of Texas

Bryan, J. L., & Laurie E. Jasinski. "Edward Dougherty." *Handbook of Texas Online*, accessed March 23, 2020. https://www.tshaonline.org/handbook/entries/dougherty-edward

Minor, David. "Collin County." 2:214-15. 1952. Revised October 8, 2020. https://www.tshaonline.org/handbook/entries/collin-county

Pingenot, Ben. "Eagle Pass, TX." 2:751-52. 1976. Revised September 5, 2019. https://www.tshaonline.org/handbook/entries/eagle-pass-tx

Tate, Michael L. "Black Seminole Scouts." 1:573. 1995. Revised September 30, 2020. https://www.tshaonline.org/handbook/entries/black-seminole-scouts

Anonymous. "Sister Grove Creek." 1952. Revised June 1, 1995. https://www.tshaonline.org/handbook/entries/sister-grove-creek

# Index

Brooking, William H., 12, 50–51, 70, 74–75

Brown, Andrew, 167

Brown, Eli, 96

Bruton family ("Bruton boys"), 5; Charles, vii, 12–13, 15, 48, 52–54, 77, 95; Wesley, 83; Wiley, 15; William Wesley, 15; W. C., 34, 83; W. T., 36

"Bud King" (by O. Henry), 178

Burditt, Jim, 83–84

Burleson, John R., 16

Burleson, Matilda Jane, 8

Burnett, Crawford ("Doc"), 132–33

Burns, John (alias John Smith), 41, 66

Burns, Pink (alias Pink Smith), 41, 66

Bushick, Frank H., 163–64

Byers, Ross, 8

## C

*Caballero's Way, The*, 178

Callison family, 45; brothers, 73–74; Frank, 74, 96; Thomas, 74

Campbell, William, 12

Canada Bill, 163–64

Canterbury, John Warner, 41

Cardwell, John, 97

Carelin, Joseph, 133

Carothers, E. A., 114, 119

Cartwright, William C., 13

Cavin, John Edward, 42, 53–54, 68

Cavin, William T., 41–42, 68, 74, 92

C. B. O. (correspondent), 95

Chadwell, J. B., 154

Charo, Cecilio, 167

Chicon Creek, 80, 85

Chinn, George Kerfoot, 29, 125

Cisco Kid, 178

Claiborne, David D., 12–13

**T**